W9-CHS-542

ExamInsight
For
A+ Operating Systems Technology

Exam 220-232

**CD-ROM practice exam provided by
BeachFront Quizzer, Inc.,
Friendswood, Texas**

Author

Tcat Houser
Network+, MCSE, Server+, CTT+

Published by

TotalRecall Publications, Inc.
1103 Middlecreek
Friendswood, TX 77546
281-992-3131

THIS IS BOOK IS GUARANTEED:
See details at www.TotalRecallPress.com

TotalRecall Publications, Inc.

This Book is Sponsored by BeachFront Quizzer, Inc.

Copyright © 2003 by TotalRecall Publications, Inc... All rights reserved. Printed in the United States of America. Except as permitted under the United States Copyright Act of 1976, No part of this publication may be reproduced, stored in a retrieval system, or transmitted in any form or by any means electronic or mechanical or by photocopying, recording, or otherwise without the prior permission of the publisher.

The views expressed in this book are solely those of the author, and do not represent the views of any other party or parties.

Printed in United States of America
Printed and bound by Data Duplicators of Houston Texas
Printed and Bound by Lightning Source in the USA and UK

ISBN: 1-59095-229-4
UPC: 6-43977-22232-9

The sponsoring editor is Bruce Moran and the production supervisor is Corby Tate.

Authors: Helen O'Boyle
Author: Tcat Houser
Subject Matter Expert: Helen O'Boyle Operating System Technology
Kenny McCready Senior Animation Specialist
Design Concepts: Bruce Moran
Edited by: KY Jurgenson

This publication is not sponsored by, endorsed by, or affiliated with CompTIA, Inc. CompTIA®, A+®, Network+™, Server+™, I-Net+™, Linux+™, Security+™ The CompTIA logos and the Network+ logo are trademarks or registered trademarks of CompTIA, Inc. in the United States and certain other countries. All other trademarks are trademarks of their respective owners. Throughout this book, trademarked names are used. Rather than put a trademark symbol after every occurrence of a trademarked name, we used names in an editorial fashion only and to the benefit of the trademark owner. No intention of infringement on trademarks is intended. This publication does not constitute an endorsement of any mentioned product by the authors or TotalRecall Publications, Inc..

Disclaimer Notice: Judgments as to the suitability of the information herein for purchaser's purposes are necessarily the purchaser's responsibility. BeachFront Quizzer, Inc. and TotalRecall Publications, Inc. extends no warranties, makes no representations, and assumes no responsibility as to the accuracy or suitability of such information for application to the purchaser's intended purposes or for consequences of its use except as described in the Guarantee.

Computers are useless.
They can only give you answers.
-Pablo Picasso

This book is dedicated to all Owls making IT better.

ExamInsight™
For
CompTIA®
A+ Operating System Technology

About the Author

Tcat Houser

Tcat Houser (Network+, MCSE, Server+, CTT+) has garnered other milestones such as IBM PSE and Microsoft MCSE/MCT. This is the result of almost 40 years of "fussing with electronics". When not writing or teaching, he is doing research. Tcat accomplishes so many tasks because to him, it isn't work, its fun, and he has fun 18 hours a day, 7 days a week. You can reach him by sending mail to Author@TotalRecallPress.com or Tcat@Tcat.net.

Looking back at the last book where I (Tcat Houser) was the lead author (i-Net+ Exam Prep 1576105989) the independent reviews were very good, and most readers understood that I had two intentions. One, ace the test. Two, supply the information to be a reference manual and/or alert the reader to upcoming technologies so as today's hero, the reader was not tomorrow's zero.

In the two years since that release, I led a number of career changers through CompTIA and wrote my own courseware. Building on that learning, you have this release.

About the Book

This study guide is designed specifically for the interim CompTIA A+ Operating System Technology certification exam (220-232), which will be given from September 12th until the new test is out. Then it will be retired and replaced by a totally new exam devoted to 2003 objectives.

The interim exam continues to score 2001 objectives and also provides you a chance to practice against upcoming 2003 objectives without having them count in your final score. Throughout this guide, we use Future Owl icons with specially boxed text to alert you to these 2003 items. Successfully answering these non-scored items insures that you are fully aware of the most recent real-world topics.

Part of the TotalRecall IT Certification System Series, this new book fills gaps existing in other study aid material and includes information found in no other book. In just reviewing the table of contents, you will see that TotalRecall Publications gave me complete freedom to build on what I have learned from running a Voc Tech school. For example, the chapter numbers are written in Base 2. This wasn't done to annoy you. The goal is to reinforce your learning binary math, since that is how much of computing works. I also include lots of real-world material so you can continue to use this book as a reference on the job. While I have kept the tone as light as possible, I incorporated a great deal of serious research to demystify some of the terms and technologies.

And we offer another exclusive—a copy of the popular BeachFront Quizzer CD with integrated eBook. The CD includes practice exams drawn from a base of over 250 questions, along with answers linked to an eBook version of this guide.

So, if you are in the game for in-depth understanding, this is the complete "certification success system" for you. However, if you are already networking and don't need a certification/reference/killer idea book, then try one of our two other guides from TotalRecall Publications. ExamInsight for CompTIA A+ Operating System Technology 220-232 is a manual with compact information and practice questions that includes a $20 discount for a BeachFront Quizzer online exam. ExamWise for CompTIA A+ Operating System Technology 220-232 is a great Q&A guide that uses a unique format of two questions per page, with answers and explanations on the reverse page. It also includes free access to a BeachFront Quizzer online exam.

I encourage questions from readers and want to support you in your work. To me, it is another form of networking, and I look forward to hearing from you. Tcat@tcat.net

A quick overview of the chapters in this book.

Table of Contents

Acknowledgments

Whoa

For the first time, this page (at least for me) isn't the usual yada-yada.

This book is one of a series that is part of the Total Recall System. Combining all the ways a human mind takes in information and teaching both sides of the brain has taken quite a bit of development time and patience from literally hundreds of people. Yes, I sincerely thank you all. And for those who's patience was particularly well-tested, my apologies.

Bruce Moran of TotalRecall Publications, Inc. along with the rest of his team deserves several Tips of the hat for having the courage to run with such a far-reaching concept as Total Recall System. More thank you is due to my family and friends such as Pam Fanstill. All of you may be geographically distant, and you didn't let that stop you from support by phone and email. And I cannot forget the students and interns at TotalRecall Publications, Inc., Inc. for the thousands of hours of testing and offering advice. Now we all have a better understanding of the saying, "Rome wasn't built in a day".

Tcat Houser

Tcat@tcat.net

How to Read this Book

This book at first glance appears to be a bit different than the ordinary "TECH TEXT BOOK". It is our hope that the layout and format will make it easier for you to absorb all the concepts and terminology contained herein.

We have used **icons** (pictures that represent something) and a variety of Owl's ™ to help you stay **focused** on the **critical material**.

Owl is used with **permission** from **Tcat.net,** a successful **interactive training school**. Owl™ is their **mascot** to represent what life can look like in **IT** (Information Technology). **Life** can be very **busy** and feel like once you got on the wheel the learning never stops. We would be doing you a disservice to pretend otherwise. Instead we offer **study tools** to assist you in managing your learning beginning with this book.

The first **tool** we offer in the form of **Owl's** are the **Success Owl's**.

We want you to focus on the key point contained there so you do not get sidetracked with all the other information that comes at you.

First and **foremost** you **cannot**, we repeat *cannot know it all*. **Relax, sit back** and **learn** what is critical and pertinent, then build on that information step by step. Get those basics down and then grow with that information.

We **separate** what **portions** of **information** are nice to know and are **historical** in nature, we also share **real world tips**. We know that **learning** from a book to pass a **certification exam** is **far** from all that you need to know to be **functional** in the **real world**.

We encourage questions! We find that if you are **patient**, and go **through** and **complete** the **exercises** this will reinforce your **learning** and the **information** will **stick** with you.

We ask the average student to plan on a **minimum** of **10 hours** of **study time** after **completing** the **course**.

You will also **notice** that many **words** are **bolded** for you. Concentrate on the bolded words to get the main topic points. This system is known as **Learning At a Glance** and is part of the **Reading At a Glance Total Recall System**™.

The **highlighting** is **pre-done** for you to **eliminate** any **confusion** as to what **points** are key. Learn to **focus** on just the **bolded words** and your **reading** will **move** along more **quickly**. The **emphasis** of the **bold words** will stay with you **longer**.

A **visual person** you say? We have included lots of **pictures** and **screen shots** of the **topics** under **discussion** to help you **correlate** what you are **reading** with what you will **see** live.

We hope we have addressed all of the many learning styles out there with **SEE IT DO IT HEAR IT READ IT**™.

ReadMe.1st

Battle-scared **field** computer **engineers,** and **Information Technology (IT) Trainers, designed** this book, **ExamInsight A+ Certification.** Rest assured that while it is obviously quite **different** from the typical **book you have seen,** we had several **reasons** for any variation from the typical tech book.

We strongly **suggest** that **regardless of** your **experience level, read** casually from this page **forward to the end** for the first time through.

One **difference** you will find is **how text** is **bolded.** The **logic** behind how **this process** was applied is to known as **Reading at a Glance.** Try it. **Stop** here, and **go back** and **read** just the **bolded words.**

Notice that while some of the conversational tone disappears, logical **facts stand out.** In short, we **embedded highlighting** into the typeface. So, if you must highlight, feel free. And if you **never learned** how to properly **use** a **highlighter,** you can **use this book** to **learn.**

When cramming for the **test,** just **review** the **bolded words.**

Our philosophy continues with blending **humor, real-world lessons learned,** and **continued support.** This is expanded on next paragraph.

Humor – All the facts and figures can be boring, by themselves. Wherever possible, we **explain** the **economic politics** from a **historical** perspective.

At least this way, you know **why** sometimes **our industry** can be **both brilliant** and **"FUBAR'd"** all at the same time. No that is one acronym we won't spell out for you! :-)

The tone is informal, slightly publicity incorrect, at least more so than other books, less so than Maximum PC magazine.

Real-world Lessons for the Classroom

If you purchased this book in **paper media,** you will notice it was designed **compact size,** and in some versions, **loose leaf.** This is so it takes **less space** on an already crowded computer **desk** and **lays flat.** Also by not binding, we can quickly effect changes for errors, omissions, and outright changes in the industry. For more information on educational and customization contact TotalRecall Publications at 281-992-3131.

Since you the reader are attempting to learn the ins and outs of the IT industry, we have brought you what it looks like to "eat your own dog food." This book **doesn't have** the traditional label of **introduction**. Instead, we used a **popular** form **in IT** as your first clue to **look for** whenever you are **unpacking** a new piece of computer **hardware** or **software**. It is **called, Readme.1st**, READ.ME, or Read.ME!, or other clearly labeled warning that is too often ignored.

The bottom line for ANY PC is, either On or Off. Early in this book, you will learn that this is a Binary option. Binary means two. Computers work in binary. So, to assist you in thinking in binary, the chapter numbers are in binary.

We have included high-resolution close up pictures to help identify what is being discussed, or used large clear graphics to help convey the message.

Continued Support

As a purchaser of this work, you are automatically entitled to join your fellow readers and authors on a private email list. Experience tells us that learning is more fun and easier when done with a group. You are encouraged to join the students from our physical (brick and mortar) school who are using this book in a classroom, and who keep in touch via email.

To join the others, send an email to: Success@Tcat.net

Subject: Subscribe APlus

If everything goes right you will get an email telling you to respond. (This is to prevent someone else from using us for creative revenge, on you.)

If you don't get a reply, check your email to see if you sent Plain Text (that helps).

Got a thought about this book? Praise us or pan us by writing to: Authors@Tcat.net

We always read each email, and unless we are teaching a class, we respond within hours.

The Why of this book

Tao is Chinese for "how". The how of **ExamInsight** reflects elements of our Tao in the classroom are reflected in this book. The old saying, "Tell them what you are going to tell them. Then tell them. Finally tell them what you told them" has merit. The way the human mind works best is by as many different input styles as possible, and repeat as much as possible.

With that in mind, you will hear some points, said one way, then referred to or re-stated again. This is not because we all hid in our corners and typed away. We compared notes throughout the process quite frequently. And when we felt that a point was a 'gotcha', in the real world, we each spoke our peace. A wise person could consider the repetitions a 'gotcha meter'.

Icon Alerts

These are the symbols or keys to information alerts; use them as another study aid.

Historical Owl

This is material that is not directly testable by CompTIA and the A+ test, but may either help you 'pull on the thread' so you can see why something is.

Geek Owl

This is material that is too deep for CompTIA and the A+ test. And knowing it will help you put the topic together.

Future Owl

This indicates a topic that should be on your radar screen. CompTIA generally only tests for what are 'commonly accepted' items in the industry. Future Owl tells you about something coming up because you will look good in a job interview and/or should know about something that will make something hot today, not tomorrow.

Real World Owl

RW Owl (a.k.a real world) describes tips for understanding the difference between by the book and the real world out there in IT.

Who is the Owl?

Owl is a registered trademark of TotalRecall Publications, Inc., Inc. *Owl* is an honest presentation of how the computer industry looks to us. It is a reflection of the continued learning that is necessary to be a success in this business. That is what this industry is about. IT is in a constant state or refreshment and therefore a lively, never boring chosen field.

With this, we warmly welcome you to an exciting life in IT!

Yours truly.

Helen O'Boyle with Tcat Houser & the Development Team

Exam Details

What you need to know about the exam.

Who may take the tests?

A+ Certification is open to anyone. The A+ exam is targeted for entry-level computer service technicians with at least 6 months on-the-job experience. No specific requirements are necessary, except payment of the fee.

Exam Title & Number; OS/Windows Exam

Exam #220-232

- approximately 80 Questions
- 469 Passing Score, based on a range of 100-900
- 90 Minutes Exam Time

Taking the Test

Please arrive at the testing center at least 15 minutes before the test is scheduled to begin. The administrator of the testing center can demonstrate how to use the computer-based testing system before the actual test begins. Two forms of identification must be presented to the test center administrator. One form should be a photo ID, such as a valid driver's license. The other can be a major credit card, or a passport. Please be aware that both forms of identification must have a signature. Books, calculators, laptop computers, or other reference materials are not allowed during the test. Because the test is computer-based, pens, pencils, or paper will not be needed. It is CompTIA's policy to make reasonable accommodations for individuals with disabilities.

After the Test, how it works!

As soon as you finish the test, you receive the final score. You will see the results immediately on the computer screen. In addition, a hard copy of the score report is provided at the testing center. The score report shows whether or not you passed the certification. It will also show all objectives related to every item not answered correctly. It can be used to verify your certification until your certificate arrives.

If you pass the examination, a certificate will be mailed to you within 4 to 6 weeks. Should you not receive your certificate and information packet within 6 weeks of passing your exam, please contact CompTIA at fulfillment@comptia.org . You can also contact the fulfillment department for replacement certificates.

Exam Assessment:

A+ Certification is a CompTIA-sponsored testing program that certifies the competency of entry-level (6 months experience) computer service technicians. The A+ test contains situational, traditional, and identification types of questions. All of the questions are multiple choices. The test covers a broad range of hardware and software technologies, but is not bound to any vendor-specific products.

Major computer hardware and software vendors, distributors, resellers and publications back the program. A+ certification signifies that the certified individual possesses the knowledge and skills essential for a successful entry-level (6 months experience) computer service technician, as defined by experts from companies across the industry.

Domain 1.0 Operating System Fundamentals 30%

1.1 **Identify the operating system functions and structure and major system files to navigate the operating system and how to get to needed technical information.**

Major Operating System functions

- Create folders
- Checking OS Version

Major Operating System Components

- Explorer
- My Computer
- Control Panel

Contrasts between Windows 9X and Windows 2000 Major system files:

- What they are
- Where they are located
- How they are used
- And what they contain

System, Configuration, and User Interface files

- IO.SYS
- BOOT.INI
- WIN.COM
- MSDOS.SYS
- AUTOEXEC.BAT
- CONFIG.SYS
- COMMAND LINE PROMPT

Memory management

- Conventional
- Extended/upper memory
- High memory
- Virtual memory
- HIMEM.SYS
- EMM386.exe

Windows 9x

- IO.SYS
- WIN.INI
- USER.DAT
- SYSEDIT
- SYSTEM.INI
- SETVER.EXE
- SMARTDRV.EXE
- MSCONFIG (98)
- COMMAND.COM
- DOSSTART.BAT
- REGEDIT.EXE
- SYSTEM.DAT
- RUN COMMAND
- DriveSpace

Windows 2000 Computer Management

- BOOT.INI
- REGEDT32
- REGEDIT
- RUN CMD
- NTLDR
- NTDETECT.COM
- NTBOOTDD.SYS

Command Prompt Procedures (Command syntax)

- DIR
- ATTRIB
- VER
- MEM
- SCANDISK
- DEFRAG
- EDIT
- XCOPY
- COPY
- FORMAT
- FDISK
- MSCDEX
- SETVER
- SCANREG

1.2 **Identify basic concepts and procedures for creating, viewing and managing files, directories and disks.**

This includes procedures for changing file attributes and the ramifications of those changes (for example, security issues).

Content may include the following:

- File attributes
- Read Only, Hidden, System, and Archive attributes
- File naming conventions (Most common extensions)
- Windows 2000 COMPRESS, ENCRYPT
- IDE/SCSI
- Internal/External
- Backup/Restore
- Partitioning/Formatting/File System
- Fat
- Fat 16
- Fat 32
- NTFS4
- NTFS5
- HPFS
- Windows-based utilities
- ScanDisk
- Device manager
- System Manager
- Computer Manager
- MSCONFIG.EXE
- REGEDIT.EXE (View information/Backup registry)
- REGEDT32.EXE
- ATTRIB.EXE
- EXTRACT.EXE
- DEFRAG.EXE
- EDIT.COM
- FDISK.EXE
- SYSEDIT.EXE
- SCANREG
- WSCRIPT.EXE
- ASD.EXE (Automatic Skip Driver)
- Cvt1.EXE (Drive Converter FAT16 to FAT32)
- HWINFO.EXE

Domain 2.0 Installation, Configuration and Upgrading 15%

This domain requires knowledge of installing, configuring and upgrading Windows 9x, and Windows 2000. This includes knowledge of system boot sequences and minimum hardware requirements.

2.1 Identify the procedures for installing Windows 9x , and Windows 2000 for bringing the software to a basic operational level.

- Start Up
- Partition
- Format drive
- Loading drivers
- Run appropriate set up utility

2.2 Identify steps to perform an operating system upgrade.

- Upgrading Windows 95 to Windows 98
- Upgrading from Windows NT Workstation 4.0 to Windows 2000
- Replacing Windows 9x with Windows 2000
- Dual boot Windows 9x/Windows NT 4.0/2000

2.3 Identify the basic system boot sequences and boot methods, including the steps to create an emergency boot disk with utilities installed for Windows (x, Windows NT, and Windows 2000.

- Startup disk
- Safe Mode
- MS-DOS mode
- NTLDR (NT Loader), BOOT.INI
- Files required to boot
- Creating emergency repair disk (ERD)

2.4 Identify procedures for loading/adding and configuring application device drivers, and the necessary software for certain devices.

- Windows 9x Plug and Play and Windows 2000
- Identify the procedures for installing and launching typical Windows and non-Windows applications. (Note: there is no content related to Windows 3.1)
- Procedures for setting up and configuring
- Windows printing subsystem Network printing
- Setting Default printer
- Installing/Spool setting
- Network printing (with help of LAN admin)

Domain 3.0 Diagnosing and Troubleshooting 40%

<u>3.1</u> **Recognize and interpret the meaning of common error codes and startup messages from the boot sequence, and identify steps to correct the problems.**

- Safe Mode
- No operating system found
- Error in CONFIG.SYS line XX
- Bad or missing COMMAND.COM
- HIMEM.SYS not loaded
- Missing or corrupt HIMEM.SYS
- SCSI
- Swap file
- NT boot issues
- Dr. Watson
- Failure to start GUI
- Windows Protection Error
- Event Viewer - Event log is full
- A device referenced in SYSTEM.INI, WIN.INI, Registry is not found

<u>3.2</u> **Recognize common problems and determine how to resolve them.**

- Eliciting problem symptoms from customers
- Having customer reproduce error as part of the diagnostic process
- Identifying recent changes to the computer environment from the user
- Troubleshooting Windows- specific printing problems
- Print spool is stalled
- Incorrect/incompatible driver for print
- Incorrect parameter

Other Common problems

- General Protection Faults
- Illegal operation
- Invalid working directory
- System lock up
- Option (Sound card, modem, input device) or will not function
- Application will not start or load
- Cannot log on to network (option NIC not functioning)
- TSR (Terminate Stay Resident) programs and virus
- Applications don't install
- Network connection

Viruses and virus types

- What they are
- Sources (floppy, emails, etc.)
- How to determine presence

Domain 4.0 Networks 15%

This domain requires knowledge of network capabilities of Windows and how to connect to networks on the client side, including what the Internet is about, its capabilities, basic concepts relating to Internet access and generic procedures for system setup. The scope of this topic is only what is needed on the desktop side to connect to a network.

4.1 Identify the networking capabilities of Windows including procedures for connecting to the network.

Content may include the following:
- Protocols
- IPCONFIG.EXE
- WINIPCFG.EXE
- Sharing disk drives
- Sharing print and file services
- Network type and network card
- Installing and Configuring browsers
- Configure OS for network connection

4.2 Identify concepts and capabilities relating to the Internet and basic procedures for setting up a system for Internet access.

Content may include the following:

Concepts and terminology
- ISP
- TCP/IP
- IPX/SPX
- NetBEUI
- E-mail
- PING.EXE
- HTML
- HTTP://
- FTP
- Domain Names
- (Web sites)
- Dial up networking
- TRACERT.EXE
- NSLOOKUP.EXE

Ability is what you are capable of doing.

-Lou Holtz-

Chapter 0000: How to get there

The objective of this chapter is to provide the reader with an understanding of the following:

How Operating Systems work
     Anatomy of an OS
Operating System Features
     CDI vs. GUI Interface
     Command-driven interface
     DOS Prompt CDI Interface
     Graphical User Interface
A Window IS?
     Mouse clicks
     Mouse Adjustment
     Mouse Control Chart
     The TAB Key
     TAB Key Table
     The Keyboard
     Shortcut Keys
     Basic Shortcut Keys for Desktop
     The Windows Key & The Start Menu
The Desktop Navigation
     Navigating the desktop
     What is a cursor?
     Customizing the Desktop
     Pop Up Menus?
     What's This?
     Context
     Create Shortcut
     Send To > Desktop
     Windows menus and dialog boxes
My computer, and Version information
     Create a folder
     Drag and Drop
     The Recycle Bin
     The Task Bar
     Multiple Windows
     How to get there from here
     The Open Option
     Explorer

Introduction

This section of the A+ Training manual prepares you for the **Operating System**s and software CompTIA A+ exam, which is the second of the two exams required for CompTIA A+ certification.

Getting Ready - Questions

1. What must be loaded to boot Windows 9x?
A: MOUSE.SYS
B: HIMEM.SYS
C: SETVER.EXE
D: EMM386.EXE

2. What does ATTRIB.EXE allow? (Choose two)
A: multiple file types
B: modification in file attributes
C: modification in folder attributes
D: attribution of file types to unknown files
E: changes in the attributes of Windows programs

3. The function key which, when pressed as Windows is starting up, causes
    Windows to start in safe mode is:
A.   F5
B.   Alt-F1
C.   F3
D.   F8

4. Actions you can perform with Windows Explorer include: (Choose all that apply)
A.   Reinstall device drivers
B.   Copy files
C.   Create files
D.   Check the Windows OS for problems
E.   Drag and drop folders

5.   Which of the following statements are true of shortcuts?
A.   Deleting a shortcut does not delete the original file it points to
B.   You can create a shortcut to a web page using Internet Explorer
C.   A shortcut always uses as much disk space as the original file it points to
D.   A shortcut can only be created by a Windows Administrator

Getting Ready - Answers

1. Correct Answer: B

2. Correct Answers: B&C

3. Correct Answer: D

4. Correct Answers: B, C and E

5. Correct Answers: A & B

II How Operating Systems work

To be functional with a computer it is necessary to understand how the interface operated by the computer user works. This interface is known as the **Operating System** (OS).

An **Operating System controls** the **hardware** and the **applications** (programs) used on a computer. Understanding how the OS works assists us in making informed decisions regarding **hardware** and **software** purchases.

Anatomy of an OS

Before we get into the details of *specific* **Operating Systems**, it is useful to understand what an **Operating System** is, and what it does.

In your A+ Core studies, you learned that the CPU is the heart of the computer, responsible for controlling the activities that occur on it.

When the CPU is shipped to you from the factory, it knows how to perform various simple activities like "add 1 to this memory address" or "move 1 byte from this memory address to this memory address".

By themselves, these instructions aren't very interesting. Most people probably wouldn't wander down to the local computer store and give someone $1000 for a couple really big boxes whose talents consisted of the ability to move 8 bits from one location in memory to another.

However, the instructions become interesting when they are combined by a computer programmer into step-by-step sequences consisting of hundreds of instructions, and the step-by-step sequence is given to the **CPU** (central processing unit), the computers brain.

With the right sequence of instructions, the **CPU** knows how to accomplish many complex activities, that computers are known for today - sending email, playing the latest computer games, surfing the net, and even formatting the resume you want to send out as soon as you become A+ certified.

These sequences of CPU instructions are called **computer programs**.

A program is an **ordered set** of **instructions**, generally in a **binary** machine language specific to the **CPU** type on which it will run, which tells the **CPU** which steps to take, to perform one or more useful actions.

An **Operating System** (OS) is a **collection** of **special programs** running on your computer, which sits between the computer hardware, which you learned about in A+ Core, and application (task-oriented) programs such as word processors, Internet browsers, email programs and spreadsheets.

The Operating System is the set of **utility functions** and **programs** that make it possible for applications to access your computer hardware, and for you to manage the use of your applications and the hardware.

Because it must perform many hardware-specific functions, an **Operating System** is **specific** to the **type** of **computer** on which it will be run.

For example, there are Operating Systems which run on standard PC's, with Intel or AMD processors, and motherboards with PCI or ISA slots.

There are also Operating Systems for Macintosh computers, and other Operating Systems for larger mini-computers and mainframes.

Some Operating Systems like Linux are available for multiple different types of computers. However, it is more common for an Operating System to be associated with a certain type of computer. For example, Intel and AMD CPU-based PC's generally run some version of Windows.

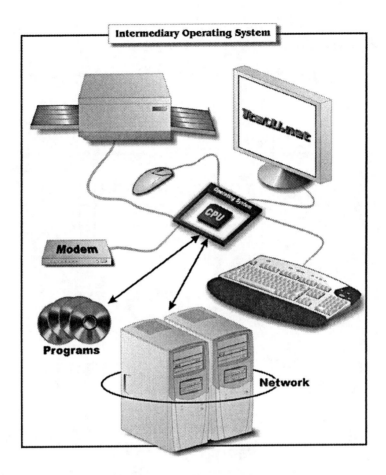

Figure 1 Intermediary Operating System

A+ Focus

The A+ test focuses on standard PC architecture

As a reminder to how a computer functions, we have included our binary chart here.

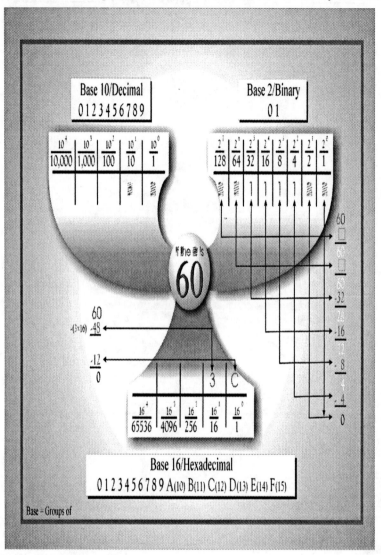

Figure 2 The Binary Chart

The Operating System knowledge requirements for A+ certification focus on the most common PC Operating Systems. In prior years, these were MS-DOS, Microsoft Windows 3.1 and Microsoft Windows 95. As of 2001, the computer Operating Systems an A+ certification candidate should be familiar with are:

DOS

Microsoft Windows 95

Microsoft Windows 98

Microsoft Windows NT

Microsoft Windows 2000 Professional

The latest release of Windows for PC desktops, known as Windows XP (available in "Professional" and "Home" versions), has been out for a while. Windows XP questions are currently being incorporated into the A+ OS certification but are not being scored at this time. Similarly, the next release of Windows known as Windows 2003 servers or Windows .NET Server, has not yet been incorporated into the exam as of late 2003.

Just like any other program, to be used, an Operating System has to be installed on your computer.

Sometimes an Operating System is "pre-installed" on a new computer's hard disk; other times, particularly if you are building a computer from parts, you must purchase the Operating System software, and install it yourself.

Either way, the Operating System is the first piece of software installed on your computer, before applications like Microsoft Word, Netscape, Lotus Notes or Quake.

Usually it is provided on CD-ROM media, like any other software package. We'll look at understanding and configuring, or personalizing each of the Microsoft Windows Operating Systems one by one.

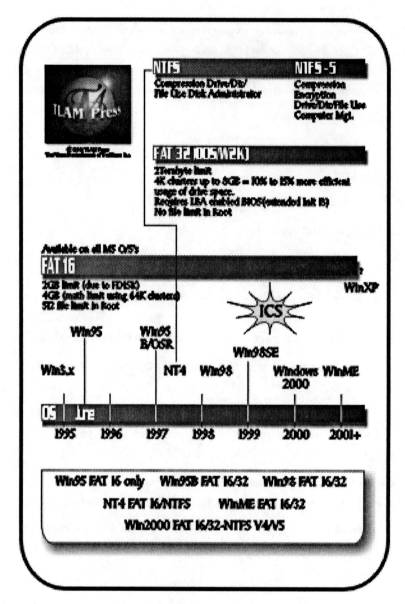

Figure 3 Operating System Family & File Structure Timeline

III Operating System Features

An Operating System has several features and requirements. Navigational ability is required to understand the features of a menu and some sort of organizational structure as in a file structure. We also need to understand as part of the navigation the differences between the look of the Operating System we are working with.

CDI vs. GUI Interface

The Operating System also provides the user interface that you use to communicate with the Operating System. For example, you install and configure the Operating System, troubleshoot it if things go wrong (of course, that wouldn't ever happen to you, would it?), identify yourself to the system (log in), start programs and switch between multiple programs The user interface simply put it what the Operating System looks like to you, on the computer screen.

There are two primary types of computer user interfaces:

Command-driven interface (**CDI**)

Graphical user interface (**GUI**)

Command-driven interface

The command driven interface or **CDI**, is navigated via the keyboard. It can display and accept as input, ASCII text characters like A-Z, a-z, 0-9, !#*$&@^, etc., but does not handle graphics. You communicate with the OS by typing commands like "copy A:*.* B:" or "dir". It communicates back to you by displaying the results of your command, generally directly below the area of the screen in which you typed the command.

What CompTIA calls the **CDI** is more usually referred to in the real world as a **CLI**, or command-line interface. But as far as the A+ certification goes, they want you to call the non-GUI user interface, a **CDI.**

DOS Prompt CDI Interface

```
Command Prompt                                         _ □ X
               0 Dir(s)   5,734,723,584 bytes free         ▲

C:\>cd mydata

C:\mydata>copy d:ocp.doc .
        1 file(s) copied.

C:\mydata>dir
 Volume in drive C has no label.
 Volume Serial Number is 5018-281C

 Directory of C:\mydata

01/13/2001  06:30p    <DIR>          .
01/13/2001  06:30p    <DIR>          ..
11/16/1999  04:34p          1,914,368 appx408.exe
01/13/2001  06:31p    <DIR>          n990-firmware1.1
11/30/2000  07:55p            647,168 ocp.doc
             2 File(s)      2,561,536 bytes
             3 Dir(s)     950,509,568 bytes free

C:\mydata>copy ocp.doc ocp-new.doc
        1 file(s) copied.

C:\mydata>_
```

Figure 4 The CDI Interface

Users are required to type in the exact format of the command expected by the Operating System, which means that it's difficult to walk up to a command-driven interface for a new type of Operating System, and accomplish anything productive without a bit of study beforehand. The other side of this is that once you do master using an OS from the command line, you can often be more productive than you would be if you limited yourself to the GUI.

In general, a **CDI** also requires that user be fairly familiar with keyboard use, in order to be productive. And if your fingers slip and you type one character incorrectly, the **Operating System** is likely to respond with an error message like, "**Bad command or file name**" or "**File does not exist**", and you'll have to type the command again.

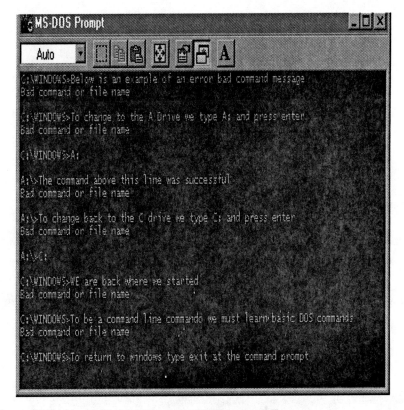

Figure 5 Windows MS-DOS Prompt with Command Errors

Older Operating Systems such as **MS-DOS** depended on **command-driven interfaces**. An MS-DOS style **CDI** is still available in Windows 2000 Professional. This is an example of how to use Windows 2000's **MS-DOS** style **CDI** to manage files (don't worry if this looks like a foreign language - it is!) To find the (nicely generically named) Command Prompt in Windows 2000, go to Start, Programs, Accessories, then choose Command prompt.

In Windows 95 and 98, the same functionality is found in the **MS-DOS Prompt** menu option. To find the **MS-DOS Prompt** MS-DOS Prompt in Windows go to start, programs then choose MS-DOS.

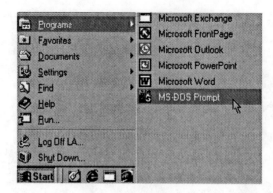

Figure 6 Windows MS-DOS Command Prompt

Why different names for what looks like the same OS function? There are actually subtle differences between the capabilities of **Command Prompt** and **MS-DOS Prompt** that matter to Microsoft's programmers, so Microsoft opted to name them differently. Besides, Microsoft likes to make the point that its NT-based operating systems (NT, 2000) are not built on top of MS-DOS, and this is yet another way of saying, "There is no MS-DOS in this operating system."

Graphical User Interface

A **graphical user interface**, or **GUI**, is usually navigated by a combination of a **keyboard** and pointing device like a **mouse**, touch pad or track ball. This type of interface presents information in a **graphical manner**, and uses its ability to easily display lists of commands, programs, and data files, to replace much of the typing required in a CDI.

The graphic shows us how to use the Windows 98 GUI to view files. Most file management functions can be accomplished by moving the mouse; in a GUI very little typing is required.

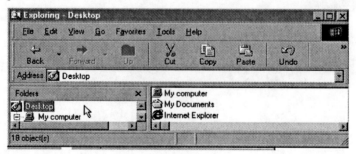

Figure 7 Windows Explorer GUI Interface

Pop Quiz 0000.0

 Pop Quiz 0000.0 *Questions*

1. The type of user interface navigated by the keyboard is:

    A. Windows

    B. RMI

    C. CDI

    D. Mouse-driven

2. The first piece of software you install on a computer is:

    A. Anti-virus program

    B. BIOS

    C. Whichever application you need most

    D. Operating system

3. Windows 2000 includes an MS-DOS Prompt feature

    A. True

    B. False

4. What is an operating system?

    A. The set of computer programs that sit between computer hardware and application programs

    B. A set of productivity programs including Microsoft Word

    C. The only program which runs directly on a computer's CPU

5. Microsoft Windows runs on which types of CPU's? (Choose two)

    A. AMD

    B. Sparc

    C. PowerPC

    D. Intel

Pop Quiz 0000.0 *Answers*

1. Correct Answer: C

2. Correct Answer: D

3. Correct Answer: B

4. Correct Answer: A

5. Correct Answers: A & D

IV A Window IS?

Our primary focus in this chapter will be on navigating around the most common **GUI** interface, referred to as a Window.

Windows or rectangles of information display areas, open up in the Windows family of Operating Systems, when we are accessing information or even when we receive an error message. We need to understand how to **resize, open, close,** and **move** these windows to increase our functionality and navigational ability in the Windows Operating Systems.

At the upper right hand corner of every window, you will see three small squares, called buttons, which always appear in the same order:

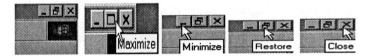

The 3 small squares are navigational keys to managing a window. If you lose track of which button does what, you can always move your mouse pointer over each button, and hold it there for a few seconds. This will cause windows to display a **Tool Tip** describing that button's function, to jog your memory.

The ⬜ square is used to **minimize** a window, temporarily removing it from the main desktop, but leaving it accessible via the tool bar at the bottom of the screen. (Minimize appears). The ⬜ square is used to **restore** a window to its original size and position. (Restore appears). The ⬜ square is used to **maximize** a window, making it take up the full screen (Maximize appears). The ⬛ square is used to **close** a window, which ends the program. (Close appears).

Looking very closely at the screen shots above, you can see that the middle button sometimes displays a picture of a single square, for the **maximize** action, and sometimes a picture of two squares, for the **restore** action. Why did Microsoft use the same buttons for two different actions? Because if a window is already maximized, taking up the full screen, it doesn't make sense to maximize it again... but it does make sense to restore it to its smaller size. And if a window is already small, taking up only part of the screen, restoring it to the same size and position doesn't make sense... but enlarging it to full-screen with the **maximize** function does.

Cursor Help

When the **cursor** is held over one of the **options** a small window will pop up and tell you what the function is.

The information that pops up is called a **Tool Tip**. This works for many function buttons

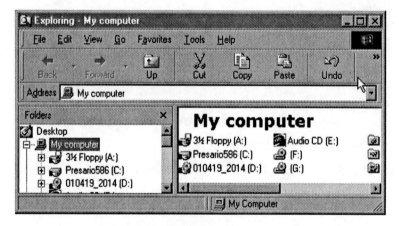

in Windows programs, like Internet Explorer and Microsoft Word.

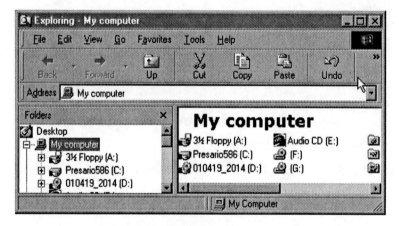

Figure 8 Windows Explorer open window.

There can be many windows open at the same time. We will show you how as we get further along. First we need to understand how to **navigate** Windows with the **keyboard** and **mouse**.

Mouse clicks

The mouse is known as a peripheral device. It is a piece of hardware attached to our computer to make challenging keyboard navigation easier. The mouse has its own **IRQ** and most computer users consider it a vital piece of hardware. They come in many flavors and styles but basically the setup is the same.

The two basic styles you might see are a traditional mouse, which is operated by rolling the device around your desk, and a trackball, which is operated by using your hand or fingers to position the ball in the device, without moving the device itself. The graphics that follow are of a typical trackball and mouse.

The mouse must be configured to use the menu features of an OS. Configuring the mouse is done through the Control Panel. If it is a mouse with special features and functions the manufacturer will include special software and drivers to utilize the special features. You'll find them in the Control Panel along with basic mouse adjustments. If those features are not available, and you know your mouse "should" support them, check to make sure that you have the manufacturer's most current drivers and software installed.

Mouse Adjustment

To use the mouse we must first decide how we want our buttons to be set. These are the buttons that we use to "click" on various menu options.

To adjust the mouse in Windows, go to start, settings, Control Panel then double click on mouse to adjust mouse properties.

Figure 9 Mouse and Mouse icon on taskbar

Notice that the mouse is highlighted on the **task bar** above. To accomplish this (it doesn't usually appear there automatically), this option was selected on the **mouse properties** Window.

This option allows you to click on the **mouse** and adjust settings as necessary, instead of going through the Control Panel to make changes. If your mouse properties allow you to configure the mouse settings to be accessible from the task bar's system tray, seriously consider doing so.

The properties window allows for left or right hand control. For those wishing increased accessibility features there are commands to customize in addition to the basic controls.

Make notes as necessary on the mouse graphic. If you are left-handed you can change how your mouse is setup in mouse properties.

The keys are to learn to double click and single click, and learn which button is which for fast navigation.

The **mouse control chart** will help you with some of the **keys** you can **press** on the **keyboard** along with a **mouse click** for faster navigation. Be aware that in newer versions of Windows, the user can select whether the mouse requires a double-click to open documents (as in "classic Windows"), or will open documents on a single-click (a newer option, designed to save on mouse button-clicking). By default, the mouse will usually be set to "classic Windows" double-click behavior. If you wish to change it to single-click behavior (which will frustrate all visitors to your PC, since the single-click option is not commonly used!), the mouse properties page lets you do that. Look for options like "Single-click to open an item (point to select)" and "Double-click to open an item (single-click to select)".

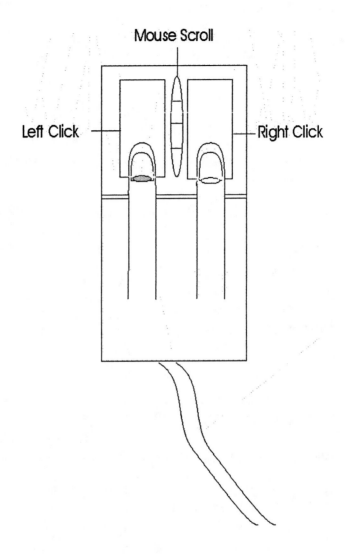

Figure 10 Make a note as to how your mouse is setup.

Mouse Control Chart

Windows Task	Set for Single Click	Set for Double Click
Choose item	Point to the item	Click the item
Open item	Click the item	Double-click the item
Select items in range	Press & hold SHIFT key, & point to the first and last items to select	Press & hold SHIFT key, & click the first and last items to select
Select multiple items	Press & hold CTRL key, and point to each of the items	Press & hold CTRL key, & click each of the items
Drag and drop	Point to selection, Click mouse button, hold it down while dragging then release to drop	Point to selection, press & hold mouse button, and drag item, release to drop

Table 1: Mouse Control

The table above shows how to accomplish various common Windows tasks using either the "Single-click to open" or "Double-click to open" setting. Note that when the mouse is set to use single-click to open, that merely pointing the mouse to an item, which would normally do nothing without the user explicitly clicking a mouse button, selects the item.

The **three** following **options**, the pointer, the hourglass, and the pointing hand, are default icons that show the position of the mouse/pointer. Besides showing you where the mouse pointer is on the screen, the different icons tell you what's going on, on the computer. The icons change with the function at hand. The plain **arrow** means the system is **idle**. It is ready for you to do something like start a program or type a paragraph. The **hourglass** means the system is **busy**. You can move the mouse now but please wait a minute before clicking.

The **pointing hand** means the mouse pointer is currently over a **link** (like a Web link), so click here if you want to activate the link.

Figure 11 The various changes of the cursor/mouse pointer

Single Clicking

If single-click operation is confusing to many users, why is it there? The single click feature is to help use the desktop like the Internet or Web, and is meant to make the PC easier to use by those whose primary interaction with it is through a web browser like Internet Explorer, where typically single-clicking on a hyperlink causes a new web page to open. For more information on this feature go to help in Windows or the View menu in Explorer and review the folder options.

☞✏ Practice using the mouse functions

☞✏ Practice testing your mouse in the Control Panel

The TAB Key

The **TAB** key is designed to make keyboard navigation faster and easier. It also serves one vital function. When the mouse hardware device dies, you need a means of menu navigation until you are able to troubleshoot the mouse or buy a new one. This is where the **TAB** key comes in.

We can go from **icon** to **icon** or **menu** selections. Each time the **TAB** key is pressed you will see each **icon highlighted**. Each time you press the **TAB** key you will **jump** to the next **icon** or **menu** item. Just keep jumping until you get to where you want and use the **Enter** key to select the item.

Notice that the **Yes** button has dots around the button (box) this means you are currently in the highlighted button (box) and can click or use the enter key to select. If the **TAB** key is used, you will jump to the **No** button and back and forth with the **TAB** key until a selection is made.

Figure 12 Highlighting Buttons

The Table includes some examples TAB key use:

TAB Key Table

KEY	FUNCTION
ENTER	**Clicks** the selected button/icon
TAB	Move **forward** through options
SHIFT+TAB	Move **backward** through options
CTRL+TAB	Move **forward** through **Tabs**
CTRL+SHIFT+TAB	Move **backward** through **Tabs**

Table 2The TAB Key Table

☞🖑 Practice the TAB key to move through the options (icons) on the desktop.

The Keyboard

The keyboard shown is an example of a keyboard designed for use with a **Windows Operating System**.

Becoming familiar with the various keys will make a difference in the speed and efficiency with which you can work through documents, play games or surf the Internet.

There are quite a variety of keyboard tutorials and practice programs available. You are encouraged to make use of some of the **shareware** programs (free to try until you decide to buy) that can be found by simply typing in "typing shareware" in your Internet search engine.

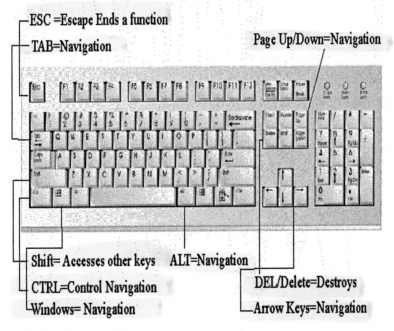

Figure 13 The Keyboard Functions

Notice the **key** that shows the Windows icon. The **Windows key** when pressed, will **display** (geeks will say bring up) a **menu**. For the **keyboard** driven user this eliminates a mouse click to get the menu open.

Why does this matter in 2002, since you can use a GUI instead? When the **mouse** does not work we need to know how to **drive** with the **keyboard** alone. Also, as you use the computer more frequently, you may find that it's faster for you to do certain actions with the mouse, and certain ones with the keyboard. And as an A+ technician, you may one day have to troubleshoot a system with a malfunctioning keyboard. So knowing how to use both effectively can be very useful.

Also, it is important to note that before a mouse driver is loaded, we must perform various functions without a mouse, such as **BIOS** settings and changes. Becoming keyboard driven is also an ergonomically sound practice.

Shortcut Keys

The keyboard has several keys used in everyday navigation. They are the **Ctrl** (control) key, the **Alt** (alternate) key and the **Del** (delete) key.

The **delete** key is found in more than one place on the standard keyboard. We also use the **Backspace**, **Shift** and **Tab** keys. The **arrow keys** ←↓→↑ found next to the number keys to the left of the main keyboard area are also used for navigation, and make traversing the **CDI** Operating Systems easier.

While some CDI's require that you type in commands on a virtually-blank screen with a "command prompt", some features accessible only by **CDI** can be reached by a text-based menu that tells you which keys to use to navigate through the choices on the screen. For example in the Core portion of the A+ studies we used the **plus +** and **minus** – and Page Up/Page Down keys to navigate the BIOS menus.

Basic Shortcut Keys for Desktop

KEY	FUNCTION
ESC Escape	Cancels ("escapes from") a function
F3	Recall entry (displays last command in MS-DOS prompt or Command Prompt mode)
F5	Refresh (when used in Explorer or Internet Explorer)
F8	Safe Mode/bypasses GUI (when used during system startup)
TAB	Navigation
Shift	Accesses other keys
CTRL Control	Navigation
Windows/Start	Navigation
ALT	Navigation
DEL Delete	Destroys
Page Up/Down	Navigation
Arrow Keys	Navigation

Table 3 Basic Key Chart Functions

☞ Practice using the keys

The Windows Key & The Start Menu

The **Windows key** [img] is a key found on most of the newer keyboards or so-called Internet keyboards. Pressing this key will display the **Start Menu** for Windows, activating the **desktop** and **Operating System** menu, which can also be activated by clicking our mouse on the **Start button** icon, **Start**, or using the Alt-Esc key combination.

Start is found most usually (by default) in the lower left hand corner of the desktop screen. If you place your cursor (mouse pointer) over this start button and use a single right mouse click, a menu of options appears. They are **Open**, **Explore**, **Find**.

To be sure we are on the desktop, rather than in a program Window, look for the **cursor** |. If nothing is happening, **left** clicking the mouse in an empty area (area without an icon) of the desktop once will **activate** the **desktop**.

When you right click, you will see a menu of options for the desktop like this:

Figure 14 Start menu right click

☞ ✍ Practice_right clicking the menu options

The **Start** menu of programs can be rearranged to suit. To do this, go to then choose the **Taskbar** and **Start Menu**.

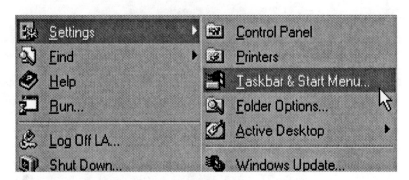

A screen similar to the following will appear:

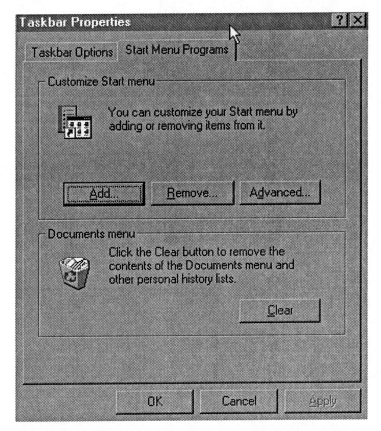

Figure 15 Task Bar Start Menu Programs

From this Window, Start Menu Programs can be arranged or removed to suit.

☞✍Practice arranging the Start Menu

As we go along, we will learn a bit more about how to use these basic keys, as well as a few others.

The following charts are designed to help you learn to use the keys on your keyboard for faster navigation and fewer mouse clicks. The chart is only for the Windows Key.

 KEY Shortcuts

Press the	Function
	Display the Start menu
+TAB	Moves through buttons on the taskbar
+F	Displays Find: All Files
CTRL++F	Displays Find: Computer
+F1	Displays Help
+R	Displays the Run command
+BREAK	Displays the System Properties dialog box
+E	Displays Windows Explorer
+D	Minimize or restore all windows
SHIFT++M	Undo minimize all windows

Table 4 Start ShortcutsKEY	FUNCTION
ESC Escape	Cancels a function
Backspace	Delete typing
F2	Rename
F3 + Key	Display Find (application key)
F4	Open Save/Dialog box
F5	Refresh Window (when used in Explorer or Internet Explorer)
F6	Switch Left & Right Panes Display Window
F8	Boot to Safe Mode/Bypass GUI startup (when used during system startup) Line by line confirmation
F8 + Shift	Refresh the Desktop
F10	Activates menu bar
TAB	Navigation
Shift	Accesses other keys
CTRL Control	Navigation
Windows	Navigation
ALT	Navigation
DEL Delete	Destroys
Enter	Make a selection
Page Up/Down	Navigation
Arrow Keys	Navigation ← Left ↑ Up →Right ↓ Down
Spacebar	Add Space in typing

Table 5 Start ShortcutsKEY	FUNCTION
Shift + DEL	Permanent Delete (No Copy to Recycle Bin)
ALT + F4	Close a Window
ALT + TAB	Switches Windows
CTRL + C	Copy
CTRL + X	Cut
CTRL + V	Paste
CTRL + P	Print
CTRL + ESC	Start Menu
CTRL + Z	UNDO
CTRL + A	Select All
Shift + F10	Display Shortcuts Options Menus
TAB	TAB Forward
CTRL+TAB	TAB Forward Options
CTRL+TAB	TAB Backward
CTRL+SHIFT+TAB	TAB Backward thru Options
Left Arrow ←	Collapse Selection In Explorer
Right Arrow →	Expand Selection In Explorer

Table 6 Shortcut Keys

Pop Quiz 0000.1

 Pop Quiz 0000.1 *Questions*

1. The key used to bring up the Windows Start Menu is:
   A. Windows key
   B. Alt-F1
   C. Alt key
   D. Coke-bottle key

2. Most windows include a button with an X in the upper-right-hand corner. What does this button do when mouse clicked?
   A. Minimizes the window
   B. Shuts down Microsoft Windows
   C. Closes the window
   D. Moves the window

3. The Control Panel can be found under the _____ option on the Windows Start Menu:
   A. Settings
   B. Programs
   C. Help
   D. Printers

4. Windows is usually set up so that a _____ click opens a file in Windows Explorer:
   A. Shift
   B. Single
   C. Double
   D. Control

5. Alt-TAB performs what function in Microsoft Windows?
   A. Brings up Performance Monitor
   B. Switches among running windows tasks
   C. Shuts down Microsoft Windows
   D. Brings up the menu in Windows Explorer

Pop Quiz 0000.1 *Answers*

1. Correct Answer: A

2. Correct Answer: C

3. Correct Answer: A

4. Correct Answer: C

5. Correct Answers: B

V The Desktop Navigation

Blueprint: Major Operating System Components

Explorer

My Computer

Control Panel

The **desktop** is the screen you see after booting your computer to the Operating System. We generally refer to this as the display after the **splash** screen. The splash screen is the screen you see announcing the Operating System is loading.

Navigating the desktop

Navigating the desktop and managing the desktop is one of the secrets to becoming a successful Operating System power user.

The desktop has preset **icons** (graphical representations) to help you organize the content of the computer's hard drive. Think of this area just as you would your desk. Your desk has areas where you store messages, file folders, tape, staples and even pictures.

The computer desktop is organized for navigation ease. The desktop icons, appearance and content can be customized. We have already learned to navigate through the desktop by using the tab key.

Main items on the desktop by default are: **My Computer,** a **Network icon, Recycle Bin.**

Figure 16 The Default Desktop Icons

What is a cursor?

The **cursor** is a navigational place marker usually depicted as a blinking vertical bar such as the one after this arrow➔ | . For example, the blinking bar lets you know where you are in a document you are editing. The cursor is moved by using either the **keyboard** (by typing characters or using the arrow keys to move the cursor without adding or changing existing characters) or the **mouse** to point to the next place to input a command or some text.

Cursor Settings

To change the rate the cursor blinks; click start, settings, then Control Panel then keyboard

The Keyboard properties Cursor Blink rate Windows

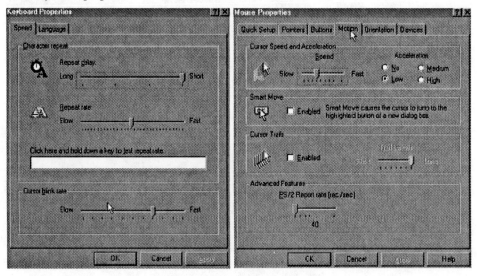

Figure 17 The Keyboard & Cursor Properties Windows

Note: To adjust the slider bars, place cursor on the bar and hold the mouse button down and drag the bar or click repeatedly.

☞✒ **Practice adjusting the cursor rate**

Customizing the Desktop

We can change the look and feel of our desktop by going to the Control Panel.

To open the Display Properties dialog box (menu) begin by clicking Start, **Start** pointing to Settings, **Settings** clicking Control Panel, **Control Panel** and then

double-clicking Display. Display The example you will see is shown below.

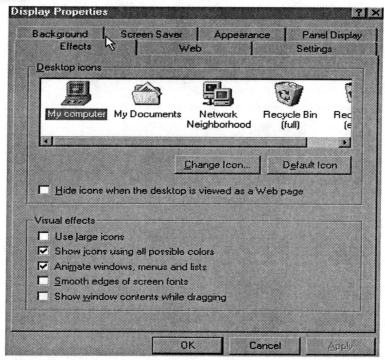

Figure 18 Display Properties Window

All the adjustments that need to be made to the background and icons on your desktop can be made in the **Display Properties** box.

Sometimes after changing the icons it might appear that icons look odd. You might notice that rebooting clears up the odd appearance. It is easier to use the **Shift +F8** keys to **refresh** (update changes) the desktop settings and appearance.

Refresh Key

Use the SHIFT + F8 keys to refresh the desktop.

☞✍ Practice refreshing the desktop

Pop Up Menus?

There are various types of menus hidden within the Windows system and Windows applications designed to assist you in navigation. Many of these windows have shortcut commands designed to help you navigate to tell you what an item is about. One of these types of menus is a pop-up menu, so named because it can "pop up" anywhere on the screen to give you information or let you choose an action to perform. A pop up menu looks like: A text box that pops up with information, as we see in the graphic below.

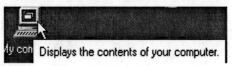

Figure 19 Pop Up menu/Mouseover

Let's look at some common types of pop-up menus now.

What's This?

A **What's This?** Menu 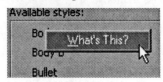 appears when you **mouse over** (or hold the mouse pointer over an item). If you click on the **What's This?** menu you will receive a description of the item. Try hovering the mouse over an area and you will see an example of the mouse over help feature. This example shows the result of hovering the mouse over the "my computer" icon on the desktop.

Figure 18 Mouse over help

☞✍ Practice using the mouse over help feature

Context

A **Context** menu appears when you right click on the desktop or in a program. It shows you actions that make sense in that particular situation, or Context. For example, you've already seen that when you right-click on the **Start** button, you receive a pop-up menu that offers the **Open**, **Explore** and **Find** actions.

☞⤸ **Right click** on the **desktop** and see what actions are available to you

☞⤸ **Right click** on desktop **icons** like **My Computer** and see that they have different actions on their Context menus

Now let's look at some useful Context menu options.

Create Shortcut

A **shortcut** is a convenient path to another program or folder that's usually more difficult to find. A simple means of making a shortcut to a folder or program on your desktop is by right clicking on the folder or program and using the pop up **Context** menu's **Create Shortcut** option. (These are different from the menu shortcuts discussed later.) When you right-click the item, you'll see a pop-up Context menu similar to this one:

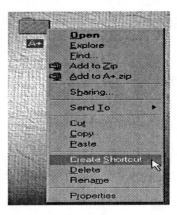

Figure 21 Shortcut Option

Right-click on **Create Shortcut**, and Windows will place on your desktop a special "Shortcut to" icon.

A **shortcut** displays as a small icon with an arrow or pointer to let you know that it is a directional shortcut *not* the *actual* program or folder. A **shortcut** can *safely* **be deleted** without destroying the program or file that it points to.

Using the A+ folder created for the writing of this book as an example, a shortcut was created. The example shows the appearance of the folder before and after the shortcut was created. It is the same folder icon but now has a directional arrow. Shortcuts for programs will display as the program's original icon, with a small directional arrow just like the folder shortcut icon.

Figure 22 The second graphic shows the shortcut icon renamed.

Notice that we can rename a shortcut after we've created it, just like we can rename a file. The **icon** is renamed by **right clicking on the icon**. You might want to do this if you can come up with a better name for the item than the one Windows creates itself, which is usually "Shortcut to" followed by the original program or folder name. Just like deleting a shortcut doesn't delete the program or folder it points to, renaming the shortcut doesn't change the name of the folder or program. In our case above, the original folder is still called "A+".

Shortcut cleanup

You can delete shortcuts by right clicking and choosing Delete.

Highlighting the shortcut and pressing the DEL key will also delete the shortcut.

CTRL+SHIFT + dragging the file or folder will create a shortcut.

Right clicking on an icon in Explorer will create a shortcut.

Send To > Desktop

You can also create a shortcut using the Context Menu's **Send To > Desktop** function. This is useful for creating shortcuts to programs and folders which are not already visible on the desktop. To use this feature, right click on a program or folder, then move the mouse pointer to **Send To**.

As you do this, notice that the highlighted option changes as you move the mouse up and down the menu. Hold the mouse over the **Send To** option until another pop-up menu displays, then click on **Desktop (create shortcut)**.

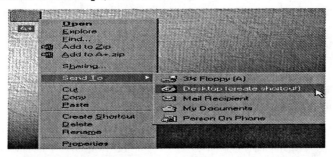

Figure 19 Send To Option

☞✍ Practice creating shortcuts

Windows menus and dialog boxes

In Windows there are many submenus and commands, designed for increased functionality.

You can click on the **title bar** of the window itself, which is the section at the very top of the Window. It's usually one row high and dark blue, to differentiate it from the rest of the window, unless the user has changed their Windows desktop color scheme. Below that is the **menu bar** which lists various submenus of functions you can access, such as **File, Edit, View, Window** and **Help.**

An <u>underlined</u> letter on a menu bar denotes the keyboard shortcut for the menu. To use a keyboard shortcut to bring up a menu, hold down the **ALT** key and press the underlined letter. For example, the "File" menu in many programs is accessed by holding down ALT, pressing the **F** key, and then releasing ALT. Also, an underlined letter on a menu option denotes the keyboard shortcut for that menu item. You may also see a combination next to the menu item consisting of keys on the keyboard that are pressed in combination to access the selected (highlighted) item on the menu. The **SHIFT, ALT** and **CTRL** keys can be held down while pressing other keys such as F4, to access different functions. Refer back to our shortcut key chart regarding functions you can access by pressing multiple keys.

Notice the menu of the screen shot of this work in progress, where right-clicking on the top (above the menu bar) of the open window produced a **context menu** that offers the **ALT + F4** choice.

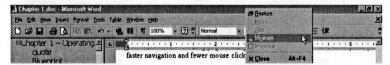

Also notice that there are icons beside **Restore** and **Minimize** to remind you how to manipulate the open window, in addition to the underlined command (control) letters to be used with the **ALT** key or in some cases the **SHIFT** key. The + sign in between the ALT and F4 keys means to press F4 while holding down the ALT key. Grayed out areas mean that the option is not currently available in the menu.

The menus and shortcut keys that are available depend on the application being run. For example, the screen shot above shows the menus available in Microsoft Word. Refer to the help file in the application or for Windows commands use the Windows help file for information on keyboard shortcuts. Most applications have **File**, **Edit** and **Help** menus, with contents appropriate to the application. The other top-level menus vary depending on what the application does and how one uses it.

Notice that the R̲estore command is bolded (available) and the R̲ is underlined. The C̲lose command is also bolded and the C̲ is underlined and also offers the option of using the ALT + F4 key to close the window.

Notice also that the **Close** command has an X beside it. This reminds you that you can close the window by clicking the X at the right hand top corner of the window, with your mouse.

Pop Quiz 0000.2

 Pop Quiz 0000.2 *Questions*

1. Common Windows 2000 desktop items include: (Choose all that apply)

    A. File Shredder

    B. Recycle Bin

    C. My Computer

    D. My Printer

    E. Network Places

2. Which Control Panel applet lets you adjust the cursor blink rate?

    A. Mouse

    B. Display

    C. Regional options

    D. Keyboard

3. You can rename a shortcut by?

    A. Right-clicking on it

    B. Left-clicking on it

    C. Dragging and dropping it

    D. Shift-clicking on it

4. What is a Context menu?

    A. The menu that appears when you right-click an item, giving you options for things to do with it

    B. The help menu that explains when a command is used

    C. The item-specific menu that appears when you press F1 while pointing the mouse at an item

    D. The menu that appears when deleting a file, that lets you choose whether to save a copy of it in the Recycle Bin folder

5. After you change Display Properties, sometimes the desktop icons will appear garbled. To fix this, use:

    A. Ctrl-F8

    B. Shift-F8

    C. Ctrl-F5

    D. Shift-F5

Pop Quiz 0000.2 *Answers*

1. Correct Answers: B, C and E

2. Correct Answer: D

3. Correct Answer: A

4. Correct Answer: A

5. Correct Answers: B

VI   My computer, and Version information

To check which version of an Operating System you are using, go to the desktop and

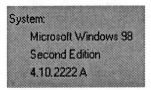

right click on the 'My Computer' icon

Then choose **Properties** from the menu that pops up. The next window that appears will show you the name and version number of your Operating System.

For example, on our work system, we see:

System:
    Microsoft Windows 98
    Second Edition
    4.10.2222 A

Figure 20 Operating System Version Information

Version numbers are important because there can be changes in the same Operating System from the original release date.

Knowing your exact version number is helpful when adding updates or upgrades to new software or even a new Operating System.

The information here will contain the OS name and version. The registration number of the OS license and details of who the OS is registered to which also be displayed.

If your computer was built by a major manufacturer or is a brand name then you will see the information about that as well.

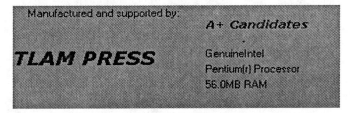

Manufactured and supported by:

A+ Candidates

TLAM PRESS

GenuineIntel
Pentium(r) Processor
56.0MB RAM

Figure 21 The Details on Version Information Screen

One major detail you will find here is the type of processor your Operating System is running on as well as the amount of RAM (memory) your computer has. These are details critical to the optimum performance of your Operating System.

☞✓🖐 Practice checking the OS version

So now we are all on the same page let's practice a bit of functionality.

Create a folder

Creating a folder on your desktop is similar to creating a shortcut. To create a folder on the desktop, place your cursor on an empty area of the desktop and then right click your mouse once. A context menu will appear.

Moving your cursor (mouseover) over the menu will allow submenus to appear (remember we are not clicking again, just moving the cursor over the menu items that appeared). This is also known as highlighting. Notice the appearance change of the area.

The menu you see in the graphic below is an example of this.

Figure 22 The resulting new folder on the desktop

Highlighting the area that says **new** will bring up a submenu and some choices of items that you can create. The choice you want is **Folder**. Notice that the shading changes as we navigate. Clicking on this option will place a new folder on the desktop. Going to the folder and double-clicking it will show that the folder is empty.

This is because the new folder is simply a placeholder, right now -- we have not yet placed any information into it. Closing the folder by clicking on the X, will close the window that appeared to show us the contents of the folder, or in this case the lack of.

After we close the folder and return to the desktop to look at the folder named NEW, we can place our cursor over the folder name NEW and right click to display the context menu for that folder. Choose the **Rename** option, by highlighting and clicking this option once.

Type in the text box, My New folder and then click to release. (This releases the cursor to new commands).

Now we have a folder named My New folder. 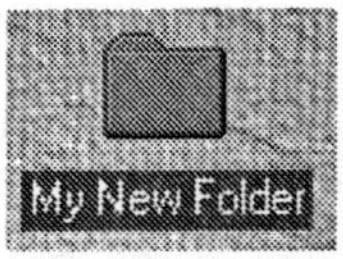

If you noticed on the submenu under Rena<u>m</u>e there was an <u>M</u> underlined in the word rename. If you had used your **Alt** key on the keyboard and pressed the <u>M</u> key at the same time this would have also allowed you to rename your folder, as this is just another way of navigating.

As mentioned earlier, it is often easier and for some faster to be keyboard driven for navigation rather than mouse driven. An example of a user who might prefer keyboard navigation is a data entry clerk who types very fast, and doesn't like to waste time by taking his hands off the keyboard to find and move the mouse.

Returning to our new, let's take a closer look at the context menu that appears when we right click on the folder. The default menu is as follows: Open, explore, find, sharing, send to, cut, copy, paste, create shortcut, delete, rename, properties.

One of these options looks a bit different than the others.

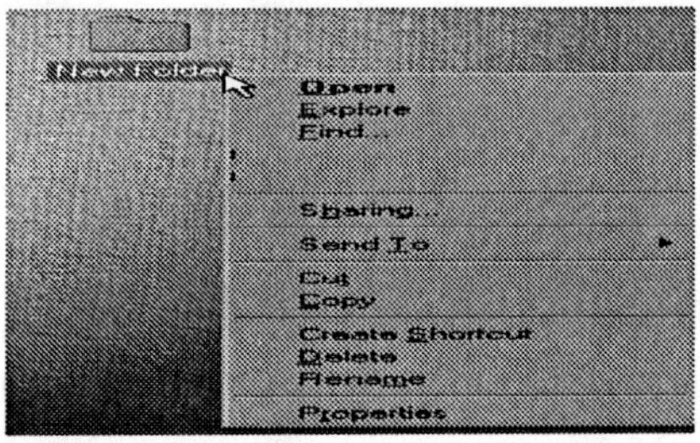

Figure 23 Send To Arrow

If you notice the **Send To** has an arrow 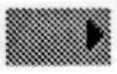 after it meaning that there is yet another sub-menu of choices, which you can reach by pointing the mouse to the **Send To** item, and holding it there momentarily, until another menu appears, to the right of this menu. In this case, the other items that show up, include types of places to which you might want to send this folder, including This is an example of pop-up menu functionality you are likely to see elsewhere in Windows, as you use the system. If you see the arrow 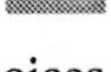 at the edge of a menu item, holding the mouse over that item will display more choices within that action category.

☞🖱 Practice right clicking folders & view a sub menu

SUBMENU

Whenever you see this arrow, ▮▶ remember there is a submenu.

Drag and Drop

Before we continue looking at the Windows Desktop, let's look at one important activity you can perform with the items on the Windows desktop, and elsewhere in Windows.

Drag and drop is a key Windows user interface function to master, because it is used in many places in Windows and in application programs, to move or copy files, text, pictures, etc. from one place to another. Let's look at how drag-and-drop works in Windows. For files and folders, you'd typically use drag and drop to move information from one folder to another, or from the Desktop to another folder (or back).

There are several ways to perform drag-and-drop. As with most keyboard-vs-mouse choices in Windows, which one you use largely comes down to personal preference and convenience.

The most basic drag and drop will **move** a file from one location to another. This means, the file will disappear from its original location, and reappear in the new one. To move a file, place the mouse pointer over the item (a folder, shortcut, program file, document, etc.), highlight it and then click the **left** mouse button. Now, while holding the left mouse button down, move the mouse over to the top of the Recycle Bin and release the mouse button. This is known as drag (moving the mouse with the button pressed) and drop (letting go of the button when the mouse pointer is somewhere else).

If you want to get fancy, and **copy** rather than **move** the file or folder, which means that you'll then have copies of the file in two locations, use the **right** mouse button to drag instead. When you release the mouse button, Windows will pop up a menu asking you what you would like to do – move, copy or create a shortcut. Choose the action you'd like. This is also a good option to use if you just can't seem to remember whether the default drag and drop action is move or copy. (One of the authors has done it just fine this way for years.)

That's the mouse-driven way to drag and drop. Now, let's get the keyboard involved. Remember that using the **left** mouse button to drag will **move** a file? You can instruct Windows to **copy** it instead, by holding down the **CTRL** key and the **left** mouse button as you drag the file to a new location.

There's one exception to the **"left click moves"** rule. If you **drag** a **file** or a folder to a location on a **different disk,** the file will be copied to the other disk, and the original will remain on the first disk.

Shortcut Keys

You can choose whether to move or copy the file, as long as you right-clicked the mouse when you drag it. If you left-click instead, Windows will usually move the file. When you left-click, you can use Windows short-cut keys to tell the system to do something different:

CTRL + Dragging will **Copy** a file

CTRL + SHIFT + Dragging will create a shortcut

☞✍ Practice creating and renaming a folder
☞✍ Practice dragging and dropping (moving and creating files and folders)

There are a few other things to know about the icons we see by default on the Windows desktop.

The Recycle Bin

The Recycle Bin is used to hold files or programs or any data we wish to delete from the computer until we are *sure* we want to delete the information permanently.

The icon for the Recycle Bin is a trash can which appears empty unless there is data in it. If the Recycle Bin contains one or more items, it appears as a trash can holding crumpled pieces of paper.

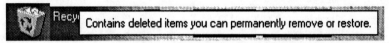

Notice the information that appeared when the pointer was hovered (mouse over) the Recycle Bin.

To delete something from the desktop or a file list in Windows Explorer, we can move it to the **Recycle Bin** with drag and drop. To review drag and drop, here's one way to do it. Place the mouse pointer over the item (a folder, shortcut, program file, document, etc.), highlight it and then right click the item. Now, while holding the right mouse button down, move the mouse over to the top of the Recycle Bin and release the mouse button. This is known as drag (moving the mouse with the button pressed) and drop (letting go of the button when the mouse pointer is somewhere else).

After you've put something into it, the **Recycle Bin** displays as a trash can with crumpled paper. To see what's in it, double click on the **Recycle Bin** like you double clicked on the new folder earlier. A window will open, containing a list of all the items currently in the **Recycle Bin.** If you place the mouse pointer on one of those items and right-click, a context menu will open, giving you the option to **Restore** that item to its original location (un-delete), or to permanently **Delete** the item from the system. In general, you probably don't want to permanently delete items unless you're absolutely sure you don't need them. (This author tends to let things sit in the Recycle bin for at least a month, just in case they're needed later.)

When you drag and drop an item or items into the Recycle Bin you will sometimes be asked if "you are sure that is what you really want to do?" Chose to click on the Yes button to confirm this or try using the ALT + Y keys to confirm the move.

Figure 24 Confirm with ALT + Y

Figure 25 Confirm with TAB key + enter

When you choose to empty the Recycle Bin (which permanently deletes **ALL ITEMS** in the Recycle Bin), you will see one more window popping up to ask you "if you are sure you want to delete those items?"

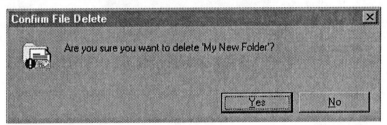

Figure 26 Confirm with TAB key+ enter

RECYCLE BIN DELETES

Once deleted from the Recycle Bin the item *cannot* be restored. Delete or empty a file from the Recycle Bin and it is permanently deleted! This is because all associated entries in the FAT (file allocation Table) are deleted.

If we right click on the Recycle Bin we have a sub-menu that appears. The menu is as follows:

Figure 27 The Recycle bin submenu

Open (this menu opens the bin)

Explore (this option allows viewing of the bin contents)

Empty Recycle Bin (this option empties the contents)(not an option if empty)

Paste (this option lets us drop in a copy of information)

Create Shortcut (this creates a shortcut to the Recycle Bin)

Properties (this option allows us customization of bin properties)

Be sure and set the properties to a size large enough to hold most files or oversize files will be auto deleted. The bin needs to be regularly emptied. If the bin is too full once again auto delete will take place and you will not have the option to recover files.

Recycle bin caution!
Know that changing the size of the recycle bin can save you in the event of an accidental file deletion. If the programs, files or folders are too large for the bin they will be automatically deleted and irretrievable. Increase the size of the recycle bin to allow it to hold more, larger files.

☞✍ Practice exploring the Recycle Bin sub menus
☞✍ Practice deleting and confirming deletion of a folder

The Task Bar

The **task bar** is also found on our desktop and is used for managing several task at a time. By default it is at the bottom of our desktop.

Clicking on the task bar allows us to manage our open windows and what information we want to appear on the taskbar.

The different areas of the Task Bar correspond to different functions available on it. You already know that the Start button displays a menu of programs and other features of your system. Immediately to the right of that area are shortcuts to frequently-used programs and areas of your system. The items in the individual boxes, in the middle of the task bar, are tasks that are underway.

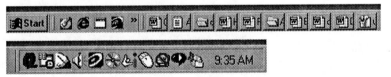

You can see there are 2 folders open, ⌗, plus a number of Word documents and other programs in the middle of the task bar. You can also see the start, [Start] and frequently-used programs to the left, and the time, and the mouse [Mouse] and cd-rom (and other) options to the right. These are all programs either running or items open on the computer. By Clicking on one of these icons will take you directly to the item or to a menu.

To display the taskbar:

> **To permanently display the taskbar**
>
> 1.   Click **Start**, point to **Settings**, and then
>   click **Taskbar & Start Menu**.
>
> 2.   Click to clear the **Auto hide** check box.
>
> **Note**
>
> • You can also open the **Taskbar
>   Properties** dialog box by right-clicking a
>   blank area on the <u>taskbar</u>, and then
>   clicking **Properties**.

To move the taskbar, simply click and drag the taskbar to a different location, at the top, or the left or right side of the screen. Drag while holding the mouse button down.

Notice that in the Windows help information shown above, the word <u>taskbar</u> is underlined. This means you can click on that word for more information. This information is found in the help file in Windows.

The taskbar can also be used to switch between tasks (programs).

> **To switch between running programs**
>
> ▸ Click the program button on the <u>taskbar</u>.
>
> > The taskbar is the bar on your desktop that includes the **Start** button. Buttons
> > representing programs currently running on your computer appear on this bar.

The help menu in Windows will assist you in remembering how to use the <u>taskbar</u>.

Sometimes a program will stop responding due to a variety of reasons. When this happens we can use the CTRL+ALT+DEL keys by pressing them at the same time to bring up a menu listing all the tasks or programs running. We can then end the program or task from the menu that appears without having to reboot our computer to get the computer to respond again. To end a program highlight and click the one you wish to close on the menu to end the task.

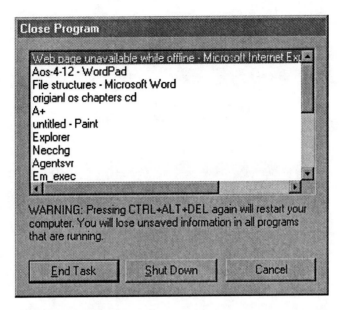

Figure 28 The Task Manager at work

Make special note of the warning listed in the menu. It is also good to know that if you do press the keys that brought up this menu you will reboot your computer.

WARNING: Pressing CTRL+ALT+DEL again will restart your computer. You will lose unsaved information in all programs that are running.

Figure 29 The End program Keys in combination.

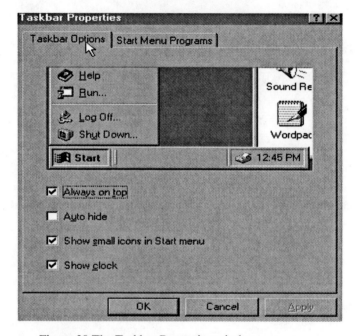

Figure 30 The Taskbar Properties window

The Reboot End Program Key Combination

Press **CTRL + ALT +DEL** to **end** a **program** or to **reboot** the computer

☞✍ **Practice the CTRL+ALT+DEL keys**

☞✍ **Practice changing & moving the task bar**

Multiple Windows

If we have multiple windows open as shown below, we can close them by using the task management feature. Each time we minimize a window, then open another program or file,(in this case it was Explorer) we had multiple windows open.

These windows can be managed from the task bar with the options to cascade or tile. This way we can view several documents or pictures at once and easily navigate through each one right clicking on the task bar (not on an icon) will bring up the help menu as we see in the graphic.

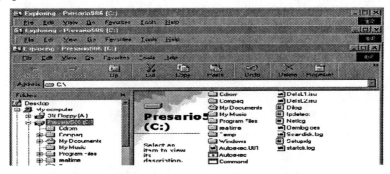

Figure 31 Multiple Open Windows

As you can see there are 3 Windows open. Each window can be opened, closed or minimized. The windows are designed to let us move through views and to let us compare information. Practice opening and closing several windows, you can't hurt anything just close each window when you are done to get back to a normal view.

☞🔖 Practice cascading/tiling windows

How to get there from here

There are other navigational basics we need to have before we move on to the other major components of an OS.

We already learned a bit about **My Computer**. If we go back to the **My Computer** icon on the desktop we see that by right clicking we have other choices from the context menu that appears. We can change the name of our computer; we can find the details about our computer in properties.

The other choices, some of which you've seen on other menus when you've right-clicked on desktop items, are:

Open

Explorer

Find

Map Network Drive

Disconnect Network Drive

Create shortcut

As with other desktop menu actions, we can use each of these choices by highlighting the choice (or placing our cursor over the desired option) and clicking -- right or left click of the mouse is ok here. Each of the choices is designed to get us where we want to go and if we do not know where something is located we can use a navigation process to look around and try to find it and then get there.

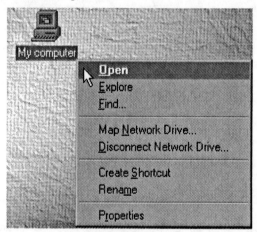

Figure 32 The Open option from My Computer

The Open Option

Right click or Double Click on 'My computer" will produce this Window.

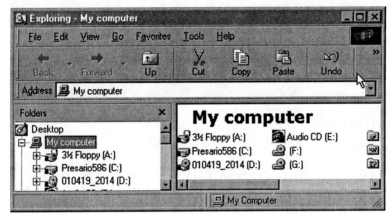

Figure 33 Exploring My Computer

When we choose the open command from "My Computer" we will see all the floppy, hard drives and cd-rom drives represented by icons. We can also click on the folders there for printers, the Control Panel, Control Panel, networking and the task scheduler in Windows 9x. In Windows 2000 we see all of the drives and have links to

See also:

My Documents

My Network Places

Network and Dial-up
Connections

click on for networking   and the control panel Control Panel

Double-clicking on any of these drives or folders will take us directly to the options or contents. Right clicking on any of these icons or folders will also bring a sub-menu of options. As usual, the options vary depending on what we click on.

If we double click on "My Computer" 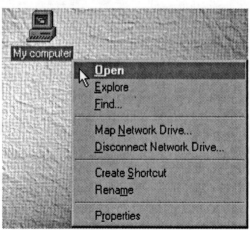 we will also be brought to a window like the screen example shown above.

☞✍ Practice the open command

☞✍ Practice ALT +underlined letter keys to open

☞✍ Practice TAB on the desktop to the open command

From this we can see the start menu **Start** and open command is another navigation option.

Explorer

To open the Explorer option from the **My Computer** context menu, **right click** and a window will appear.

Notice that graphically to the right of the list on the left that the contents appear just as they did by double-clicking on my computer.

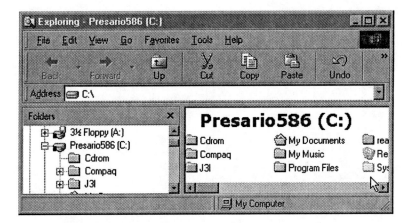

Figure 34 Explorer Menu Expansions

Notice the '+' and '-' signs next to each option, in the **Explorer** window. This will expand your menu or file options further by clicking on the + sign to expand the menu and the minus - sign to contract or close the menu.

F6 KEY

Use the **F6** key to switch between panes of the Window Display. Using the arrow ← **left** key will collapse a selection, using the → **right** expands a selection.

The contents displayed on the right are now displayed here. If we then click on the plus + sign next to each drive we will see the contents of that drive.

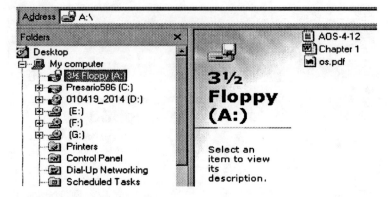

Figure 35 The Full Explorer View

Notice that each time we click on a drive or folder in the Explorer display, the contents of the **Address** area of the window we are in changes. In addition to the name of the drive or folder, an icon is also displayed. The icon is included in the address to identify if we are in a folder or a drive. Some folders are represented by special icons, such as the **Control Panel:**

Figure 36 The Address Bar.

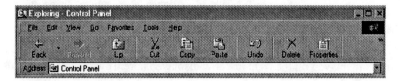

Figure 37 The menu bar.

Notice that there is a **menu** at the top of the **screen**, where we can **change** the **view** of the **files**. This changes what is displayed in the Explorer.

Open the **View** menu and then choose **Folder Options** from the submenu that appears.
In the Folder Options window, click on the **View** tab and then click **Show all files,** which
is an option under the "Files and Folders", "Hidden files" section.

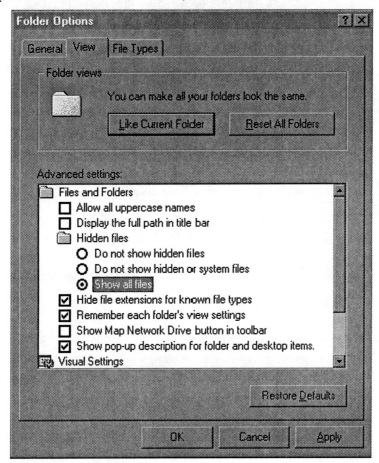

Figure 38 The View Tab.

When we choose to **view all files,** then all **files associated** with whatever we clicked on,
will appear in the **right pane (portion)** of the window. Without this option selected,
only SOME files will appear. Windows will not show operating system files and other
special files in Explorer, unless you have selected this option. You might think, "Why do
I need to see all the operating system files? I didn't create them, so why do I care?". The
answer is that this is very handy when troubleshooting system problems.

You've seen that you can open Explorer from **My Computer** by right clicking the menu option or double-clicking on Explorer. To open Explorer from the start menu, ![Start] choose **Programs**, then **Windows Explorer**. Explorer is intended to be the navigation menu that allows you to see all the files and file details in your computer.

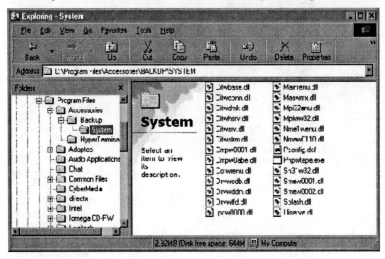

Figure 39 The Explorer Window with detail view.

Notice all the information contained in the window. The bottom of the window tells us how much disk space there is and that we are exploring the "my computer" portion of the desktop.

The information in the split window (panes) is designed to tell you what drive or folder you are exploring and what information is contained in there.

You can see by going to this menu that you can choose from your hard drive to floppy to cd-rom drive or any other drive options on your computer.

Once in the drive you can click on any program or file you wish to view further or open and even a program to start.

☞🖱 Practice Opening Windows Explorer

Pop Quiz 0000.3

 Pop Quiz 0000.3 *Questions*

1. To find the version of Windows a computer is running:

    A. Right-click on the desktop and choose Version

    B. Run the System Version Info applet in Control Panel

    C. Open a Command Prompt and use the "version" command

    D. Right-click on the My Computer icon and choose Properties

2. What does Control-Alt-Delete do?

    A. Immediately reboot your computer

    B. Close the current application

    C. Start Program Manager

    D. Start Task Manager

3. By default, Windows displays all the names of all files in a folder, when using Explorer:

    A. True

    B. False

4. In Explorer, the + sign to the left of an item in the left panel of the window means:

    A. You must press page-down to see more files

    B. The item listed next to the + sign is an archive file containing more files

    C. The item listed next to the + sign is a folder, and clicking on the + sign will expand the list of subfolders under that folder

    D. The contents of the item listed next to the + sign are displayed in the right panel of the window

5. To rename a file on the desktop, click on the file to select it, then press:

    A. Alt-M

    B. Alt-R

    C. Ctrl-Shift-R

    D. Alt-N

Pop Quiz 0000.3 *Answers*

1. Correct Answer: D

2. Correct Answer: D

3. Correct Answer: B

4. Correct Answer: C

5. Correct Answers: A

VII **Creating Folders In Explorer**

We can also create folders in the Explorer window. To do this we bring up the E window.

Then click on blank space on the right hand side (or "pane") of the split display window. Refer to the example below.

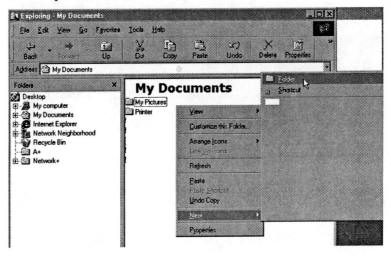

Figure 40 The Split Pane, folder creation.

Creating a folder in the split display window

Another way to create a new folder in Explorer is to go to the **File** menu and select **New**, as we see in the example below. As when you create a file from the Windows Desktop, selecting **File -> New** brings up a submenu of different types of files that you can create.

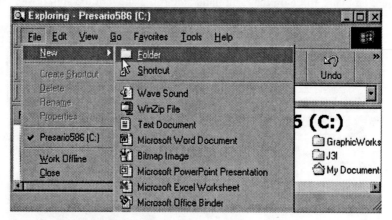

Figure 41 Creating a new folder from the file menu in Explorer

☞✍ Practice creating a new folder in split display
☞✍ Practice window & file menu

Arranging the Start menu

Start menu programs can also be arranged in **Explorer** by going to the **Start menu** and dragging the **start folders** to arrange the order they will appear.

VIII Control Panel Features

The Control Panel is the "car dashboard" for your computer. It has all the information to "drive your computer". In the Control Panel we look for hardware conflicts, make a boot disk, add/remove programs, set display and user settings. We also configure our network information here.

To go to the Control Panel, **we choose** start, settings **and** Control Panel. **We can also double-click on "my computer" on the desktop and open the** Control Panel.

If we happen to be in Explorer, viewing My Computer, we can also navigate to the Control Panel from there.

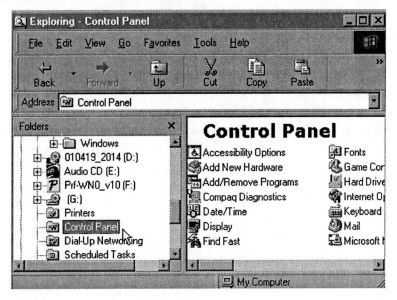

Figure 42 The Control Panel in Explorer

Some of the main areas of the Control Panel we need to familiar with, are discussed below.

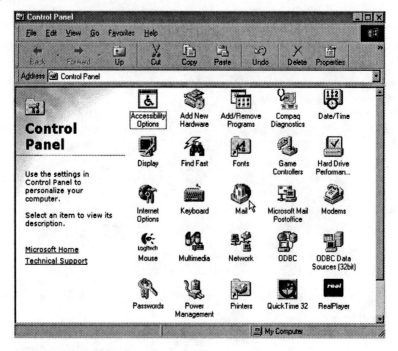

Figure 43 The Control Panel in Default View

From here we can change settings for our monitor, sound, modem, network. As you can see from the menu on the left side of the screen shot that this is where we use settings to personalize our computer. We can even change the view of our Control Panel to a list of items. You can choose **Large Icons**, **Small Icons**, **List** or **Details**. The first two give more screen space to the icon for the function, while the second two give more screen space to the text name of the function and information about it. Let's choose the **List** option. Note in the screen shot of the Control Panel the result of this change.

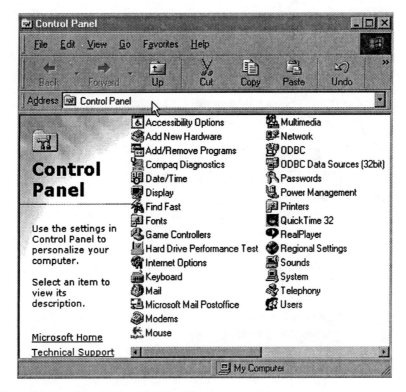

Figure 44 The Control Panel in List View

☞ Practice changing Control Panel Views

Control Panel Icons

This whole section is all about how to get there from here. Noticing our options in the Control Panel we can change the system time and the system time appearance.

Options available to a customized or manufactured system will also be found here. We will cover the main features in the Control Panel.

Figure 45The Control Panel Default Icons

Changing the Time

To change the time and time zone (regional settings) properties, go to Start, Settings, Control Panel, then choose Regional Settings. Clicking on the time display on the task bar will also take you to the regional settings window.

Figure 46 The Date/Time/Regional Settings Icons

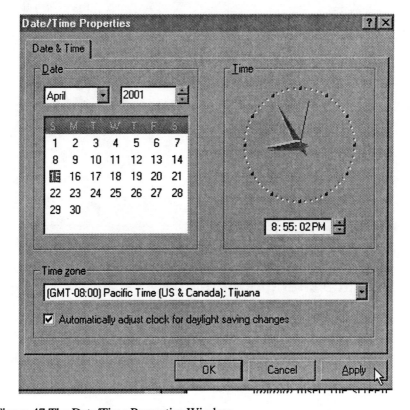

Figure 47 The Date/Time Properties Window

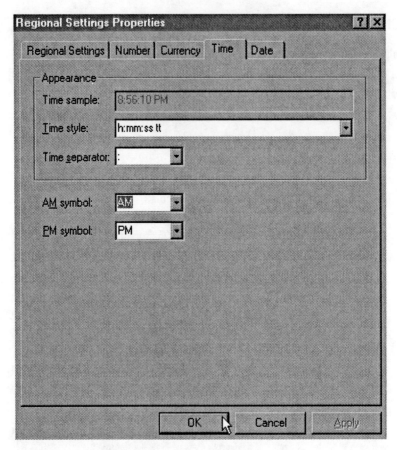

Figure 48 The Regional Settings Properties Window

☞✍ Practice changing the time

Power Management

Power
Management

Adjusting the power settings can be critical to computer function. Setting the power scheme to "always on" can be the key to troubleshooting a computer that spontaneously reboots. Using the power settings for the monitor can save energy. Let's take a look at some of the options found in power settings. We need to go to start, Control Panel, and choose power management. Mouse over on the power icon on the task bar and we see: Power Management

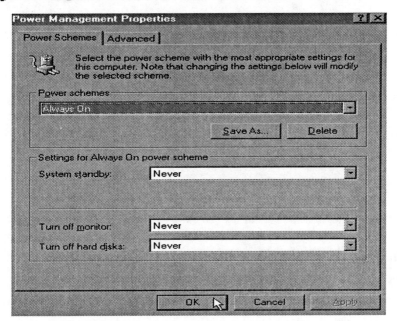

Figure 49 The power Management Properties Window

Power Settings

Changing the power setting to **"Always On"** may help troubleshooting spontaneous rebooting.

☞ Practice adjusting the power settings

Modem Properties

Modems

The modem is key for many to access to the outside world.

Running a diagnostic on each modem installed is key to understanding the settings and making changes or updating drivers to get the modem talking.

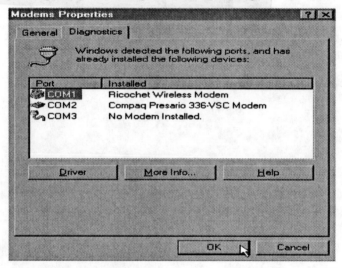

Figure 50 The Modem Diagnostics Tab

☞🖱 Practice viewing the modem properties

Display Properties

Display

To adjust display settings for your video card and monitor go to the display icon in the Control Panel. Clicking on the display icon will produce a display similar to the one shown below. The first screen shows us where to adjust the color. Choosing the Settings tab, we can make the adjustments.

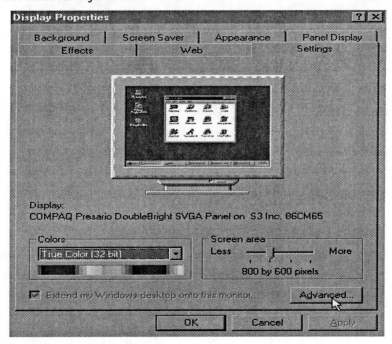

Figure 51 The Display Properties Tabs

If we choose the **Advanced** tab, we can change the refresh rate and any other settings particular to the video card and monitor installed.

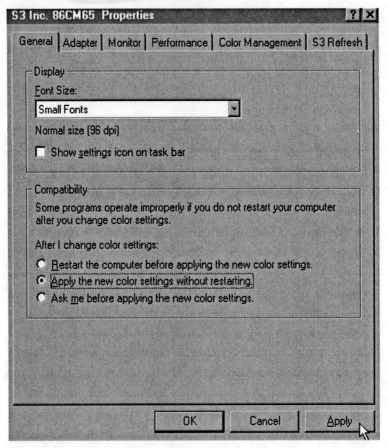

Figure 52 Video Adapter properties Tabs/options.

☞✎ Practice changing display settings

Safe Mode Video Troubleshooting

If you make a mistake in the refresh rate settings and cannot see the screen, reboot the computer in **safe mode** and adjust the display settings, and reboot.   **Safe mode** starts the computer with a minimal set of (hopefully known working) drivers. It's not pretty, but at least it lets you see the screen!

Display troubleshooting

We can have various installation or configuration issues with a display adapter or a monitor. Sometimes we need to make adjustments to the graphics accelerator. To do this, go to System Properties, point to Display Adapters, click the plus sign to display all available adapters (since on recent versions of Windows, you can have more than one adapter and more than one monitor), and double-click the adapter whose settings you wish to adjust.

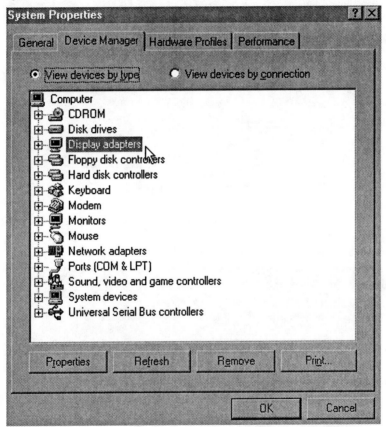

Figure 53 Control Panel View

Once in the Display Adapter the following screen appears.

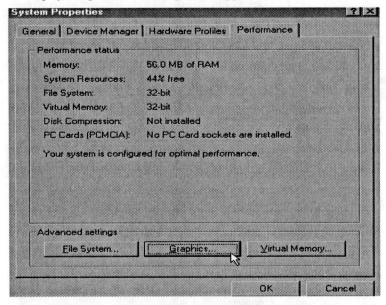

Figure 54 The Performance Tab in Display Adapter Properties

Now choose the Graphics Tab and the following screen will appear.

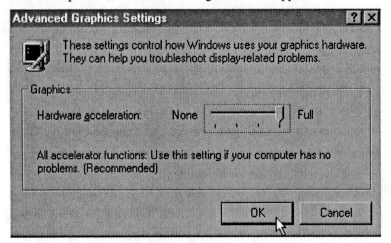

Figure 55 Graphics Acceleration Tab

Here the Graphics acceleration (hardware) can be adjusted. Having some control over the adapter will help with memory and display issues. Note that sometimes issues with a display getting garbled can be resolved by reducing the hardware acceleration.

The good news is that even if the changes we make are not right we can adjust them again after rebooting to "safe mode".

Hardware Acceleration

Know where the Hardware Acceleration Bar is located

☞✓📝 **Practice adjusting the Graphics acceleration**

Add/Remove programs

Add/Remove
Programs

This option lets you add or remove application programs via the **Install/Uninstall** tab, or add or remove Windows OS components via the **Windows Setup** tab. It is also the location that allows you to create a Startup Disk.

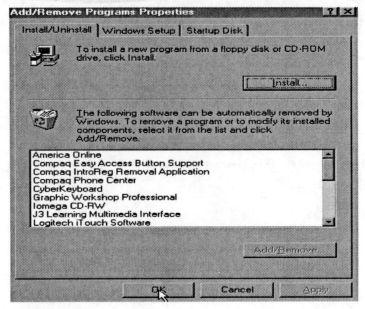

Figure 56 The Add/Remove Programs Properties Window

☞✍ Practice adding a program

Creating a boot floppy

There are several ways to create a boot floppy or startup disk. In fact there are at least 4 ways. The most common one is to go to Add/Remove Programs Properties and then choose the **Startup Disk** tab, and then choose create disk.

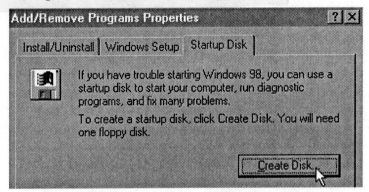

Figure 57 The Create Startup Disk Tab

The Second method is to create a disk through Windows explorer. Go to Explorer, then right-click on the floppy or A drive, then choose format.

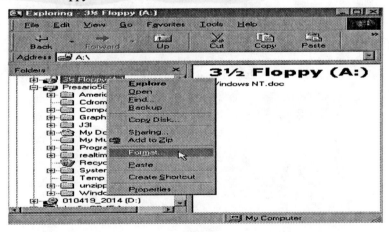

Figure 58 Exploring the A+ drive & Formatting

When the Format window appears choose the Copy system files <u>only</u> option. Be sure and have a floppy disk in the drive before you start the process, including trying to right-click on the A drive in Explorer.

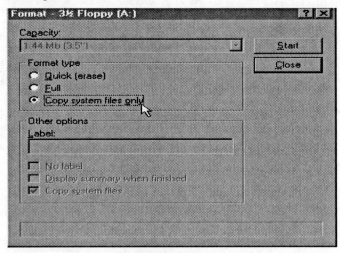

Figure 59 The Format A (floppy) drive/ with Systems Files

If we type Format a:/s at the run command, by going to start  key then

choosing type in the command. This screen will appear:

Figure 60 Formatting Drive A

The next method is similar. We type in Format a:/s at a MS-DOS  which then gives us a pop up screen with the MS-DOS prompt.

Figure 61 Formatting a system disk at the MS-DOS prompt

System Disk
format (insert drive letter): **/S** = drive format + systems files

Use **SYS.com** (insert drive letter): to transfer systems files to a disk which has already been formatted. You don't need to explicitly use **SYS** on a newly-formatted disk if you have already formatted it with the **/S**, since the **/S** option on **format** automatically runs **SYS.**

Create a **formatted system** disk by right clicking on the Drive in Windows Explorer.

From the Control Panel Select Add/Remove Programs, Startup Disk

From My Computer right click on the Drive to format

Note: Transferring system files is always optional

☞ Practice creating a boot floppy

System Properties

System

This area of the Control Panel Control Panel is most familiar to those who are experienced at troubleshooting. This feature is where most all conflicts, driver issues and configuration issues are solved. At the least this is the place to begin.

To explore System Properties, we go to the Control

Panel, Control Panel then choose system System, double-click on system (right – click once to use the open menu). The following window appears.

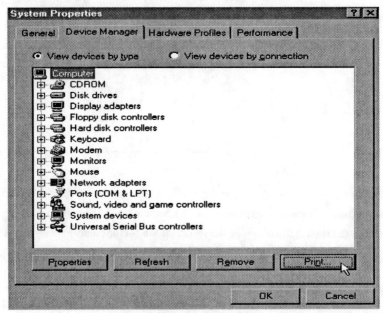

Figure 62 Devices in the system by type

Clicking on any of these **icons** will **expand** the menu to more information about the **device** and bring up windows we can troubleshoot through.

Changing the view to Connection we see the following window.

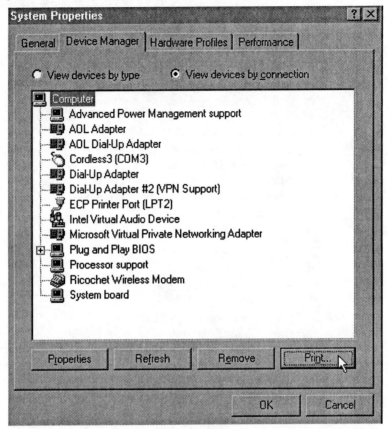

Figure 63 The change in view shows the connection relation.

Notice that we can print the information we need by highlighting and clicking the print button.

To display in detail the System Devices click the **System Devices** tab to expand the devices list, then choose the device you wish to learn more about.

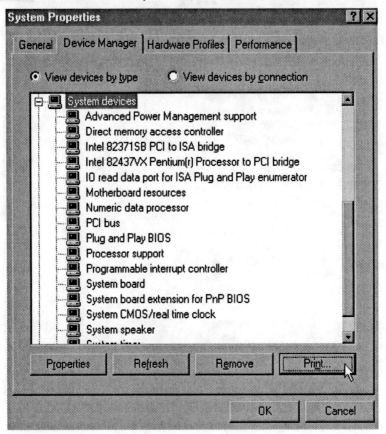

Figure 64 System Devices in Detail

To explore the troubleshooting possibilities in System Properties, an expanded group of windows are shown.

The Dial Up Adapter properties will be reviewed.

Beginning with the windows in order:

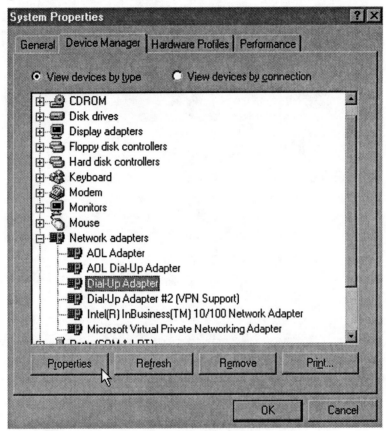

Figure 65 System Properties Network/ Dial Up Adapter choice

Choose the Properties tabor double click on the icon.

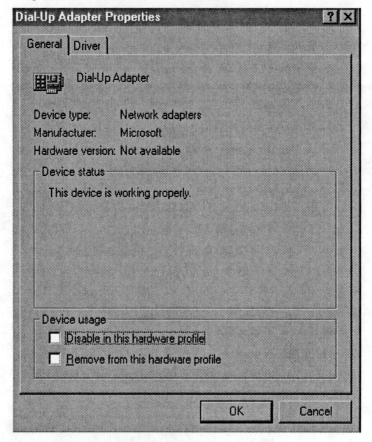

Figure 66 The General Tab in Dial-Up Adapter Properties.

The device is working properly.

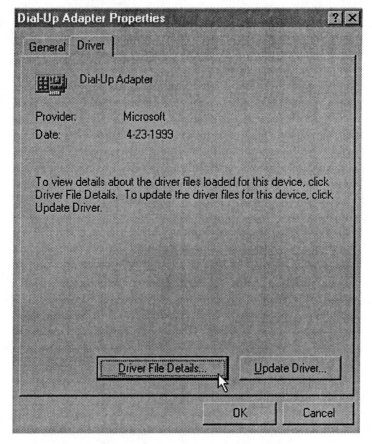

Figure 67 The Driver Tab in Dial-Up Adapter Properties.

Choose the Driver File Details **button** to learn more.

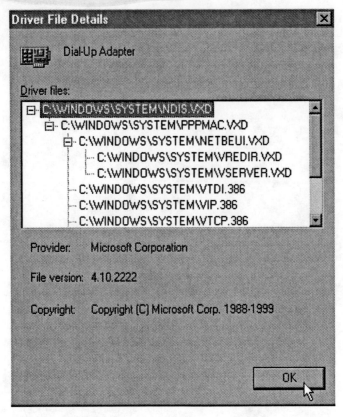

Figure 68 The Dial-Up Adapter Drive File Details Window.

All Driver Details are found here. As you can see, all files that comprise the driver are listed. Also, the name of the vendor providing the driver (Microsoft, in this case) is displayed, as is the exact version of the driver. Next we shall update the driver.

Choose the Update Driver Tab.

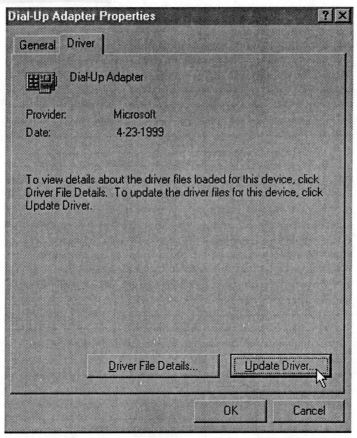

Figure 69 The Update Driver Tab For the Dial-Up Adapter

A wizard or help window will tell you to click next while it searches for information. This is only one of a number of wizards in Windows, which step you through common administrative tasks.

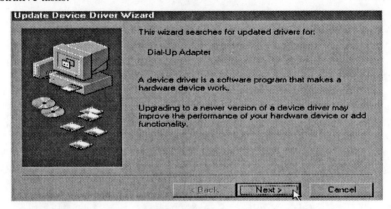

Figure 70 The Update Driver Wizard

Then choose to either have Windows search for a driver or to load a driver from a downloaded update or manufacturer's drivers disk.

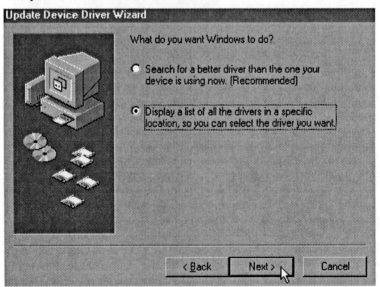

Figure 71 Choosing the manual option to dedicate a driver

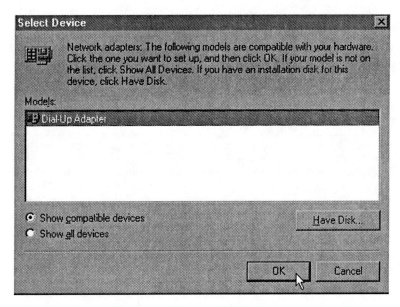

Figure 72 Choosing the Dial –Up Adapter Window

The Dial Up Adapter is listed, so select that. This is the time to use the manufacturer's driver disk or to use a downloaded driver update, by clicking the **Have Disk** option.

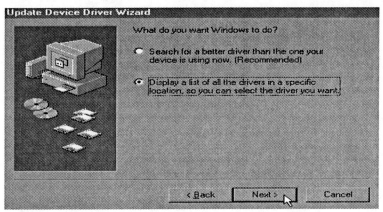

Figure 73 Update the Driver Wizard

After installing the driver, click **Finish** to complete the wizard. Often you may need to reboot your computer after installing a driver. This is less true on later versions of Windows, particularly Windows 2000 and later, than on earlier versions.

Troubleshooting Driver Updates

The process of troubleshooting and driver updates is virtually the same for all computer devices through the System Properties, in the Control Panel.

☞✍ Practice Exploring System Properties

Pop Quiz 0000.4

 Pop Quiz 0000.4 *Questions*

1. Setting the power management scheme to 'Always on' is useful for:

    A. Preserving notebook battery life

    B. Ensuring that the computer uses electric power even if a battery is installed

    C. Troubleshooting power management problems

    D. Keeping the screen saver from running

2. Which Display Properties tab is used to change the display resolution?

    A. Settings

    B. Properties

    C. Advanced

    D. Appearance

3. What command-line program can be used to make a diskette bootable by transferring system files to it?

    A. TRANSFER

    B. MAKEDISK

    C. SYS

    D. FORMATFLOPPY

4. The System Properties applet's Device Manager tab lets you: (choose all that apply)

    A. See what devices are installed in the system

    B. Adjust graphics card acceleration

    C. View disk usage log information

    D. Troubleshoot device issues

5. Driver file details lists:

    A. File version

    B. Files used by a driver

    C. Driver publisher

    D. Date driver was installed

Pop Quiz 0000.4 *Answers*

1. Correct Answer: C

2. Correct Answer: A

3. Correct Answer: C

4. Correct Answer: A&D

5. Correct Answers: A, B and C

IX   Startup Configuration

There are several ways to view the startup configuration of your computer. For the purposes of this discussion we shall view how to look at the settings in Windows 98.

Go to Start, Programs, Accessories, then System tools, then System information, then System configuration utility. From here, choose the **Startup** tab. Notice that we can also view the other critical information files here by **TAB**bing to each bit of information we desire. In the startup folder we can select how we want programs to start.

> Note: We can also arrange this information in Explorer.

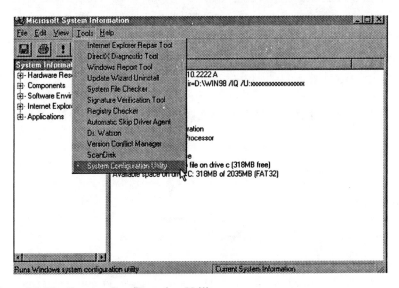

Figure 74 The System Configuration Utility

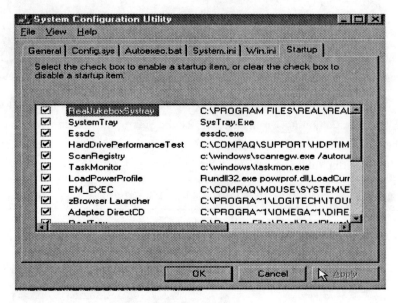

Figure 75 The Startup Tab in Windows 98

☞✍ Practice finding the startup configuration

Windows Help

The Help Feature

One feature of the Windows family is that there is a built in help system. We see evidence of this first when we mouse-over something we do not understand. We will either see a text box pop up asking us what's this and if we right click on that it will tell us, or we see a text box appear that tells us what the item or icon is.

Figure 76 The Help mouseover

For Help on an option, click the question mark ?  then click the option.

To find the full Windows Help menu itself, go to start,  then to help. Here we have options to help us find out what we are looking for or wondering about. Notice the 3 options in help. They are the contents, the index and the search. In each of the contents area we can choose from either menu of topics or in index words related to the topic we are searching or in search we can type in the topic, say Control Panel and the menu of choices relating to that topic will appear.

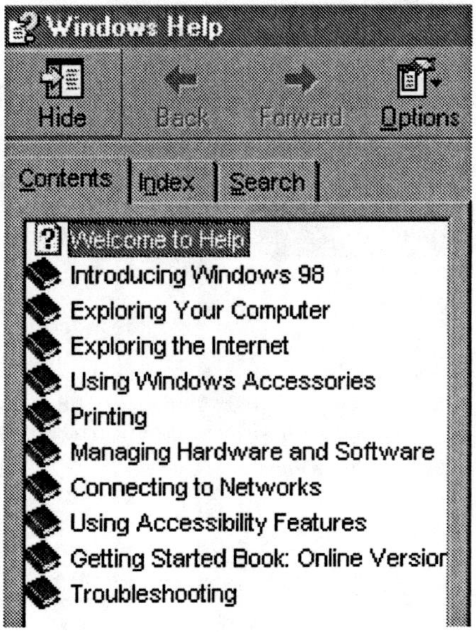

Figure 77 The Windows Help Menu

The F1 Key

To display help on any Open Dialog Box, press the F1 key.

The Troubleshooters

One feature in help is the Troubleshooter. This works quite well in asking you a series of questions to help guide you to a solution, even if you are not quite sure what is wrong. Look at the screen example of troubleshooting a sound card.

Do not forget to look in the Control Panel at the Device Manager to begin troubleshooting a conflict or driver issue as well.

To get to the Troubleshooter, go to help then select Troubleshooting from the display window and choose the area you need help.

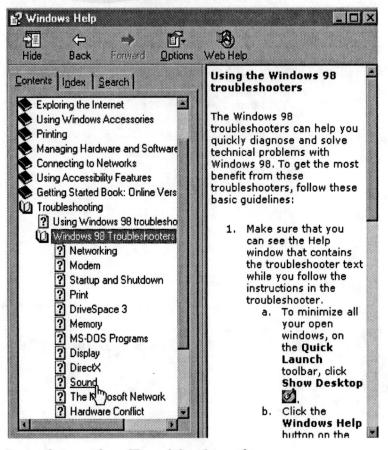

☞🔖 Practice using Troubleshooting

X   Summary

You have learned "how to get there from here." There are many ways to get to the same information in the Windows Operating System. You can use the mouse or the keyboard, or a combination of both. You can use drag-and-drop. You can use context menus which appear when you right-click an item, or you can use menu options that appear on the menu bar of an application like Windows Explorer. The key to success on the A+ Operating System test is to know the various methods of navigation and the functions of the keys to assist in making the correct choices when testing. Practice the various methods of creating folders and navigation and you too will become a desktop guru.

XI   TotalRecall: Test For Success Questions

1. What happens when you delete a file from the Recycle Bin?
    A. Clusters are flushed.
    B. The files are moved to C:\Windows\Temp.
    C. Sectors of hard drive are blanked/erased.
    D. Associated entries in the FAT are removed.

2. Your sound card is not working and when you look in Device Manager, the Sound card shows up with an exclamation mark. What should you do? (Choose two)
    A. Ensure that the speakers are compatible.
    B. Make sure the sound card is on IRQ14.
    C. Select the default multimedia CODEC device.
    D. Start the Hardware Conflict Troubleshooter from within Windows Help.
    E. Select the properties of the sound card and examine the resources tab for conflicting resource settings.

3. Your Windows 98 computer is having display-related problems. Where can you adjust the graphics hardware acceleration so that you can troubleshoot the problem?

A. Control Panel, System, Performance, Graphics.

B. Control Panel, System, Display Settings, Graphics.

C. Control Panel, System, Device Manager, Display Adapter Properties, Graphics.

D. Control Panel, System, Hardware Profiles, Display Settings, Graphics.

---

4. A customer calls you and explains that he can't display an entire web page even though he has a 17 inch monitor, and that he has to use the scroll bars to go from right side to the left side. What would you change in his display settings?

A. Click Advanced and change to large font.

B. Click Advanced and change the screen size.

C. Slide the screen area bar over to 800 by 600.

D. Adjust contrast control until the screen has shrunk in size.

Total
Recall

5. How do you make hidden files visible in Windows 95?

A. Tools, Options, Show All Files.

    ‑ B. Windows Explorer, View, Folder Options, View tab, Show All Files.

    C. Windows Explorer, File, Preferences, Unhide All Files.

    D. Control Panel, Device Manager, File Attributes, Unhide.

---

6. How do you set the system time? (Choose three)

    ‑ A. Command prompt, 'time'.

    B. Device Manager, select Clock.

    ‑ C. Control Panel, select Date/Time.

    ‑ D. Taskbar properties 'show clock.'

    ‑ E. Double-click on the clock in the system tray.

7. Home/office desk, presentation, and portable/laptop are examples of _____.

  A. Users profiles.
     B. System profiles.
     C. Hardware profiles.
     D. Power option settings.

---

8. You need to create a Windows 98 startup disk. You open the Add/Remove Programs applet and click 'Create Disk' from the _____.
     A. Install TAB.
     B. Create Disk TAB.
   − C. Startup Disk TAB.
     D. Windows Setup TAB.

9. How do you rearrange your Start Menu in Windows 9x?
    A. Click Start and choose Arrange.
    B. Click the corresponding applet in the Control Panel.
    C. Right-click on the Start button and select Explore.
    D. Right-click on the desktop and choose Start Menu.

---

10. Your customer calls and complains that sometimes his desktop icons look different, but after rebooting they return to normal. What shortcut can he use instead?
    A. <Alt>+<F4> to refresh memory.
    B. <Alt>+<TAB> to refresh memory.
    C. <Shift>+<F4> to refresh memory.
    D. <Shift>+<F8> to refresh desktop.

11. You are troubleshooting a system that has a malfunctioning mouse. You need to check the Device Manager for conflicts. Since the mouse does not work, what key toggles you from the desktop to the taskbar?

A. <ALT>
  B. <TAB>
    C. <CTRL>
    D. Arrow key.

---

12. What TAB in the System Configuration Utility displays items that are automatically run on boot?
  A. Startup
    B. SYSTEM.INI
    C. General
    D. Boot

13. In Windows Explorer, which two of the following will successfully create a new folder?

    A. File, New, Folder.

    B. Folder, Create, New Folder

    C. Triple Click in Display Window

    D. Right Click in Display Window, New, Folder.

    E. Edit, Create, New, Folder.

---

14. What should you do first to adjust your display resolution?

    A. Flash the BIOS first.

    B. Refresh your desktop.

    C. Update your Windows drivers with the latest available version.

    D. Check for 16 bit drivers loading in your SYSTEM.INI.

15. You change video resolution on your system and reboot. You cannot see anything on your screen as it boots. The hard drive finishes loading the Operating System. How can you safely reboot the computer so you can access Safe Mode?
   - A. Press CTRL+ALT+DEL twice.
   B. Reset power to the computer.
   C. Press Alt + F4. and then press Enter.
   D. Press and hold CTRL+BREAK.

16. How can you close a program that has quit responding without shutting down Windows 95?
   A. Press CTRL+ALT+ DEL twice.
   B. Run unlock.exe.
   C. Open another instance of the application and close it.
   - D. Press CTRL+ALT+ DEL. Select program listed as not responding and click the 'End Task' button.

17. You uninstall an application. When looking at the Start Menu, its shortcut is still
    there. What two methods can be used to remove the shortcut?
    _ A. Reboot the PC and allow the uninstall to complete.
    _ B. Delete the item from the Device Manager.
    C. Refresh Windows Explorer using the F5 key.
    D. Right click the taskbar and choose Properties. Click Remove on the Start Menu
    programs TAB.

_____

18. Which key can you hold down after seeing the Windows logo to stop an application
    in the startup folder from executing?
    A. F8
    _ B. ESC
    C. CTRL
    D. SHIFT

19. A long file name in Windows 9x can be changed using which method? (Choose two)

~ A. In Windows Explorer, choose File, Rename.

B. From an MS-DOS prompt, type 'ren <filename> <newfilename>'.

C. From the Control Panel, click System, then click Rename.

⁻ D. In Windows Explorer, choose Tools, Rename File.

---

20. A bootable floppy disk can be created in which 4 ways in Windows 9x? (Choose three)

A. FDISK A: from a command prompt.

– B. In Windows Explorer, right click on A drive, choose Format, Floppy System Files.

C. Format a: from a command prompt.

‿ D. Format a:/s from a command prompt.

⌐E. Format a:/s from the Start, run command box

⁻ F. Control Panel, Add/Remove Programs, Startup Disk TAB.

21. You are troubleshooting a computer that does not have a working mouse. You have made it into the Device Manager. Which key will move from one device to another? (Choose two)

    A. TAB
    B. HOME
    C. ENTER
    D. ARROW KEYS

---

22. Which key combination switches a user between applications that are currently running in Windows?

    A. <FN>+<TAB>
    B. <ALT>+<TAB>
    C. <CTRL>+<TAB>
    D. <SHIFT>+<TAB>

Test for Success Answers

1. What happens when you delete a file from the Recycle Bin?
    A. Clusters are flushed.
    B. The files are moved to C:\Windows\Temp.
    C. Sectors of hard drive are blanked/erased.
    D. Associated entries in the FAT are removed.

Explanation: D, Associated entries in the FAT are removed.

Recall that the Recycle Bin is a temporary holding place for deleted files, designed to
    give you one last chance to retrieve a deleted file before you empty the recycle bin,
    or specifically delete one or more files from it. When a file is deleted from the
    Recycle Bin, or the Recycle Bin is emptied, the file is removed from disk, so it is not
    true that the files are moved to a temp directory after being deleted from the Recycle
    Bin. Clusters are not flushed, and hard drive sectors are not erased – that term
    implies that the data is somehow wiped out, which doesn't (normally) happen on
    Windows. However, the clusters related to the file can no longer be accessed,
    because the FAT entries (directory entries) allowing access to the file have been
    removed.

2. Your sound card is not working and when you look in Device Manager, the Sound card shows up with an exclamation mark. What should you do? (Choose two)

A. Ensure that the speakers are compatible.

B. Make sure the sound card is on IRQ14.

C. Select the default multimedia CODEC device.

D. Start the Hardware Conflict Troubleshooter from within Windows Help.

E. Select the properties of the sound card and examine the resources Tab for conflicting resource settings.

Explanation: D, Start the Hardware Conflict Troubleshooter from within Windows Help, and **E. Select the properties of the sound card and examine the resources tab for conflicting resource settings**. If the sound card shows up with an exclamation point, then something is wrong with its configuration and you should take steps to find out what. You shouldn't be worrying about the speakers yet, since whether or not you have the right speakers won't matter until you can get the sound card to show up without an exclamation point in Device Manager, by correcting its configuration. The sound card would not normally use IRQ 14, which you can recall from A+ Core, is normally the Primary IDE channel interrupt. And CODEC's, like speakers, are not an issue until you have resolved the hardware configuration issue.

3. Your Windows 98 computer is having display-related problems. Where can you adjust the graphics hardware acceleration so that you can troubleshoot the problem?
   A. Control Panel, System, Performance, Graphics.
   B. Control Panel, System, Display Settings, Graphics.
   C. Control Panel, System, Device Manager, Display Adapter Properties, Graphics.
   D. Control Panel, System, Hardware Profiles, Display Settings, Graphics.

Explanation: C. Control Panel, System, Performance, Graphics is where this is adjusted. The other choices aren't correct. In particular, note that this is **NOT** done in the Display Adapter configuration area. It is done in the system performance area.

---

4. A customer calls you and explains that he can't display an entire web page even though he has a 17-inch monitor, and that he has to use the scroll bars to go from right side to the left side. What would you change in his display settings?
   A. Click Advanced and change to large font.
   B. Click Advanced and change the screen size.
   C. Slide the screen area bar over to 800 by 600.
   D. Adjust contrast control until the screen has shrunk in size.

Explanation: C. Slide the screen area bar over to 800 by 600 is the correct change. This question assumes that the reader will assume the user was previously using a lower resolution like the VGA default of 640x480. Increasing the resolution will allow more information to be displayed on the screen. Changing to a large font will reduce the amount of information on the screen rather than increase it. The screen size is not changed via the Advanced tab. Adjusting the contrast will only change the relative brightness of what appears on the screen.

5. How do you make hidden files visible in Windows 95?
    A. Tools, Options, Show All Files.
    B. Windows Explorer, View, Folder Options, View tab, Show All Files.
    C. Windows Explorer, File, Preferences, Unhide All Files.
    D. Control Panel, Device Manager, File Attributes, Unhide.

Explanation: B. Windows Explorer, View, Folder Options, View tab, Show All Files
    is the correct action to take.

---

6. How do you set the system time? (Choose three)
    A. Command prompt, 'time'.
    B. Device Manager, select Clock.
    C. Control Panel, select Date/Time.
    D. Taskbar properties 'show clock.'
    E. Double-click on the clock in the system tray.

Explanation: A. Command Prompt, 'time', C. Control Panel, select Date/Time and
    E. Double-click on the clock in the system tray are methods to set the time.
    There is no clock option in Device Manager, and showing or not showing the clock
    in the task bar does not change the time on it.

7. Home/office desk, presentation, and portable/laptop are examples of _____.
   A. Users profiles.
   B. System profiles.
   C. Hardware profiles.
   D. Power option settings.

Explanation: D. Power option settings. User and system profiles typically apply regardless of hardware settings or location, so the answer is between C and D. The answer **could** be C, but in this case **D** is the more likely answer. You can select names for hardware profiles, and theoretically, you **could** choose the above names for them, but that's unlikely. **D. Power option settings** is more likely to be correct because the listed terms are pre-set power schemes in the Control Panel's power management applet.

---

8. You need to create a Windows 98 startup disk. You open the Add/Remove Programs applet and click 'Create Disk' from the _____.
   A. Install Tab.
   B. Create Disk Tab.
   C. Startup Disk Tab.
   D. Windows Setup Tab.

Explanation: C. Startup Disk Tab is the correct choice. The Install Tab and Windows Setup tab don't contain an option to 'Create Disk'. There is no Create Disk Tab in Add/Remove Programs. Add/Remove Programs only contains **Install/Uninstall, Startup Disk** and **Windows Setup** tabs.

9. How do you rearrange your Start Menu in Windows 9x?
    A. Click Start and choose Arrange.
    B. Click the corresponding applet in the Control Panel.
    C. Right-click on the Start button and select Explore.
    D. Right-click on the desktop and choose Start Menu.

Explanation: C. Right-click on the Start button and select Explore is the correct
    option. The others are not valid actions.

---

10. Your customer calls and complains that sometimes his desktop icons look different,
    but after rebooting they return to normal. What shortcut can he use instead?
    A. <Alt>+<F4> to refresh memory.
    B. <Alt>+<Tab> to refresh memory.
    C. <Shift>+<F4> to refresh memory.
    D. <Shift>+<F8> to refresh desktop.

Explanation: D. <Shift>+<F8> to refresh desktop is the correct action. <Alt>+<F4> is
    used to close the current window. <Alt>+<Tab> is used to cycle among active tasks
    in the task manager.

11. You are troubleshooting a system that has a malfunctioning mouse. You need to check the Device Manager for conflicts. Since the mouse does not work, what key toggles you from the desktop to the taskbar?
    A. <ALT>
    B. <Tab>
    C. <CTRL>
    D. Arrow key

Explanation: B. <Tab> will toggle you from desktop navigation to task bar navigation (particularly, to the Start button). <ALT> and <CTRL> do nothing in this situation. The arrow keys can be used to navigate among items on the desktop.

---

12. What Tab in the System Configuration Utility displays items that are automatically run on boot?
    A. Startup
    B. SYSTEM.INI
    C. General
    D. Boot

Explanation: A. Startup is the correct tab. General and SYSTEM.INI are tabs in the System Configuration Utility, but they are not used to control which programs are run on system boot. There is no Boot tab in the System Configuration Utility.

13. In Windows Explorer, which two of the following will successfully create a new folder?

    A. File, New, Folder.

    B. Folder, Create, New Folder

    C. Triple Click in Display Window

    D. Right Click in Display Window, New, Folder.

    E. Edit, Create, New, Folder.

Explanation: A. File, New, Folder and **D. Right Click in Display Window, New, Folder** are the two ways to accomplish this from Windows Explorer. The other options aren't valid.

---

14. What should you do first to adjust your display resolution?

    A. Flash the BIOS first.

    B. Refresh your desktop.

    C. Update your Windows drivers with the latest available version.

    D. Check for 16 bit drivers loading in your SYSTEM.INI.

Explanation: C. Update your Windows drivers with the latest available version will ensure that you're using the latest (hopefully least buggy) drivers for your graphics card, before you stress it with a higher display resolution.

15. You change video resolution on your system and reboot. You cannot see anything on your screen as it boots. The hard drive finishes loading the Operating System. How can you safely reboot the computer so you can access Safe Mode?
    A. Press CTRL+ALT+DEL twice
    B. Reset power to the computer.
    C. Press Alt + F4 and then press Enter.
    D. Press and hold CTRL+BREAK.

Explanation: A. Press CTRL+ALT+DEL twice.

---

16. How can you close a program that has quit responding without shutting down Windows 95?
    A. Press CTRL+ALT+ DEL twice.
    B. Run unlock.exe.
    C. Open another instance of the application and close it.
    D. Press CTRL+ALT+ DEL. Select program listed as not responding and click the 'End Task' button.

Explanation: D. Press CTRL+ALT+DEL. Select program listed as not responding and click the 'End Task' button. None of the other options will accomplish the task. Opening another instance of the program and closing it will close that new instance, not the one that is currently listed as 'not responding'.

17. You uninstall an application. When looking at the Start Menu, its shortcut is still there. What two methods can be used to remove the shortcut?
    A. Reboot the PC and allow the uninstall to complete.
    B. Delete the item from the Device Manager.
    C. Refresh Windows Explorer using the F5 key.
    D. Right click the taskbar and choose Properties. Click Remove on the Start Menu programs Tab.

Explanation: A. Reboot the PC and allow the uninstall to complete and **D. Right click the taskbar and choose Properties. Click Remove on the Start Menu programs Tab**. Refreshing Windows Explorer and deleting the item from Device Manager would not affect the Start menu.

---

18. Which key can you hold down after seeing the Windows logo to stop an application in the startup folder from executing?
    A. F8
    B. ESC
    C. CTRL
    D. SHIFT

Explanation: A. F8.

19. A long file name in Windows 9x can be changed using which method? (Choose two)
   A. In Windows Explorer, choose File, Rename.
   B. From an MS-DOS prompt, type 'ren <filename> <newfilename>'.
   C. From the Control Panel, click System, then click Rename.
   D. In Windows Explorer, choose Tools, Rename File.

Explanation: A. In Windows Explorer, choose File, Rename and B. From an MS-DOS prompt, type 'ren <filename> <newfilename>' are the correct ways to do this. There is no option to rename, in Control Panel, System, or under the Windows Explorer, Tools menu.

---

20. A bootable floppy disk can be created in which 4 ways in Windows 9x? (Choose three)
   A. FDISK A: from a command prompt.
   B. In Windows Explorer, right click on A drive, choose Format, Floppy System Files.
   C. Format a: from a command prompt.
   D. Format a:/s from a command prompt.
   E. Format a:/s from the Start, run command box
   F. Control Panel, Add/Remove Programs, Startup Disk Tab.

Explanation: D. Format a:/s from a command prompt, E. Format a:/s from the run command and F. Control Panel, Add/Remove Programs, Startup Disk Tab are the ways to accomplish this. FDISK is used to partition hard disks, and format a: by itself will not create a bootable floppy, since a bootable floppy must contain system files.

21. You are troubleshooting a computer that does not have a working mouse. You have made it into the Device Manager. Which key will move from one device to another? (Choose two)
    A. Tab
    B. HOME
    C. ENTER
    D. ARROW KEYS

Explanation: C. ENTER and **D. ARROW KEYS** are the correct answers. Tab and Home do not do this.

---

22. Which key combination switches a user between applications that are currently running in Windows?
    A. <FN>+<Tab>
    B. <ALT>+<Tab>
    C. <CTRL>+<Tab>
    D. <SHIFT>+<Tab>

Explanation: B. <ALT>+<Tab>. This switches a user between applications that are currently running. The other key combinations given do not.

Motivation determines what you do

-Lou Holtz-

Chapter 0001: File Structure

> **The objective of this chapter is to provide the reader with an understanding of the following:**
>
> File structure
> 　　Partitioning/Formatting/File System
> 　　FAT139
> 　　Using the Windows Disk Defragmenter
> 　　To start Task Scheduler
> 　　Check for Disk Errors using ScanDisk
> 　　FAT 16146
> 　　FAT 32148
> Drive Converter Design
> 　　Using Drive Converter (FAT32)
> 　　NTFS4153
> 　　NTFS5155
> 　　HPFS156

Introduction

The composition of files is key to successfully negotiating the A+ Operating System test. Understanding the organization and file feature information is also key to managing a hard drive efficiently Realizing that not all file structures are alike can also aid in preparing for installation of a new drive.

Getting Ready - Questions

1. Which files need to be reviewed to troubleshoot an error encountered during installation of Windows 9x?
   A: ERROR.TXT
   B: ERROR.LOG
   C: FAILLOG.TXT
   D: DETLOG.TXT
   E: DETLOG.LOG
   F: SETUPLOG.TXT

2. In order to create a new-mirrored volume in Windows 2000, what type of partition must the disk have?
   A: basic
   B: primary
   C: dynamic
   D: extended

3. A file system which is not supported by Windows NT is:
   NTFS
   FAT32
   FAT16
   HPFS

4. Scandisk is used for:
   Searching a disk for a specific word
   Formatting a disk
   Checking a disk for errors
   Displaying a list of all files on a disk in alphabetical order

5. An advantage of FAT32 is:
   FAT32 is compatible with all versions of Windows
   Converting a FAT16 disk to FAT32 will save disk space
   FAT32 includes encryption capabilities
   FAT32 can be used by the original Windows 95

Getting Ready - Answers

1. *Correct Answers*: **D & F**

2. *Correct Answer:* **C**

3. *Correct Answer:* **B**

4. *Correct Answer:* **C**

5. *Correct Answer:* **B**

◆ II   File structure

Each operating system has a file structure that allows the hard drive to organize information. There are features and benefits to each type of structure. Understanding those features allows the user to make informed installation choices.

Partitioning/Formatting/File System

Understanding a **file system** and **file allocation table** is key to managing the hard disks' structure and directory structure of files.

FAT

The File Allocation Table is the keystone of DOS or the Disk Operating System, the basic operating system that PC's have used for many years. While DOS handles other tasks, such as orchestrating printers, keyboards, and monitors, the bulk of the effort is managing how a single file is stored (and sometimes scattered) on the magnetic bits of a floppy or hard drive. This same concept is still in use in modern "file systems", which organize the manner in which bits are stored on disk.

An analogy of FAT can be found in a library that uses a card system to look for a book.

You can search by book title and the card will tell you where in the library to look for the book. Take the concept further by visualizing a book is still in the library, however the different chapters are scattered through different parts of the library.

The index card would tell you that 1) the book is there, and 2) where you would find the different chapters or even pages of chapters in the library. This is how FAT works.

If you delete a book from the library because the book was out dated, you could insert a new book in whatever spaces were available in the library. Over time, your library would become quite scattered and it would take a bit of time to get the data together on one entire book. In a computer file system, this is known as **fragmentation,** and it slows down the computer much like you'd be slowed down getting a book in the far corner of your library.

Improve performance by Defragmenting

You can improve easily improve performance by running a defragmentation program.

This program is also known as disk defragmenter. In "geek shortspeak" we refer to this as Defragging or Defrag. Microsoft includes a defrag utility in Microsoft Windows. Other software vendors also sell enhanced defrag utilities, which do a more thorough job or perhaps have more features ('bells and whistles') in the program. For most users, though, the Windows defrag program is all that you need.

Using the Windows Disk Defragmenter

From Windows Help Files:

Using Disk Defragmenter to speed up access to your hard disk. You can use Disk Defragmenter to rearrange files and unused space on your hard disk so that programs run faster.

To start Disk Defragmenter:

Click Start, point to Programs, point to Accessories, point to System Tools, and then clicking Disk Defragmenter.

The following screen will appear. Choose the drive you want to defrag.

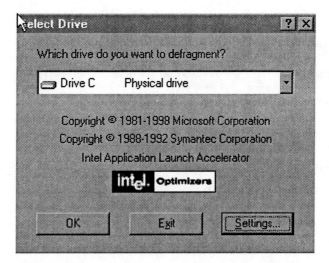

Figure 78 The Screen to choose the drive to Defrag.

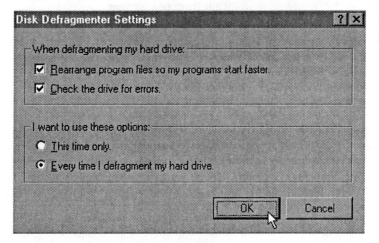

Figure 79 The screen to adjust settings for Defrag.

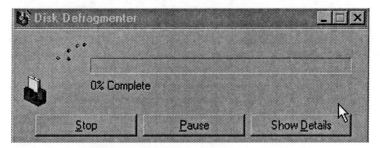

Figure 80 The beginning of the Defrag Process.

Note: Choosing the show details button will show progress of the process.
Note: Defragmentation programs do face several challenges.

If a computer has been in serious use, files may be very scattered, and it could take a substantial amount of time to run the first time. Each time you delete or move a file or folder or program, the related entries in the FAT are also jostled about.

Other programs may interfere with defragmentation. If any program writes to the drive while the defragmentation program is running, the process must begin again.

Stopping and Starting Defrag Process

Anti-Virus **software and** Screen Savers **may prevent the** defragmentation **program from completing.**

Defragmentation programs can be set to run automagically (say at night) either through the program itself, or the free defragmentation program that comes with some version of Windows can be set up as a scheduled task with the built in program called the Task Scheduler.

To start Task Scheduler

You can start Task Scheduler by double-clicking My Computer, and then double-clicking Scheduled Tasks.

Scheduled
Tasks

This will open the Scheduled Tasks folder. Double-click Add Scheduled Task to open the Scheduled Task wizard, which walks you through scheduling a task.

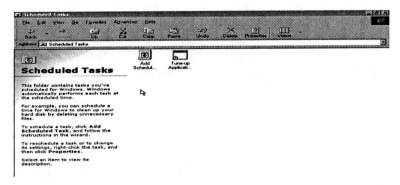

Figure 81 The Task Scheduler Screen

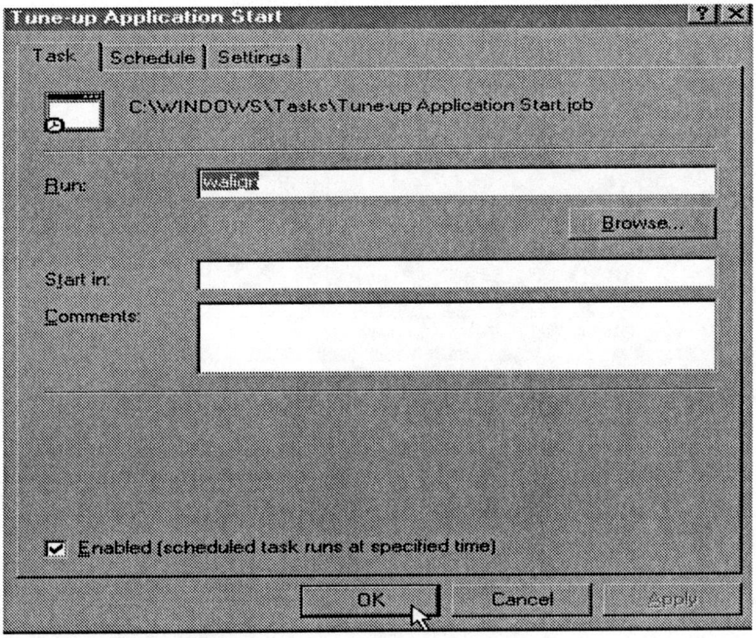

Figure 82 The Task Scheduler Option Screen.

This disk error checking program is known ScanDisk.

ScanDisk was designed to find and repair problems in the disk file system.

From Windows Help Files:

Check for Disk Errors using ScanDisk

You can use ScanDisk to check your hard disk for logical and physical errors. ScanDisk can then repair the damaged areas. This is important to do, because a damaged disk may cause your files to be stored improperly so that you won't be able to pull them up on your computer again.

To add ScanDisk to your StartUp folder:

On the task bar, ight click on the **Start** button, and select the Open command.

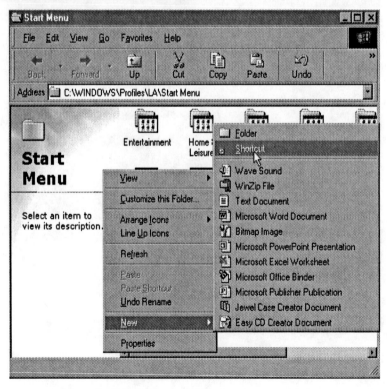

This will open a list of the contents of your Start Menu.

From there, right click on a blank area of the window, and choose **New** from the pop-up menu, then **Shortcut** from the next submenu.

Figure 83 The Shortcut command.

This starts another Windows wizard, to walk you through the steps involved in creating a shortcut.

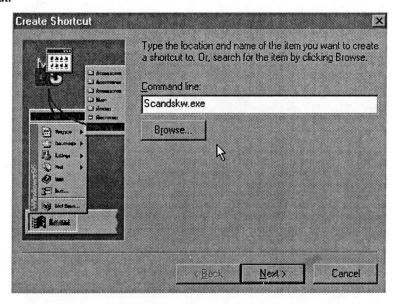

Figure 84 Screen prompt with Command Line.

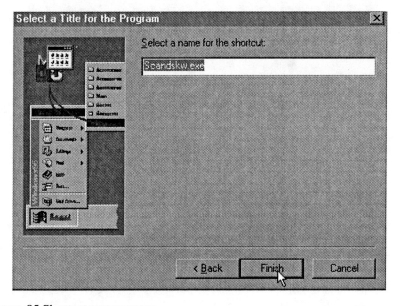

Figure 85 Shortcut name screen.

Figure 86 Shortcut

Shortcut result on the start **Start** menu.

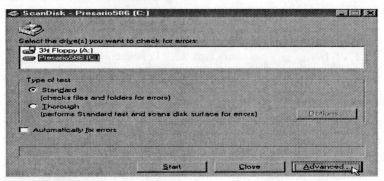

Figure 87 Starting ScanDisk

Figure 88 ScanDisk Options

FAT 16

Fat 16 was introduced with DOS Version 2. Technically, it supports up to **4 GB** of hard drive space.

Due to a bug in (MS) FDISK, the limitation for Windows 3.x/9.x Operating System1, the **limit** is stated to be a **2 GB** limit2

Fat LIMITS

This explains why there is a **4GB** limit for FAT 16 in **Windows NT** and a **2GB** limit when using **DOS** based **Windows.**

FAT 16 has other limitations as well. For example, *no more* than **512 entries** (that is, 512 files and folders) can be in the **root directory** of a hard drive.

Also with **FAT 16,** each **cluster,** or section of the FAT, gets larger **large** as **drive size** increases in each partition. This is important, as files are stored in groups of clusters much like you might store speech notes on 3x5 index cards. Whether there's one word or 5 lines on an index card, it still takes an entire card (unless you break with convention and tear off the part of the card you're not using!). The same is true with clusters. You can store an entire (small) program in the amount of disk space it takes to store the word "hello", because one entire cluster is used for each file. At the maximum size of 2 GB, each cluster becomes 64K. Since the cluster is the smallest area DOS can address (without additional software assistance) saving a 1 or 2 KB (Kilobyte) file wastes 62 to 63 KB of space. Storing a one-word file that contains the word "hello" wastes even more. For this and other reasons, FAT 32 is preferable.

Fat 16 Limits

FAT 16 is limited to 2 Gigabytes (GB) and is limited to 512 entries in the root.

Cluster Size

A cluster is the smallest area DOS can address.

Foot Note:
1 Some argue that Windows is not an Operating System. There is some merit to the statement, as Windows really operates on top of MS-DOS. And Microsoft calls Windows an Operating System. Since this is a course on preparing for the A+ O/S test from CompTIA, and Microsoft is a CompTIA member, it is considered an Operating System. So, your authors are referring to Windows as an Operating System. If you desire our personal opinion on the matter, drop a line to Authors@Tcat.net
2 With a non-MS FDISK, you can reach the hard math limit of 4 GB with FAT 16. If for some odd reason you 1) Need FAT 16, and 2) Need to exceed the 2 GB limit, send email to Tcat@Tcat.net with a reply address that can accept a file attachment, and he will send you a non MS-FDISK to accomplish your needs. The FDISK program is licensed under the GNU guidelines.

The good news about FAT 16 is that disk partitions in the FAT 16 format can be accessed by virtually every PC Operating System written.

OS & Fat 16

FAT 16 can be accessed by: Windows 95, Windows 95B (OSR 2), Windows 98, NT 4 and Windows 2000

Drive Converter

Drive Converter will convert from **FAT 16** to **FAT 32**. It will **Not convert!** from **FAT 32** to **FAT 16**

The less than stellar news about FAT16 beyond the limitations mentioned is *it is not* reliable. Some would call it down right fragile. For all these reasons, unless you have a specific need, avoid FAT 16 where possible. If you need FAT and can use FAT 32, it is a superior choice.

FAT 32

FAT 32 removed the 2 GB limit on file system size. Up to 2 TB (Terabytes) can be addressed with FAT 32. The cluster sizes in FAT 32 are much smaller (given 2^32 can address a much higher number), allowing more efficient use of disk space, with less wasted space. The 512 file limit for the root directory is gone, and the indexing system in FAT 32 is much more s table than FAT 16.

Other technical improvements in FAT 32 over FAT 16 abound. There are enough changes to fill a white paper (which Microsoft did). Everything from the stability via redundancy (2nd FAT) to more stable drive mapping can be found in FAT 32.

FAT 32 is supported by Windows **95B,** Windows **98** and Windows **2000.** Note that it is not available in Windows 95 (original release) or NT 4.

To make it easy to convert to FAT 32, Microsoft included in Win 95 B, Win 98, and Windows 2000 the Drive Converter.

This program will convert FAT 16 to FAT 32, but not backwards, so be sure when you use it, that you won't need to go back – or that you have a good backup of your FAT 16 data!

Pop Quiz 0001.0

 Pop Quiz 0001.0 *Questions*

1. The Disk Defragmenter utility is used to:

    A. Rearrange files and free space on disk to speed up access to the hard disk

    B. Convert from FAT16 to FAT32

    C. Delete small fragments of files left on disk after files were deleted

    D. Resolve driver issues causing data transfer problems

2. What is the limit for disk (file system) size using FAT16 in Windows 98?

    A. 540 megabytes

    B. 2 gigabytes

    C. 4 gigabytes

    D. 2 terabytes

3. A disk cluster is:

    A. A set of disks which make up a file system

    B. A server used as a file server

    C. The smallest area of disk that DOS can address

    D. The set of related files in a folder

4. The program used to convert a drive from FAT16 to FAT32 is:

    A. Disk Defragmenter

    B. Drive Converter

    C. Scandisk

    D. Disk Upgrade

5. Disk Defragmenter may have problems if _____ is running:

    A. Microsoft Office

    B. Internet Explorer

    C. Windows Explorer

    D. Anti-virus software

Pop Quiz 0001.0 *Answers*

1. Correct Answer: A

2. Correct Answer: B

3. Correct Answer: C

4. Correct Answer: B

5. Correct Answers: D

▶ Drive Converter Design

Drive Converter (FAT32) **converts** your drives **from** the original File Allocation Table **(FAT16) to FAT32,** a very efficient system for storing files on large disk drives (over 512 MB). Converting to FAT32 may create some free disk space.

Be aware that you *cannot* compress drives that use FAT32.

Using Drive Converter (FAT32)

Drive Converter converts your drive to the FAT32 file system, an enhancement of the File Allocation Table (FAT or FAT16) file system format. As noted previously, when your drive is in this format, it stores data more efficiently. If you're currently using FAT 16, you'll probably find that you "create" up to several hundred MB of extra disk space on the drive by converting to FAT 32.

The bonus is that programs load faster and your computer uses fewer system resources.

Start Drive Converter by clicking Start, point to Programs, point to Accessories, point to System Tools, and then clicking Drive Converter.

Figure 89 How to get to the Drive Converter.

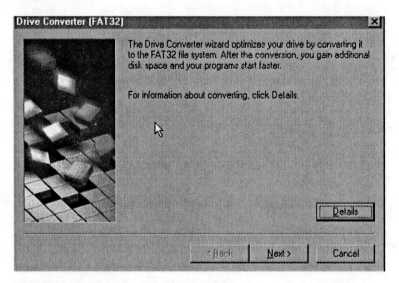

Figure 90 Screen prompt for Drive Converter

OOPs! The Drive Converter will also tell you if you can accomplish the task, or if it was already done!

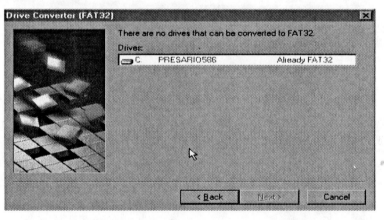

Figure 91 Drive Conversion or not screen

There is a lot to know before beginning a drive conversion. The following tips should be your guides.

Fat 32 Conversion Lookout!

Once you convert your hard drive to FAT32 format using Drive Converter, you cannot return to using the FAT16 format unless you repartition and reformat the FAT32 drive.

Windows 98 Conversion

If you **converted** the **drive** on which **Windows 98** is installed, then you must *reinstall* **Windows 98** after **repartitioning** the **drive**.

Caution!

Older disk compression software is not compatible with **FAT32**. If your drive is already **compressed,** you *may not be* able to convert to **FAT32**.

FAT 32 Compatibility

If you convert a removable disk and use the disk with other operating systems that *are not* FAT32-compatible, you cannot access the disk when running the other operating system.

Drive Converter Caution

If you convert your hard drive to FAT32 using Drive Converter, you can no longer use dual boot to run *earlier* versions of Windows (Windows 95 [Version 4.00.950], Windows NT 3.x, Windows NT 4.0, and Windows 3.x). However, if you are on a network, earlier versions of Windows can still gain access to your FAT32 hard drive through the network.

FAT 32 Space finder

If a computer has limited drive space, and the Operating System supports FAT 32, changing (converting) the drive to FAT 32 will improve usable drive space.

FAT 32 is born

FAT 32 was introduced with Windows 95 (B), sometimes called OSR2.While there are a great many new improvements to FAT with FAT 32, there is a downside. FAT 32 cannot be seen by Windows 95 (a) or NT 4.

Can you see the FAT?

Moving a drive or dual booting without regard to this limitation (FAT 32 not recognized by all OS) may result in volumes or partitions not being recognized.

Now, after that roundup of FAT 32 tips.... As cool as FAT 32 is, even it has it limitations, as seen when you review the features of NTFS.

NTFS4

The New Technology File System (NTFS) is the child of HPFS (High Performance File System) that was born with OS/2 Lan Man.

The last O/S that supported HPFS was NT 3.51. Beginning with NT 4, it was possible to convert to NTFS from either FAT 16 or HPFS. It could not create a HPFS *volume*.

NT4 can create a FAT 16 *volume*, (up to 4 GB), since it doesn't need FDISK. Frequently, you will see NTFS4 referred to simply as NTFS. The 4 got hung on the end with Windows 2000, when a new and improved version of NTFS was introduced in Windows 2000.

There are a great many features of NTFS that give good reasons to use this over FAT. File integrity is greatly increased, and guarding against a flaky hard drive may be a great reason for choosing NTFS over FAT anything.

NTFS File Structure Support

NTFS 4 supports FAT 16, NTFS 4 and CDFS.

Another reason for the existence of NTFS is the ability to hold on to more than the 4 file attributes available in FAT (archive, hidden, system, read-only). NTFS has a greatly expanded indexing system, which allows for security attributes to be attached to each file.

This can protect sensitive data from prying eyes, if the users login access does not allow reading of the file, they *cannot* read the file.

The down side to all this extra stuff is the indexing system (called the Master File Table or MFT) is so huge, it *cannot* fit on a 1.44 MB floppy.

Lost and Restored

Should files be backed up (saved) from NTFS and restored to a FAT based drive, the extra data, such as; security information is *lost*. Only the **4 file attributes** and **long file names** will be transferred.

NTFS Features

NTFS 4 allows for compression of data at the volume, directory or file level.

NTFS5

Without reasons to spend money on an upgrade OS, few would upgrade the OS just because something was new.

Microsoft gave a great many reasons to upgrade to Windows 2000 and NTFS V5. Beyond the features of NTFS V4, Microsoft created the concept of the dynamic disk.

A dynamic disk is akin to "storage in the sky" at least as far as the user is concerned.

To the A+ technician, a dynamic disk *can be* a series of physical drives that are located on different PCs and even be in different locations.

That leaves the question, "What to call a drive that is set up in the traditional format?"

The answer is they are referred to as Basic Volumes.

Windows 2000 File Structure Support

Windows 2000 supports FAT 16, FAT 32, NTFS 4, NTFS 5, and CDFS.

If a laptop or notebook computer is in the mix, and it has the resources to support Windows 2000, your authors strongly advise considering the use of Windows 2000. (PRO)

While support for new features such a USB and other features are very nice, one feature of Windows 2000 for mobile use is sufficient reason for the upgrade.

Windows 2000 supports all the features of NTFS 4, and adds the ability to encrypt data at the volume, directory or file level.

Since data is the real 'crown jewel' of any business, this is sufficient reason to go W2K on a mobile computer.

While NT 4 *does not* allow access based on permission, installing a new copy of NT would allow anyone to become the administrator and 'take' the file or entire drive volume, rendering security on a mobile computer no security at all.

Encryption (encoding data so that it is unreadable without a password or other proof by a user that they are authorized to see the data) on W2K can be made rather tight, making a 'lost' laptop tough to crack open to discover business secrets.

NTFS5 Supports

NTFS 5 supports Compress and Encryption at the volume, directory or file level.

HPFS

As mentioned above, HPFS was born with OS/2 LanMan. OS/2 was a joint venture between Microsoft and IBM to replace DOS.

This project dates back to the mid 1980's. While tension increased between the two corporations, the final rift occurred over the fate of the AT (80286).

IBM wanted to support the 286, and Microsoft insisted on leaving it behind, and set the baseline (minimum) with the 386.

They parted ways, with IBM creating its own GUI interface with *TopView*, and supporting the 286, and Microsoft working on NT (New Technology) that required a 386.

Today, there are few drives running HPFS.

IV Summary

Understanding file structure and how the FAT works or not with each operating system will assist us in planning installation and setup of the hard drive. Understanding the various features of each type of FAT will help in troubleshooting file sharing and drive space issues.

By learning about drive fragmentation and defragmentation we can mange hard drives more efficiently. The various utilities mentioned to install and maintain our FAT should be explored through further practice. This chapter was an introduction to the concepts and further study is encouraged.

V TotalRecall: Test for Success Questions

1. What happens when you delete a file from the Recycle Bin?
    A. Clusters are flushed.
    B. The files are moved to C:\Windows\Temp.
    C. Sectors of hard drive are blanked/erased.
    D. Associated entries in the FAT are removed.

---

2. You back up files on an NTFS partition using the Backup utility, and then later restore them to a FAT32 partition. Which file properties are retained? (Choose two)
    A. Encryption.
    B. Permission.
    C. Compressions.
    D. File attributes.
    E. Long file names.

3. Which advantages does FAT32 have over FAT16? (Choose three)

   A. Programs load faster.

   B. Fewer resources required.

   C. Greater file security allowed.

   D. Drive mappings are more reliable.

   E. Increase storage efficiencies.

---

4. What do you need to do to make a Windows 98 system dual boot with Windows 2000 on a single partition?

   A. Install Windows 2000 in NTFS.

   B. Install Windows 2000 in FAT 32.

   C. Delete any FAT32 partitions and install.

   D. Run Windows 2000 Setup: Dual Boot version.

5. A technician needs to convert a FAT16 partition to NTFS from a DOS prompt. Which command should the technician use?

 A. SYS C:A:C:

 B. FDISK /MBR

 C. FORMAT C:/S

 D. CONVERT C:/FS:NTFS

---

6. Your client reports that he is running Windows 98 and has a 2GB hard drive. It is formatted as FAT16; he is nearly out of disk space. What is the simplest and quickest way to increase his disk space?

 A. Convert the drive to FAT32.

 B. Run the Space Recovery utility.

 C. Replace the hard drive with a larger one.

 D. Back up the data, format the drive and restore the data.

7. In Windows 98, which of the following conversions is possible?

    A. FAT16 to NTFS.

    B. FAT32 to FAT16.

    C. FAT16 to FAT32 and FAT32 to FAT16.

    D. FAT16 to FAT32 but not FAT32 to FAT16.

---

8. You have set up a dual boot computer. Your Windows 2000 installation has been tested, and has no problems. However when in Windows 98 you cannot see the files in the NTFS partition. Windows 98 resides on a FAT 32 partition and Windows 2000 operates on an NTFS partition. Why?

    A. The partition has not been made active.

    B. File sharing between the drives has not been enabled.

    C. Windows 98 is not compatible with NTFS.

    D. NTLDR is not set to load when starting Windows 98.

9. In Windows 98, what will ensure that you have created a FAT16 partition?

    A. FAT 16 is not supported by Windows 98.

    B. Select N when prompted to enable large disk support running Fdisk.

    C. Select N when prompted to create an Extended partition when running FDISK.

    D. Select Y when prompted to implement a large partition when running FDISK.

10. After you install NT Workstation 4.0 on your Windows 98 computer, you find that in NT Workstation you cannot see your Windows 98 partition. Why?

    A. The NT partition is formatted with FAT16.

    B. The Windows 98 partition is formatted with FAT32.

    C. Windows 98 was deleted during the installation.

    D. The Windows 98 partition has not been set as active within NT Workstation's settings.

11. What advantages does FAT32 have over FAT? (Choose two)
   A. Faster file access.
 * B. More efficient compression.
   C. Reduced cluster size.
   D. Increased logical drive size.
 * E. Increased security attributes.

---

12. Which file system in Windows 2000 supports compression?
   A. CDFS
   B. HPFS
   C. FAT32
 * D. NTFS

13. You have taken a hard drive from a computer using Windows 98 and installed it into a computer running Windows 95 as a second drive. The BIOS recognizes the drive but the drive does not appear when you open My Computer. Why?

    A. You forgot to run Convert32.exe.

    B. The new drive is partitioned with FAT32.

    C. You forgot to install a new driver for the drive.

    D. The new drive is write protected.

TotalRecall: Test for Success Answers

1. What happens when you delete a file from the Recycle Bin?
    A. Clusters are flushed.
    B. The files are moved to C:\Windows\Temp.
    C. Sectors of hard drive are blanked/erased.
    D. Associated entries in the FAT are removed.

Explanation: D, Associated entries in the FAT are removed. Recall that the Recycle
   Bin is a temporary holding place for deleted files, designed to give you one last
   chance to retrieve a deleted file before you empty the recycle bin, or specifically
   delete one or more files from it. When a file is deleted from the Recycle Bin, or the
   Recycle Bin is emptied, the file is removed from disk, so it is not true that the files
   are moved to a temp directory after being deleted from the Recycle Bin. Clusters are
   not flushed, and hard drive sectors are not erased – that term implies that the data is
   somehow wiped out, which doesn't (normally) happen on Windows. However, the
   clusters related to the file can no longer be accessed, because the FAT entries
   (directory entries) allowing access to the file have been removed.

---

2. You back up files on an NTFS partition using the Backup utility, and then later restore
    them to a FAT32 partition. Which file properties are retained? (Choose two)
    A. Encryption.
    B. Permission.
    C. Compressions.
    D. File attributes.
    E. Long file names.

Explanation: D. File attributes and **E. Long file names** are retained.
Encryption, Permission and Compression are not. FAT32 does not offer encryption or file
   access permissions.

3. Which advantages does FAT32 have over FAT16? (Choose three)

   A. Programs load faster.

   B. Fewer resources required.

   C. Greater file security allowed.

   D. Drive mappings are more reliable.

   E. Increase storage efficiencies.

Explanation: A. Programs load faster, D. Drive mappings are more reliable and **E. Increase storage efficiencies** are found in FAT32 vs. FAT16. Neither FAT32 nor FAT16 offer file security.

---

4. What do you need to do to make a Windows 98 system dual boot with Windows 2000 on a single partition?

   A. Install Windows 2000 in NTFS.

   B. Install Windows 2000 in FAT 32.

   C. Delete any FAT32 partitions and install.

   D. Run Windows 2000 Setup: Dual Boot version.

Explanation: B. Install Windows 2000 in FAT 32. Windows 2000 understands FAT32. You cannot install a dual-boot Windows 2000 and Windows 98 configuration on an NTFS drive, because Windows 98 does not understand NTFS.

5. A technician needs to convert a FAT16 partition to NTFS from a DOS prompt. Which command should the technician use?

A. SYS C:A:C:

B. FDISK /MBR

C. FORMAT C:/S

D. CONVERT C:/FS:NTFS

Explanation: D. CONVERT C:/FS:NTFS is the correct command in Windows 2000 to convert a FAT16 partition to NTFS. Sys transfers system files but does not reformat the drive. FDISK/MBR will sometimes help recover a corrupt disk. Format c:/s will reformat the hard drive, erasing all of its contents.

6. Your client reports that he is running Windows 98 and has a 2GB hard drive. It is formatted as FAT16; he is nearly out of disk space. What is the simplest and quickest way to increase his disk space?

A. Convert the drive to FAT32.

B. Run the Space Recovery utility.

C. Replace the hard drive with a larger one.

D. Back up the data, format the drive and restore the data.

Explanation: A. Convert the drive to FAT32 is an easy way to get some more disk space quickly, if the disk is currently formatted as FAT16. There is no "Space Recovery" utility. Replacing the hard drive and backup/format/restore both take far more time than running convert.

7. In Windows 98, which of the following conversions is possible?
    A. FAT16 to NTFS.
    B. FAT32 to FAT16.
    C. FAT16 to FAT32 and FAT32 to FAT16.
    D. FAT16 to FAT32 but not FAT32 to FAT16.

Explanation: D. FAT16 to FAT32 but not FAT32 to FAT16 is the correct answer.
Windows 98 does not support NTFS. And, you cannot convert from FAT32 back to
    FAT16 using the standard utilities available within Windows 98 (although there are
    third party packages that will allow this).

8. You have set up a dual boot computer. Your Windows 2000 installation has been
    tested, and has no problems. However when in Windows 98 you cannot see the files
    in the NTFS partition. Windows 98 resides on a FAT 32 partition and Windows
    2000 operates on an NTFS partition. Why?
    A. The partition has not been made active.
    B. File sharing between the drives has not been enabled.
    C. Windows 98 is not compatible with NTFS.
    D. NTLDR is not set to load when starting Windows 98.

Explanation: C. Windows 98 is not compatible with NTFS.

9. In Windows 98, what will ensure that you have created a FAT16 partition?

   A. FAT 16 is not supported by Windows 98.

   B. Select N when prompted to enable large disk support running FDISK.

   C. Select N when prompted to create an Extended partition when running FDISK.

   D. Select Y when prompted to implement a large partition when running FDISK.

Explanation: B. Select N when prompted to enable large disk support running FDISK is the proper answer. "Large disk support" is the code phrase that indicates a version of FAT that will work on larger drives than are supported by FAT16.

---

10. After you install NT Workstation 4.0 on your Windows 98 computer, you find that in NT Workstation you cannot see your Windows 98 partition. Why?

   A. The NT partition is formatted with FAT16.

   B. The Windows 98 partition is formatted with FAT32.

   C. Windows 98 was deleted during the installation.

   D. The Windows 98 partition has not been set as active within NT Workstation's settings.

Explanation: B. The Windows 98 partition is formatted with FAT32. NT does not support FAT32, so it will not see the contents of a disk formatted with it. If the NT partition is formatted with FAT16, that would not prevent it from seeing a Windows 98 partition unless that partition was FAT32. When you set a partition active, it is across all systems, not just per OS, so if you can use Windows 98 on the computer but can't see its partition when running NT Workstation, 'active partition' is not the issue.

11. What advantages does FAT32 have over FAT? (Choose two)
    A. Faster file access.
    B. More efficient compression.
    C. Reduced cluster size.
    D. Increased logical drive size.
    E. Increased security attributes.

Explanation: C. Reduced cluster size and **D. Increased logical drive size** are two advantages. FAT32 doesn't support security attributes. Additionally, faster file access and more efficient compression are not necessarily attributes.

---

12. Which file system in Windows 2000 supports compression?
    A. CDFS
    B. HPFS
    C. FAT32
    D. NTFS

Explanation: D. NTFS supports compression.

13. You have taken a hard drive from a computer using Windows 98 and installed it into a computer running Windows 95 as a second drive. The BIOS recognizes the drive but the drive does not appear when you open My Computer. Why?

A. You forgot to run Convert32.exe.

B. The new drive is partitioned with FAT32.

C. You forgot to install a new driver for the drive.

D. The new drive is write protected.

Explanation: B. The new drive is partitioned with FAT32. Windows 95 (a) does not support FAT32. Running Convert32 will convert a drive from FAT16 to FAT32, so that won't help. Windows 95 includes IDE drivers automatically. It's unlikely that the drive is write-protected (some high-end SCSI drives offer this feature, but most don't).

Attitude determines how well you do it

-Lou Holtz-

Chapter 0010: File Attributes

Introduction

The attributes or properties of a file will dictate how we can access or use those files. Understanding the various file properties is key to successfully negotiating the A+ Operating System test. Understanding the properties associated with the various attributes will also aid in managing file security, and file sharing.

Getting Ready - Questions

1. What is the possible reason that, when booting, an error message " Current driver is no longer valid" appears?

   A: boot disk does not contain CONFIG.SYS

   B: boot disk does not contain AUTOEXEC.BAT

   C: AUTOEXEC.BAT command attempted to access a drive that is not valid

   D: CONFIG.SYS command line attempted to access a drive that is not valid

2. An application is uninstalled on a system. The next time the system boots up, an error message stating that a device file may be needed to run Windows or a Windows application cannot be found. Which program should be used to fix the problem? (Choose two)

   A: DEFRAG

   B: SYSEDIT

   C: REGEDIT

   D: SCANDICK

   E. DISKCLEAN

3. What does Drive Compression do?

   A. Decrease the amount of space it takes to store each file on disk

   B. Compress drive commands to speed up the drive

   C. Copies multiple small drives onto one larger drive

   D. Delete files not used in the past 3 months

4. The process of copying data back to disk from a backup is called:

   A. Recover

   B. Replace

   C. Unbackup

   D. Restore

5. What backup stragegy involves a backup of everything on the system, followed by backups of everything that has changed since the last backup?

   Full + incremental

   Full + differential

   Differential

   Incremental

Getting Ready - Answers

1. *Correct Answer:* **C**

2. *Correct answer:* **B&C**

3. *Correct answer:* **A**

4. *Correct answer:* **D**

5. *Correct answer:* **A**

II   File Attributes

All computer files have **attributes.** Those **attributes** are **properties** of a **file,** which determine what we can do with a **file.** These **properties** are **permissions,** the manner in which we can **view, read, share, print,** or **copy** a **file.**

Attributes and Permissions

To view the properties of a file:

Open   My Computer, or Windows Explorer, and double-click on the C Drive. Look for

the Program Files folder, Program Files and right-click on the folder, to bring up the

menu. Click on Properties,

Program Files Properties   ? X

    General | Sharing |

            Program Files

    Type: File Folder
    Location: C:\
    Size: 488MB (512,324,977 bytes), 523,304,960 bytes used
    Contains: 4,894 Files, 331 Folders

    MS-DOS name: PROGRA~1
    Created: (unknown)

    Attributes: ☑ Read-only   ☐ Hidden
                   ☐ Archive   ☐ System

                   ☐ Enable thumbnail view

                   OK   Cancel   apply

Figure 92 File Properties Window

As you can see there are several options to check regarding the properties of this file folder. In this instance the **Read-only** property  is checked and therefore defined. (More about what this means, later!) This is a **file attribute**.

If we click on the **Sharing** Tab, the following window appears. This is a **file property**.

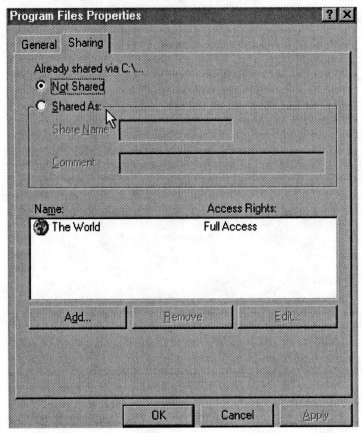

Figure 93 The Sharing Tab Window

Notice that this folder is not shared. This means that **permission** is not granted to network users on other computers, to view the file. This is known as **network file permission** or **network share permission**. Share permissions apply to users accessing network files from Windows 9x machines in addition to NT machines.

Note: Be aware that these are permissions for network users on other computers in your network. On Windows 9x, even if a file or folder is not shared, it doesn't mean that no one except you can ever access it – anyone logging on to your computer will be able to access your files or folders. Remember that only NTFS has additional attributes to specify file permissions that apply to local users as well as network users.

If we click on Shared As, we will see the following Window appear.

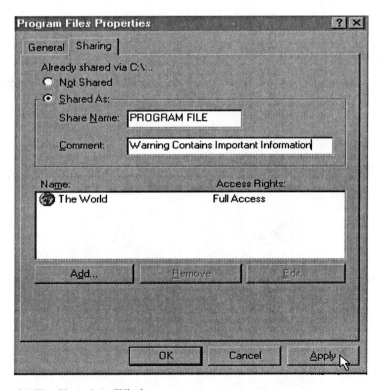

Figure 94 The Shared As Window

To add sharing, we click on the **Shared As** button and then add any comments we may have. An example of this appears in the Window.

We must then **choose whom** to **share** this folder **with**.

When the folder or file is shared we will then see a graphical depiction of this when we

view the folder as an icon. Program Files

File/Folder Properties

To get to File/Folder Properties, you can also right-click a folder or file
that is on the desktop, and then click Properties.

Changing file or folder properties

Like many other activities in Windows, there's more than one way to change the
properties of a file

From My Computer 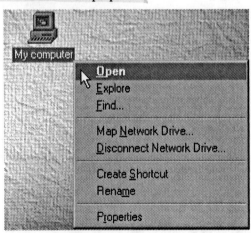 , you can view files by using the Open or Explore
options, and right click to access their properties.

Figure 95 Open from My Computer

Right-Click works

You can also right-click a folder or file that is on the desktop, and then click Properties.

From Windows Explorer, 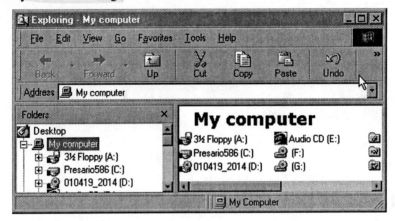 you can also click the file or folder whose properties you want to change.

Figure 96 Windows Explorer

On the **File** menu, click **Properties**.

Enter changes in the **Properties** *dialog box.*

Window Panes

You can also go to **Windows Explorer**, choose the **folder** in the left window **"pane"**, **right-click** the folder to **change** the **properties**

So we have learned how to get there from here. Now let's learn what these **file permissions** and **properties** mean.

File properties and Permissions

Permissions are telling us what we **can** or **cannot do** with a **file**. Most commonly **permissions** are **used** on a **network** where **files** are **shared**.

The main file permissions are:

Read Only

Hidden

System

Archive

Read Only attribute

The **read only** permission means just that! This file is to be **read, but not changed** in anyway. Right clicking on the folder options **Folder Options...** will produce the window to make the **read only** permission change.

Hidden attribute

Hidden 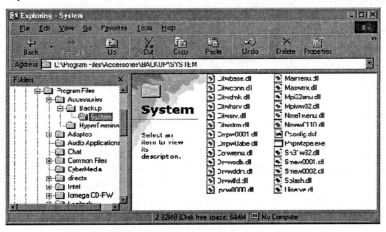 Hidden files files are typically the files that we do not need to access when viewing a program. These might be **driver files** for example. Typically most **system** files are **hidden.** Remember how we set the system to "Show all files" earlier? Without this option set, files which have the "hidden" attribute are not displayed in the Windows Explorer and other programs. Hidden files can cause much fun for a support professional when troubleshooting. Be sure to set the system to show all files, from Windows Explorer's Folder Options -> View menu.

> 📁 Hidden files
> ○ Do not show hidden files
> ○ Do not show hidden or system files
> ⦿ Show all files

Figure 97 The Choices from the View menu

To remind you how to do this...

Figure 98 Hidden Files In Windows Explorer

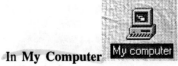

In **My Computer** or **Windows Explorer,** 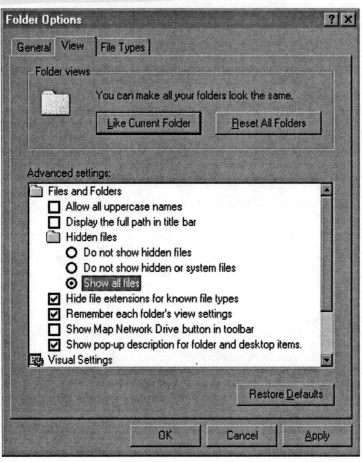 click the folder you want to look at.

Program Files   On the **View** menu, click **Folder Options**.

Click the **View** Tab, and then click **Show all files**.

Figure 99 All Files Option in Windows Explorer

If you want to see *all* file name extensions, click to clear the **Hide file extensions** for known **file types** check the following box. ☐ Hide file extensions for known file types. We'll talk more about this in the section on file naming conventions.

System attribute

System files are the files that relate to the **engine** of the **Operating System**. These files might be **driver** or similar types of files. The **Dynamic Link Library files** (.DLL) ▭ .dll are some of the most common. These are **files** found in the **Operating System**.

Typically we can view these files by going to Explorer and then the Windows folder, then the system folder. ▭ System Address ▭ C:\WINDOWS\SYSTEM

Archive attribute

The archive attribute is set by the system to indicate that the file has changed recently and should be included on the Administrator's next backup of the system. Typically, this is set when a new file is created or if a user modifies an existing file, say, by updating a word processing file of company policies.

Remember the RASH

As we have already learned FAT has 4 attributes that can be assigned to a file. The attributes <u>R</u>ead only, <u>A</u>rchive, <u>S</u>ystem, <u>H</u>idden, can be remembered by the acronym, **RASH**.

There is much to know about files, as we have already learned. The basics of saving a file are quite straightforward. There are several ways to do this.

III   Saving Files

To save a file we typically will be in a Window and use the **Save** command from the menu. The **CTRL + S** key can accomplish the save as well.

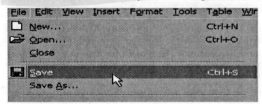

Figure 100 The Save Option

Clicking the **Save As** option will allow for saves in a particular **location** or with a **name change** of the file.

To save a file with a different name or format

On the **File** menu of the program you are working in, click **Save As**. Specify (type in) (or scroll to view the file extension options) the **name** and or **format** in which you want to save the **file**. If the **file** was **previously saved** with a different name or **format**, that version will remain **unchanged**.

File Protection
If a file was previously saved with a different name or format, that version will remain unchanged. This serves as a protection of the original file in case you make a mistake or lose the new file.

When working with graphics we can **change** the **type** of **file** (format) for instance from a **bitmap** (.BMP) to a JPEG (.JPG) and still **view** the **picture**. The properties of the file also change in this instance.

Warning!

Changing the file extension to a file type that is not compatible will render the file unreadable!

On the bright side, changing the extension back again will magically make the file readable again.

All **files** have some sort of **format** to identify the **program** they are **associated** with. These **file formats** are better understood by learning more about **file naming conventions** (methods).

File Naming Conventions (Most common extensions)

The Windows file naming convention is that a file name is made up of the main descriptive part of the name, then a dot followed by 3 letters after the filename. This dot + 3 letters (like ".ext") is referred to as the file name extension. The extension is used by Windows to determine the type of data in a file, and which programs can be used to open the file. For example, when saving a word processing document, you might see the following. Note that ".doc" appears twice, once in the name, and once to confirm that the type of data in the file is the usual ".doc".

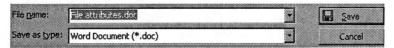

Figure 101 The File extension appears when saving a file

The most common file extensions are;

.EXE executable

.BAT batch

.SYS system

.DLL dynamic link library

.INI   initialization

.COM Command

Calc.exe   cal.ini   magicc.bat   Msdos.sys

Some of the more common document files are;

.TXT text

.DOC

Sqlsrdme.txt   Script.doc

Some of the more common graphics file extensions are;

.BMP (Bitmap)

.JPG   (JPEG)

.GIF (graphic image format)

.PNG   (Portable network graphic)

Bubbles.bmp Wave.jpg tips.gif settab.png

File Names

A file name can contain <u>up to</u> **255 characters**, *including* spaces. It *cannot* contain the following characters: \ / : * ? " < >

Remember that when we discussed how to "Show all files", we also mentioned another option on that menu page, **Hide file extensions for known file types**? As with hidden files, hidden file name extensions can be confusing when you're trying to troubleshoot, so the authors recommend that you make sure this option is turned off, by clearing the check-box as described earlier.

Lost in the Maze?

We have so many files in our computer it can be very easy to forget where we put them. We may simply not know because a program **auto saved** (to a default location) them for us. There is **help**! Windows contains a **Find** function that will help us locate files, based on what we remember about them.

Try using this method for finding a file.

Click **Start**, point to **Find**, and then click **Files** or **Folders**.

Click **Date** to look for **files** that were **created** or **modified** on or between specific dates.

Click **Find Now**.

Figure 102 Find Files or Folders

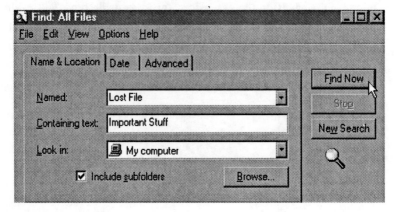

Figure 103 Find All Files

Notice we can include **subfolders**. These are the **folders** that have **associated information** such as a **viewer** for a **picture**. The search below in the **Advanced** tab is looking for a **.BMP** (Bitmap file) a type of **picture** or **graphic file**.

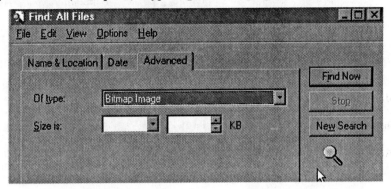

Figure 104 Find (.bmp) Bitmap File

File Search

Click the **Advanced** tab to look for files of a specific type (extension) or size.

Database lookout

Some application programs (database programs are famous for this) use their own "proprietary" file system format. If you need to use one of these applications, be aware that it's unlikely that the standard Windows tools for managing and searching disk (file) contents will work.

IV ◆ File Management

There are a few more things to know about managing files. Along with the **basic file attributes**, we can apply a few advanced features such as **compression** and **encryption**.

Compress? Encrypt?

What to do when? Let's first understand what compression is. Compression of a file occurs when a program applies algorithms to the file to make it smaller or more compact.

Hence, we have the term compression. Think of it like taking all the air out of a plastic bag. The reason compression is applied to a file most typically is to assist in disk/drive management. This means we have more storage space.

There are many 3rd party programs out there to perform this function. We commonly refer to these compression programs as zipping.

We have one compression program built into Windows. It can also be used to **compress a drive** (if the drive is not FAT 32). A hard drive contains files, and when this program is properly applied, will **compress those files** for us as we save them as part of the **file attributes**.

The program built into **Windows 9x** is called **Drive Space 3.**

Drive Space 3

To configure **DriveSpace 3** to compress files as you save them;

Start DriveSpace 3 [3 DriveSpace] by clicking **Start,** [Start] point to **Programs,** [Programs] point to **Accessories,** [Accessories] point to **System Tools,** [System Tools] and then click **DriveSpace 3.** [3 DriveSpace]

Start DriveSpace 3. [3 DriveSpace]

On the **Advanced** menu [Advanced], click **Settings.** [Settings...]

Click Standard compression. [⊙ Standard compression]

(handwritten) OR Disk Cleanup in JK

Standard Compression provides compression *without* (much) loss of speed.

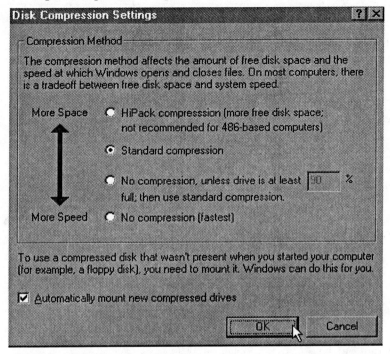

Figure 105 Disk Compression Settings

With standard compression in Windows 98, files are typically compressed to just over half their original size. With standard compression in DriveSpace 3, more of your disk is searched for repetitive data, providing even better compression while maintaining performance.

Figure 106 Standard Compression information from Windows Help files

DriveSpace is a program

To use a compressed DriveSpace 3 drive on another computer, DriveSpace 3 must be installed on it.

Compression Agent Needs DS3

You can use Compression Agent to compress files only on drives compressed using DriveSpace 3.

However, if you are low on hard disk space and have a fast processor, use HI Pack compression.

Prices to Pay

HI Pack provides more compression, *fast* reading but *slower* writing to the drive.

Hence, the need for a faster processor. This method compresses files to approximately half the original size.

Compress a Drive

When all the files on your computer are filling up your drive, try using the Windows feature called Compression Agent. This will compress *all* of the files on your drive.

Right click on a drive to view the free space.

Capacity: 1.98 GB

Used: 1.64 GB

Free: 355 MB

Using Compression Agent

You can use Compression Agent 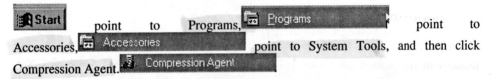 to compress selected files using the settings you specify. Compression Agent, 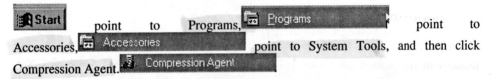 will help you save disk space by compressing files, or improve performance by changing the level of compression on your files.

During file recompression on your drive, the Compression Agent 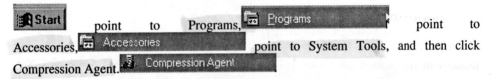 updates the information in a Table to show you how your disk space changes as files are moved from one compression method to another.

To open Compression Agent;

Open Compression Agent by clicking Start,

 point to Programs, point to Accessories, point to System Tools, and then click Compression Agent.

This feature is used primarily for compressing all the files on a drive.

Figure 107 Compression Agent Wizard

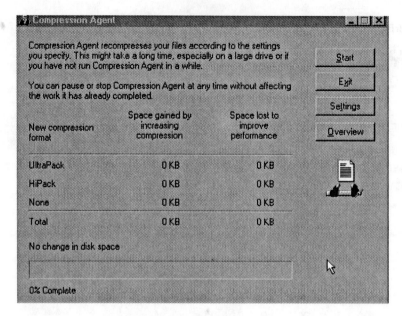

Figure 108 Compression Agent Window

Understanding disk compression

When a drive is compressed it looks and feels like a real drive. This is because after compression a *new drive letter* is assigned to the compressed space. This new space file is called a compressed volume drive (CVF).

The hard drive you compressed became a new drive letter and the CVF file is stored on the uncompressed drive. Confused?

Try picturing this; Drive C is full and needs compression. The Compression Agent will rename that to drive D then compress the contents of that drive and call it drive D. The compressed file CVF is *stored* on D and then it will become the host drive for C.

The new drive D will look and act just like your old drive C except drive C now has more space on it.

Only drives that have been compressed can have the free space available adjusted.

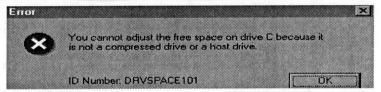

Figure 109 OOPS! Error

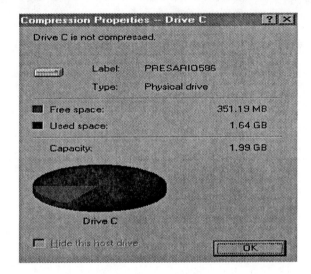

Figure 110 Compression Properties

Encryption

So what else can we do to a file or a drive? We can encrypt it.! Why encrypt? For security!

Encryption is a means of applying an algorithm to the file and making it secure.

Think of this like trying to decode hidden words in a puzzle. When applied to a file, the encryption program reassembles the information to its code, then when decrypted, assembles it back again as it was meant to be read.

PGP (Pretty Good Privacy) is one such program.

The point is to make sure that the file is secure Sometimes keys are needed to "unlock" the file encryption. A key is like having the secret code or password to open the file.

Permissions & Security
While not the same as encryption, applying strict permissions to files, at the least, deters unwanted viewers.

Pop Quiz 0010.0

 Pop Quiz 0010.0 *Questions*

1. What function is available in the Windows 98 Start Menu, to help you locate a file if you're not sure what directory it was saved in?
   A. Scandisk
   B. Checkdisk
   C. Directory
   D. Find

2. What program allows you to recover disk space by reducing the amount of space used to store each file?
   A. Compression Agent
   B. Disk Agent
   C. FAT32
   D. Device Manager

3. DriveSpace3 is available in Windows 2000
   A. True
   B. False

4. Which of the following is not a Windows file attribute?
   A. System
   B. Archive
   C. Deleted
   D. Read-only

5. Which of the following is not a common Windows file extension?
   A. .RUN
   B. .DLL
   C. .EXE
   D. .TXT

Pop Quiz 0010.0 *Answers*

1. Correct Answer: D

2. Correct Answer: A

3. Correct Answer: B

4. Correct Answer: C

5. Correct Answers: A

V **Backup/Restore**

All of these files we create everyday need to be managed Part of that management includes backing up (saving) our files. There are different types of backups and methods.

Method to the Madness

One of the simplest ways is to save the file to another disk such as a **floppy** disk. We call this **removable media**. Today with the ease of **CD-R/RW** burning, we can backup this way.

Another method is to **backup the files** on another **drive** or across a **network** to another drive. One of the most common methods is to **backup the files** to a **tape drive**. Have you heard the phrase **"restore from tape?"**

If we lose a drive or a file then we have a copy of the information to restore from.

We back up in the first place because we **lose files, corrupt files** and **drives die**. As our data is important the **method** we employ to **protect** that **data** should be carefully **considered**.

We can specify where, when and how the **files** will be backed up. If we are on a network the **system administrator** makes those decisions and uses a backup (program) **agent**. There is also **scheduling** done to determine what type of Backup will occur.

Backup Considerations
First we consider the media on which we want to back up then we decide on the method.

Archive Bit

Now that we've heard more about backup, we can talk more about the **archive bit**. What is the **archive bit**?

This is an **attribute** (remember **RASH**?) that indicates a **file status** regarding the **backup attribute applied** to the **file**. When this **bit** is **set**, the **backup utility program** (agent) keeps track of the **file attribute** information, and each time a program or file is used or opened it checks to see if the **information** has **changed** and includes this **file** or **program** in the **backup**, thus **saving** the **changes**.

The **bit** is **set** (meaning the placeholder for the information is recognized) by the **network operating system** (NOS), which in turn **alerts** the **backup utility** to include **any files** that were **changed**, when the **archive bit** "alarm" (if you will) was setoff, in a backup. The bit is **"turned on"** when a **file** is **changed**.

Archive Bit ON/OFF
The bit is "turned off" when a full or incremental backup is performed.

VI **All Backups are not created equal**

Full Backup

This choice means:

Everything selected is **fully backed up!** The **entire drive** will be recoverable in the event of a failure. Be sure all the **hidden files are checked**. Typically this is done **weekly**. The **archive bit** is then reset.

Restoring Full Backups

This method is the slowest, but most complete and reliable backup possible. To restore from a **full backup set** simply use the **full set** (complete) of tapes or other media and begin the **restoration** process.

Differential Backup

This choice means:

All files that have **changed** *since* the **last full** (complete) **backup** are saved in this backup method. Typically this is done **once a week** *concluding* with a **full backup of the week**(separate process) and then when the next week starts, the **cycle** (schedule) of **backups of all files** that have *changed* since this most **recent last full backup** begins again. The maximum number of **backup sessions** that occur in a **week** for this **method** is **five,** assuming that users work on the system five days a week. The **archive bit** is *not* touched (reset) during each backup.

Restoring Differential Backups

This method is **slower,** but not as slow as a full backup. This method is **safer** than an **incremental backup** but *not* as easy as a full backup to restore. When you need to **restore** you must use a full set (all of them!) of the **full** (complete) **backup tapes,** *and* the most *current* **differential backup tape.**

Incremental Backup

This choice means:

A **partial backup** of **files** that have *changed* , since the **last full backup**. Typically this is method is used as a **daily backup**. This means that *only* the files that have *changed* are backed up each day and since the amount of data or information is less, it is a **faster method**. The **archive bit** is cleared each backup.

Restoring Incremental Backups

To **restore** from tape using this backup method, you must use the **full backup** (complete) set of **tapes** *AND each* **daily tape**, going all the way back to the **last full backup**.

This **method** is the **fastest** backup, but **not** the **safest** as the **archive bit** is **cleared**. Do not rely on this method alone.

Backup Method for Windows 9x

The following windows will show you the typical display in Windows 98 look like for backup options.

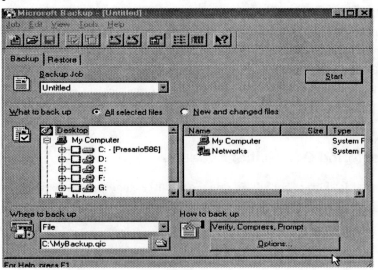

Figure 111 The Backup options window

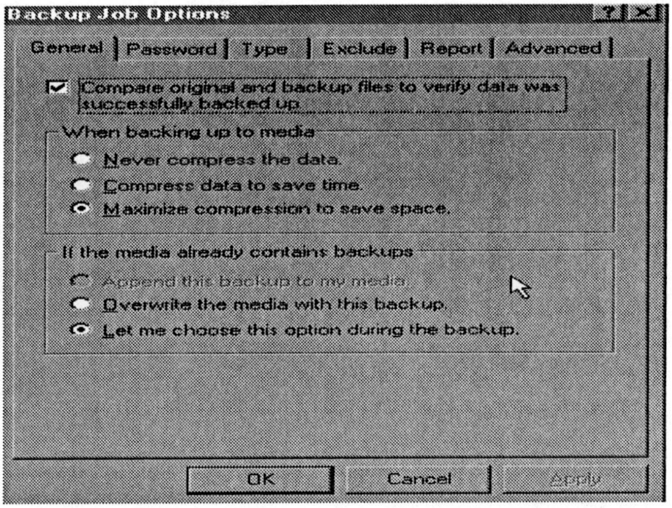

Figure 112 Backup Options General Tab

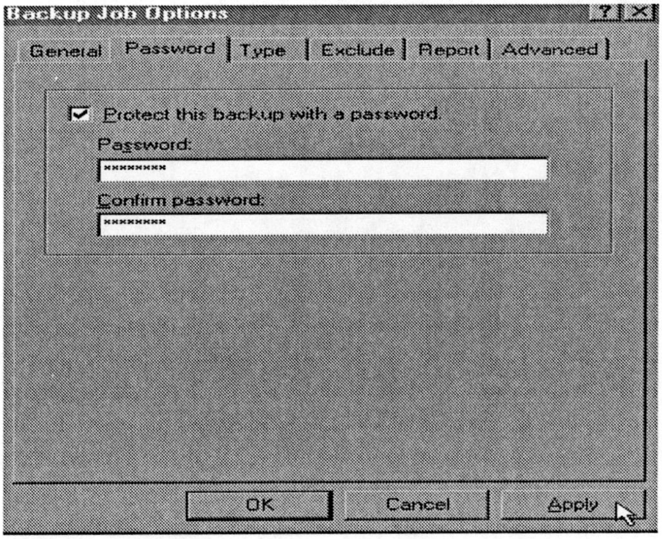

Figure 113 Backup Options Password Tab

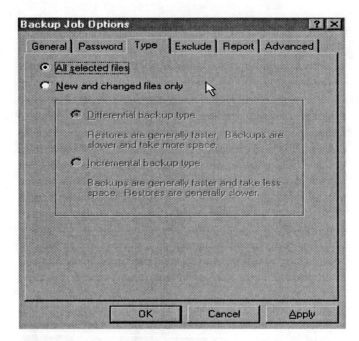

Figure 114 Backup Options Type Tab All Files

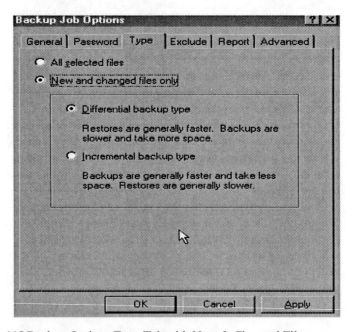

Figure 115 Backup Options Type Tab with New & Changed Files

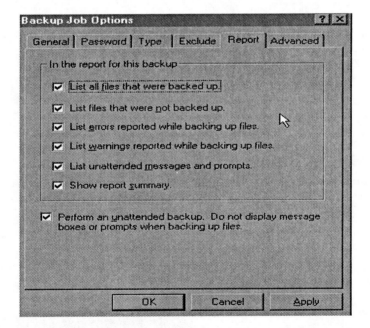

Figure 116 Backup Options Exclude Tab

Figure 117 Backup Options Report Tab

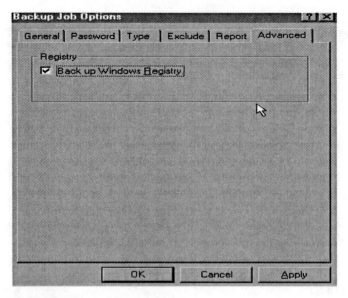

Figure 118 Backup Options Advanced Tab

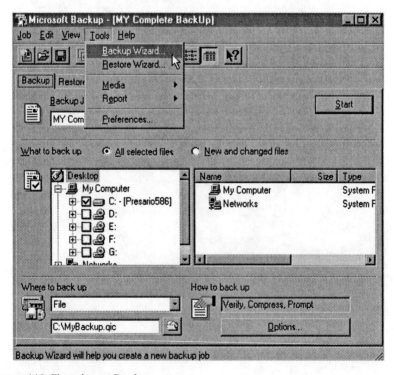

Figure 119 Choosing to Backup

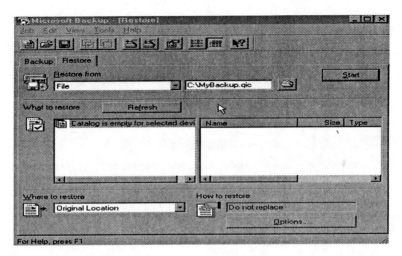

Figure 120 Choosing to Restore

To Start a Backup;

Start Backup 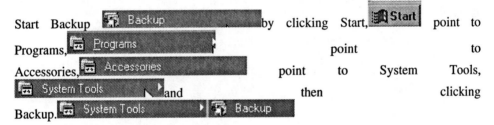 by clicking Start, point to Programs, point to Accessories, point to System Tools, and then clicking Backup.

Is it there?
If Backup is not listed on the Accessories menu, it is *not* installed.

To install Backup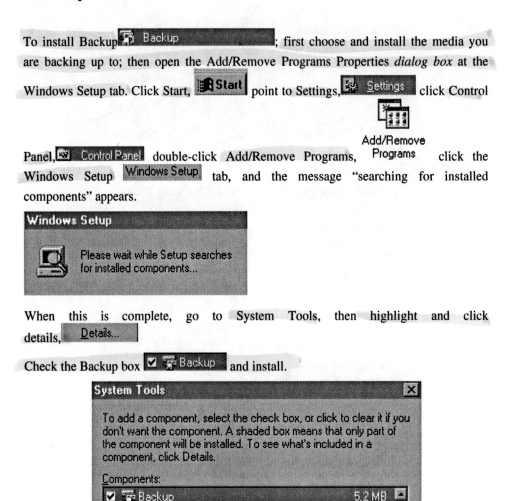 Backup; first choose and install the media you are backing up to; then open the Add/Remove Programs Properties *dialog box* at the Windows Setup tab. Click Start, Start point to Settings, Settings click Control

Panel, Control Panel double-click Add/Remove Programs, Add/Remove Programs click the Windows Setup Windows Setup tab, and the message "searching for installed components" appears.

Windows Setup

Please wait while Setup searches for installed components...

When this is complete, go to System Tools, then highlight and click details, Details...

Check the Backup box ✓ Backup and install.

System Tools ✕

To add a component, select the check box, or click to clear it if you don't want the component. A shaded box means that only part of the component will be installed. To see what's included in a component, click Details.

Components:

✓ 📠 Backup   5.2 MB

Figure 121 System Tools Installing the Backup feature

You may need your Operating System CD (software) to complete the install, because the Backup program files may not already be on your hard disk.

Running Backup via the wizard

The following wizards will guide you through the backup process.

The Backup Windows Step by Step

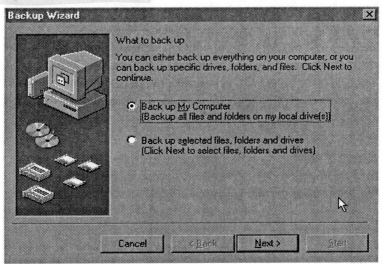

Figure 122 Choosing what to Backup

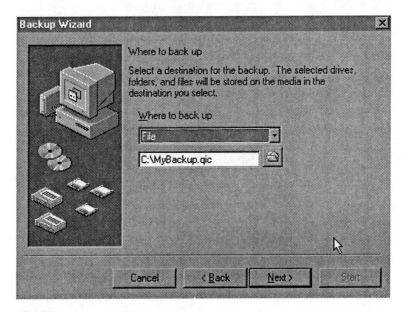

Figure 123 Where to Backup

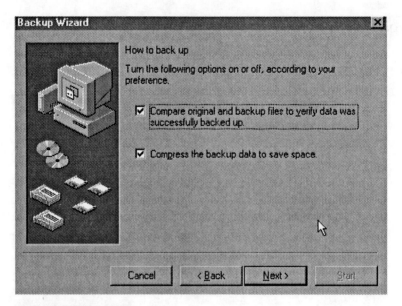

Figure 124 How to Backup

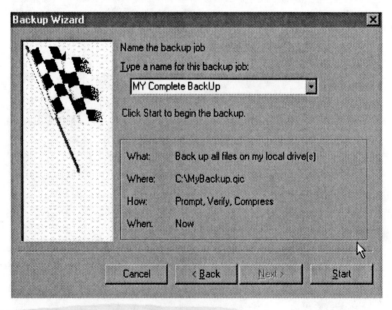

Figure 125 Who is the Backup, Naming the File

If you feel secure in your choices, choose the following.

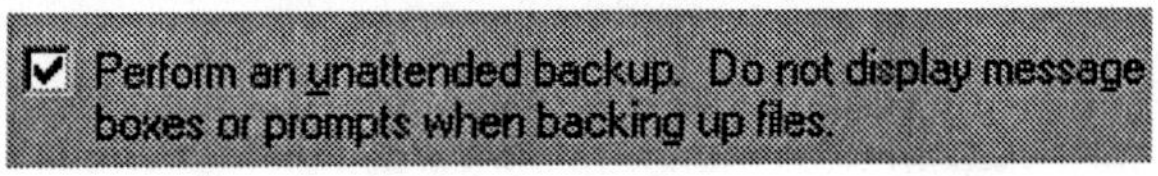

> ☑ Perform an unattended backup. Do not display message
> boxes or prompts when backing up files.

Figure 126 The unattended Backup option

Knowing how to plan backups, we are going to be as safe as possible. We expect hardware and media (drive, cable, hardware, even power) failure will eventually occur, so learning to make copies is not a bad thing. If you are not backing up to a network consider backing up to removable media. Some of us do both!

These authors are sure one day you will be glad you planned.

We *cannot* address however, the failure on the part of that between seat and keyboard to make certain the backup happens.

VII   Summary

In this chapter the types of files and file extensions were covered. The various attributes of a file and file properties were examined. You learned about various types of file, drive compression and encryption.

We also learned about the 3 types of backups. The common scandisk feature of a drive was reviewed for understanding. You are encouraged to practice the various methods of backup and use practice files and folders to change the attributes. Further explore the various types of encryption and compression available.

VIII Test for Success Questions

1. Which type of backup requires the least amount of storage space and the least amount of time to execute? (Choose all that apply)
   A. Daily
   B. Normal
   C. Differential
   D. Incremental

---

2. Why you are on-site at customer location, you need to determine which type of backup is best for your client. What does an incremental backup do?
   A. Full backup of all files.
   B. Same as a differential backup.
   C. Backs up only files that have changed.
   D. Backs up all files that have the archived option turned on.

3.An employee calls you, declaring that the taskbar is missing from Windows 98. You
   check to see that it has not been hidden, and it is not. What is the most likely cause of
   the problem?
   A. The system is running in Safe Mode.
   B. The registry is corrupt and must be restored from the backup.
   C. WIN.INI has been modified by a newly installed application.
   D. SYSTEM.INI has been damaged by a newly installed application.

4.What on the properties of a differential backup?
   A. Complete backup of all files.
   B. Back up of files with the archive bit turned off.
   C. Backs up files that differ from the first full back up.
   D. Backs up all files that have changed since the last full backup.
   E. Backs up all files that change since last full backup, and clears the archive bit

5. A user on your company's network has worked for several hours on a document that was retrieved from the network. The document was saved several times by clicking the Save icon. After returning from an absence, the user finds his computer indicating a fatal write error. Why? (Choose all that apply)

  A. The network drive is read only.

  B. The user's hard drive has crashed.

  C. The file is restricted to administrative use.

  D. The users disconnected from the network drive.

  E. The network drive is off line running a backup.

---

6. You are about to perform an operating system upgrade. What is your first step?

  A. Partition the drive.

  B. Format the drive.

  C. Backup critical data.

  D. Backup old operating system.

  E. Tell the system administrator the PC will be off-line

7.You are working on the system. What is required to make hidden files visible in
   Windows 95?
   A. Tools, Options, Show All Files.
   B. Windows Explorer, View, Folder Options, View, Show All Files.
   C. Windows Explorer, File, Preferences, Unhide All Files.
   D. Control Panel, Device Manager, File Attributes, Unhide.
   E. This is not an option in Windows 95

Test for Success Answers

1. Which type of backup requires the least amount of storage space and the least amount of time to execute? (Choose All that apply)
   A. Daily
   B. Normal
   C. Differential
   D. Incremental

Explanation: D. Incremental backup backs up only the information that has changed since the last backup, and thus requires the least storage space and least time to execute. **Daily** backups may be of any type, so that is not specific enough. Normal is not a type of backup. Differential takes less space and time than Full, but more than incremental.

---

2. Why you are on-site at customer location, you need to determine which type of backup is best for your client. What does an incremental backup do?
   A. Full backup of all files.
   B. Same as a differential backup.
   C. Backs up only files that have changed.
   D. Backs up all files that have the archived option turned on.

Explanation: C. Backs up only files that have changed is the function of an incremental backup.
A **Full backup** backs up all files. A differential backup backs up all files that changed since the last Full.

3. An employee calls you, declaring that the taskbar is missing from Windows 98. You check to see that it has not been hidden, and it is not. What is the most likely cause of the problem?

A. The system is running in Safe Mode.

B. The registry is corrupt and must be restored from the backup.

C. C.WIN.INI has been modified by a newly installed application.

D. SYSTEM.INI has been damaged by a newly installed application.

Explanation: B. The registry is corrupt and must be restored from the backup.

---

4. What on the properties of a differential backup?

A. Complete backup of all files.

B. Back up of files with the archive bit turned off.

C. Backs up files that differ from the first full back up.

D. Backs up all files that have changed since the last full backup.

E. Backs up all files that change since last full backup, and clears the archive bit

Explanation: D. Back up all files that have changed since the last full backup

5. A user on your company's network has worked for several hours on a document that was retrieved from the network. The document was saved several times by clicking the Save icon. After returning from an absence, the user finds his computer indicating a fatal write error. Why? (Choose all that apply)

A. The network drive is read only.

B. The user's hard drive has crashed.

C. The file is restricted to administrative use.

D. The users disconnected from the network drive.

E. The network drive is off line running a backup.

Explanation: D. The users disconnected from the network drive.

If the drive was read-only or restricted to administrative use, the other saves would not have completed without incident.

---

6. You are about to perform an operating system upgrade. What is your first step?

A. Partition the drive.

B. Format the drive.

C. Backup critical data.

D. Backup old operating system.

E. Tell the system administrator the PC will be off-line

Explanation: C. Backup critical data is the first thing you should do as part of an OS upgrade.

7. You are working on the system. What is required to make hidden files visible in
   Windows 95?
   A. Tools, Options, Show All Files.
   B. Windows Explorer, View, Folder Options, View, Show All Files.
   C. Windows Explorer, File, Preferences, Unhide All Files.
   D. Control Panel, Device Manager, File Attributes, Unhide.
   E. This is not an option in Windows 95

Explanation: B. Windows Explorer, View, Folder Options, View, Show All Files is
   the correct action.

If you have knowledge, let others light their candles at it.

-Thomas Fuller-

Chapter 0011: DOS

The objective of this chapter is to provide the reader with an understanding of the following:

Introduction

The most basic yet very powerful Operating System known as DOS (Disk Operating System), will be examined in this chapter. The DOS environment is still present in Windows 9x and 3.x, and the commands work in the MS-DOS window in those versions of Windows. Additionally, the commands that work in DOS also work when used at the **NT Command Prompt,** making DOS command line knowledge a valuable thing to have in your toolbox. The various methods of using DOS as a troubleshooting tool as well as learning what really goes on under the hood will be covered here.

Getting Ready - Questions

1. Why would you use the SETVER utility?

    A. To select between multiple versions of MS-DOS loaded on your computer

    B. To look up the version of the operating system

    C. To set the version of DOS reported to programs, for compatibility reasons

    D. To select between multiple versions of device drivers loaded on your computer

2. The program used to load a CD-ROM device driver in MS-DOS is?

    A: MSCDEX.EXE

    B: OAKCD.EXE

    C: MSCD.EXE

    D: LASTDRIVE.EXE

    E. CDDRV.BAT

3. What does the line BOOTGUI=1 in MSDOS.SYS accomplish?

    A. Puts up a GUI (graphical) boot screen when you reboot your computer

    B. Causes Windows to start in GUI as opposed to CDI mode

    C. Causes a GUI version of MS-DOS to run when you select MS-DOS Prompt from the Start Menu

    D. Causes Windows to start in CDI as opposed to GUI mode

4. Windows NT requires HIMEM.SYS to operate properly on computers with more than 640K of memory.

    A. True

    B. False

5. The SCANREG tool performs which functions: (Choose two)

    A. Fix registry errors

    B. Allow registry to be backed up

    C. Scan registry for the appearance of specific entries

    D. Performs a regular scandisk with no other options

Getting Ready - Answers

1. *Correct Answer:* **C**

2. *Correct answer:* **A**

3. *Correct answer:* **B**

4. *Correct answer:* **B**

5. *Correct answer:* **A&B**

II ▶ Command Line Commando

Let's begin our tour with DOS (Disk Operating System) by looking at what starts up.

On first up the **PC** doesn't know too much. The first program launched is known as the **bootstrap loader,** or **boot loader.**

This is what looks for **DOS,** or any other **operating system** that is at the **beginning** of a **diskette** or **hard drive**. Assuming that the **DOS start routine** is there, the **second step** occurs, which is *loading* **DOS**. Once *loaded,* on the screen you will see either a **CAPTIAL** letter **A** or more commonly a **capital** letter **C,** followed by a **>** symbol, looking like this **C>:** This is known as the **prompt**. The **prompt** is literally telling you it is *ready* for you to **type** in a **command**.

To get a **command** to work (do something), you **type** in the **name** of a **command** and press the **computers enter key**.

Figure 127 Press Enter

It is the job of **DOS** to find the **program** *associated* with the **name** to make it **run** **(work/do something)**.

What is DOS?

DOS is a **program** that is **divided** into several **sub-programs**. There are **three** major **portions** of **DOS**.

The first two of the portions listed below are hidden from view. The three portions are:

- MSDOS.SYS
- IO.SYS
- COMMAND.COM

The **third sub-program** is **visible** and actually **replaceable**. This **program** is called **COMMAND.COM**. The function of **COMMAND.COM** is to interface with you, the **operator (user)**; in whatever human language you are most natural in using.

COMMAND.COM takes terse **commands** in your native human communication language, and **interprets** them into something that one of the **hidden sub-programs** can use.

This is why you will sometime hear **COMMAND.COM** referred to as a **command** *interpreter*. On other occasions you may hear **COMMAND.COM** referred to as a **shell**. In the days when **DOS** was the way to *talk* to the **PC**, a firm had created a replacement to **COMMAND.COM**, known as **4DOS**. This was sold as a more powerful **command shell/interpreter**. For all practical purposes these days, though, you will be using the COMMAND.COM that shipped with your operating system.

Under the hood, the **two** hidden programs **MSDOS.SYS** and **IO.SYS** perform **functions** that the computer needs to do your bidding. **IO.SYS** is responsible for **in** and **out** functions.

This literally means **in** and **out** in ways you may not think of. As a case in point, think about the **keyboard**. Its purpose is to **input** into the computer, so it must talk to **IO.SYS**.

MSIO.SYS

MSIO.SYS *functionality* can be extended with **device drivers**. All **device drivers** are loaded in the **CONFIG.SYS** file, and are declared as such in the **CONFIG.SYS** file with the *call* **DEVICE=SOMEDRV.SYS** i.e. **DEVICE=OAKCDROM.SYS**

Identifying the files

CONFIG.SYS is called at bootup by IO.SYS

IO.SYS goes to the BIOS at boot.

Changes in **CONFIG.SYS** require a **re-boot**.

> **Boot Order (2-5-6-7-8 Characters)**
>
> The boot order of DOS is: IO.SYS, MSDOS.SYS, CONFIG.SYS, COMMAND.COM, AUTOEXEC.BAT. The 2-5678 order represents the number of characters in each filename, so if you can remember the five filenames, you can also correctly put them in the right boot order.

COMMAND.COM has some **commands** built into it.

Examples of **internal commands** include;

- DIR (short for directory)
- DATE & TIME
- COPY
- Type

Since these are built into the *interpreter*, they're known as **internal** commands.

Interestingly, other *support* **programs** exist with **DOS**, however they *do not* exist inside the **interpreter**. Rather, they're stored as separate files on the disk. This is a **compromise**, because if all the **programs** were **internal**, they would be **using** up **memory**. In general, the designers of DOS tried to put the most often used, reasonably small, programs into DOS as internal commands, and left the others as external programs.

Examples of **external programs** include:

- FDISK
- XCOPY

Since they're *not* inside the **interpreter**, they are known as **external commands**.

> **UPPER or lower?**
>
> You can *type* (in most cases) **UPPER** or **lower** case letters; **DOS** doesn't care and **internally** will **convert** them to **UPPER** case.
>
> When typing a **command**, at the **prompt** there will be **typing** either *after* a **letter** followed by a **colon,:** , for example **C:\\>**

This tells **DOS** that you wish to work with the **C** drive. This is known as the **drive specification**. To change the **drive specification**, simply enter a *valid* **drive letter** followed by a **colon**, then press the **enter** ⏎ **Enter** key.

DOS is intended to be compact and unobtrusive. This means that when the **command** has been successfully **entered**, it does the job it was asked to do, and **prompt**s for **more**.

Suppose you ask for something that doesn't exist. Perhaps you *mistyped* a **program name**. **DOS** will inform you that it *cannot* follow your desire with the message:

Bad command or file name

Figure 128 Bad Command

There's a *standard* **format** for asking **DOS** to carry out your bidding. This **format** is called the command **syntax,** and it governs the way **commands** are entered. The basic format is:

COMMAND-NAME + modifiers (if any)

Figure 129 Command Operating

Practice DIR COMMAND

Lets look at the internal **command** function, **DIR.**

The DIR Command

Typing **DIR** and pressing **enter (enter or return key)** will **display** a list of <u>**everything**</u> that is the **current area (current directory)** of the specified **drive.** A directory is really just another name for what is now called a **folder** in Windows. So, you can see that the **DIR** command is yet another way to find out the contents of a folder.

Using a modifier or a switch will change what information is displayed by the **DIR** command. A switch is a modifier that tells the command to operate in a specific way, other than its default behavior. For example:

Typing **DIR/P (Directory/ Pause)** will change the same **output** from the **DIR command** rolling off the screen. Instead, it will fill the **screen,** and pause waiting for any **keystroke** to tell it to continue. Notice the examples:

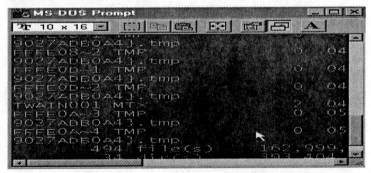

Figure 130 DIR command *without* the /P (pause) switch

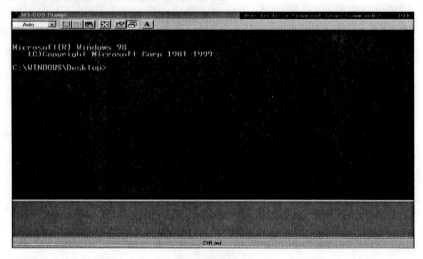

Figure 131 The DIR command

Notice the pause with the DIR command and the /P switch notice the screen display paused with the message:

"Press any key to continue"

Practice DIR COMMAND

Figure 132 Get Wild

DOS 231

There's a way to refer to more than **file** at a time with the **magic** known as **wildcards**. **Wildcards** are a way of *specifying* **part** of any **filename** to be *included* in a **command** for **processing**. Actually, there are **two wild cards**. They are;

Asterisk (*)

Question mark (?)

The *question mark* will match any single character in a filename, while the asterisk* will match any number of characters that may exist.

For example;

JAN1.DOC

JAN10.DOC

JUNE1.DOC

JUNE10.DOC

JUNE 30.DOC

JULY1.TXTEntering **COPY J*.*** would **copy** *all* the **files** listed above. Typing **COPYJ*.doc** would **copy** all *but* the file **JULY 1.TXT**. commanding **DOS** with **COPY JAN?.*** would only copy **JAN1.DOC** *not* **JAN10.DOC** .

☞✍ Practice Copying Files

Better Prompting with PROMPT

The **prompt command** can be used to modify how the operator is told the pc is ready for the users bidding. by typing the **command prompt** with a **$** sign followed by either reserved characters or a string of text, the **command prompt** instantly changes to that *'ready'* set.

Two of the most commonly used **prompt** characters are:

$P

$G

The **$P** tells the **operator** what area of a **hard drive** they are in. This is called the **sub-directory** or **folder**.

The **folder** or **sub-directory** is covered later on.

Symbols
The **$G** creates the **greater** than **symbol** (**>**)

Hiding PROMPT and CLS

A method to strike terror into the heart of almost any PC user is to **enter prompt** followed by the **$** *sign* and while **holding down** the **ALT** key, use the *number pad* and **enter 255**.

This tells the **PC** to use the **255ᵗʰ character** for the **prompt**. Character 255 is **nul (blank)**.

After entering this, type the *three* letters, **C:\ >CLS** *enter.* This is the **DOS command** to clear the screen. At this point, the screen will be completely blank. Type **prompt $P $G** *enter* **again** before the user regains consciousness.

☞✍ Practice Hiding Prompt

Figure 133 Command Line Commando

The VER command

DOS will tell you what *version* is running simply by typing **VER** & pressing *enter* at the **command prompt**.

DOS Version

Type **VER** then **press** ⏎ **Enter** at the **command prompt** to determine what version of **DOS** is running. In **Windows** from the **DOS** *Prompt* **VER** will display the **Operating System** *version*.

Mixing up *versions* of programs from **DOS** can make the program appear *corrupt*. Occasionally, the **DOS program** is smart enough to figure out what is going on.

For example, the archaic program **backup** in **DOS** will display the **error** "wrong **DOS** version."

☞✒ Practice VER command

DOS within DOS

Be cautious concern **command**.com and **DOS** *version* 5. There were actually two *versions* of **DOS** 5. *Version* **A** and *Version* **C**. The **command.com** for each are NOT interchangeable.

DATE

Do we know what day and time it is? First we have to make sure these are set before using the computer as a calendar and large wristwatch.

Typing the *word* **Date** followed by a **space** and entering numerical values will **set** the **date**. An example would be:

C:\>Date 12-25-2002

```
C:\Date 12-25-2002
```

```
C:\>Date
Current date is Sat 05-05-2001
Enter new date (mm-dd-yy):
```

Note: Remember we must change from Windows directory to the DOS directory. Notice the example. The format(entry information) is displayed on the screen to assist you.

```
MS-DOS Prompt
Tr 10 x 16

C:\WINDOWS>cd \

C:\>Date
Current date is Sat 05-05-2001
Enter new date (mm-dd-yy): sat 05-01-2005

Invalid date
Enter new date (mm-dd-yy): 06-01-01

C:\>date
Current date is Fri 06-01-2001
Enter new date (mm-dd-yy): 05-05-01

C:\>date
Current date is Sat 05-05-2001
Enter new date (mm-dd-yy): ■
```

Figure 134 Setting and Re-setting the Date

TIME

Time follows the same format and can use either 24-hour **time** or twelve-hour time with either an **A (AM)** or a **P (PM)**. Notice both entries set the same time.

For example:

C:\>Time 6:45p or Time 18:45

```
C:\Time 6:45P▌ C:\Time 18:45▌
```

☞✓ Practice Setting Date& Time

NOTE: Pressing the ESC key while in MSDOS will ENTER a BACKSLASH (\)on the screen, if you then PRESS ENTER you will ESC(ESCAPE) what you were doing and be returned to the C prompt.
Type CD \ windows to return to windows. Then at the prompt type EXIT to return to the Windows GUI.

COPY

The **COPY command** can use **wildcards** and can *rename* files in the process of copying. Follow the example:

C:\>COPY A:MY-DOC.TXT F:\>NOW-YOUR.TXT

This will copy from the **file** named MY-DOC.TXT to the F drive and rename it NOW-YOUR.TXT, and will do this while being at the drive specified as drive **C**. (Note that the only spaces in the command above are after the word "COPY" and after the first ".TXT".

☞✓ Practice Copying & Renaming

III   8 dot 3 limit/common extensions

The lineage of **DOS** dates back to the '70's. This heritage explains why there's a **limit** of **8 characters** followed by the **dot** with a **maximum** of **3 characters** for the **extension**.

The 8-character limit no longer exists in Windows, but it is definitely a part of heritage on the DOS platforms, and references to it are still present on many versions of Windows. For example, the **DIR** command on many versions of Windows will still display two name columns in its directory listings – the first column, a shorter name that Windows has made up, like "Progra~1," to make the user's file name look like one of these 8.3 format filenames, and the last column, the original long name for the file or folder, like "Program Files".

Extensions can be anything you want, or even **none** at all. The wise geek would follow commonly accepted conventions, as we discussed earlier. Some of the most common ones are:

.exe	executable
.com	command
.txt	text
.do	c document
.bat	batch file
.sys	system extension (driver)
.bak	back up
.ini	initialization
.inf	information (system setup)
.reg	registry
.pdf	acrobat (adobe)
.bmp	bit map graphic (paint)
.tif	vector graphic

This list is by no means conclusive. If you don't follow the common **conventions**, you may have a tough time getting a **data file** to work with an **associated program**.

DEL/ERASE

Both **DEL (Delete)** **ERASE** mean the same thing, they **delete** files. **DEL** is more popular than **ERASE**, simply because there are fewer keystrokes. Typing **DEL *.*** would **delete** *everything*, period. Due to user feedback, starting with **DOS** 3, when **DEL *.*** was typed, **DOS** offers,

"Are you sure?Y/N". Y (YES) N (NO)

```
C:\WINDOWS>DEL *.*
All files in directory will be deleted!
Are you sure (Y/N)?
```

```
C:\WINDOWS>ERASE *.*
All files in directory will be deleted!
Are you sure (Y/N)?█
```

	Bye-bye hard drive.

DOS 2.x **DEL *.*** no confirmation

DOS 3 **DEL *.*** confirmation

"Are you sure?Y/N".

The **DEL *.*** would silently do your bidding without confirmation in **DOS** 2.x.

Yes, this author quickly and solidly erased the root entries of a 10MG hard drive, thinking I was logged to the A drive, and cleaning up an old diskette.

In a few keystrokes, **COMMAND.COM**, and the **DOS** program extensions (.sys files) along with a painfully created **CONFIG.SYS** and **AUTOEXEC.BAT** file were sent to never-never land.

This sad fact in **DOS** 2.x made Peter Norton a great deal of money with the 3rd party utility, **Norton** *Unerase*, whose functionality (as you might expect) was to recover files lost by errant "del" or "erase" commands. **Microsoft** purchased *Unerase* from Norton and included it with **DOS** 5.

For the Practice excise create a text file in **Notepad** by going to **start, programs, accessories, Notepad** and creating a bit of text, then Practice **DEL (deleting)** the file in **DOS.**

☞✔ Practice DEL/ERASE

REN

The **REN (RENAME)** command allows for the changing of a filename. An example would be:

C:\>REN MYFILE.DOC OLDFILE.BAK

☞✔ Practice Renaming

TYPE

The **TYPE command** allows **printing** the contents of a **text** file to the **screen**.

C:\TYPE myfile.txt

☞✔ Practice TYPE command

EDIT

The **EDIT** command is a full screen text editor that permits the **editing** of a **text** file.

Edit
Early versions of **DOS** didn't have an **edit**. This full screen editor appeared with **DOS 5**. **Edit** was borrowed from another Microsoft program, known as **BASIC** (a computer language). Before **EDIT**, you needed **EDLIN**. **EDIT LINE** also allows editing, however, you must work with *one line* of text at a time. Think of writing a book with a line editor ⊗. (yes, it has been done.)

☞✔ Practice EDIT

SCANDISK

SCANDISK is used to **find** and **repair errors** on **floppy** and **hard** drives. The good news is it works most of the time, saving untold grief. It performs the same functions as the Windows version of scandisk, but without the pretty user interface. You'll be glad it's there, user interface or not, though, the first time you run into a disk so corrupt that Windows will not boot into its GUI.

Scandisk

C:\>SCANDISK/SURFACE

Finds and repairs errors

SCANDISK repairs floppy and hard drive **errors**, using the **switch, /SURFACE.** For **example:** C:\>SCANDISK /SURFACE will not only look for **errors** in the **indexing** system, it will also **test** each magnetic **bit** on the surface of the media and if it finds a weak spot, will **remove** any **data** and put it in a safer area and **mark** the weak **spot** as **bad** and unusable. Note that the /surface option increase the time it takes to run SCANDISK.

`C:SCANDISK /SURFACE`

Scandisk

SCANDISK was introduced in **DOS** 5, *prior* versions of **DOS** used **CHKDSK. CHKDSK** could not perform a **surface scan.**

`C:/CHKDSK`

☞📖 **Practice SCANDISK**

SETVER

So far we have mentioned a number of major changes occurred with **DOS** 5. The changes were drastic enough that it gave digital heartburn to some programs written before **DOS** 5. To keep them running, the **SETVER** program was created.

Without **SETVER**, many older programs instead of running, would give up with **DOS** declaring tersely, **"packed file corrupt"** or **exe corrupt**. It is the job of **SETVER** to "fake" the older program into thinking it was running on the **DOS** version it was intended for.

`C:/SETVER` notice the message below when **SETVER** was not loaded into **CONFIG.SYS**

```
NOTE: SETVER device not loaded. To activate SETVER version reporting
      you must load the SETVER.EXE device in your CONFIG.SYS.
```

Pop Quiz 0011.0

 Pop Quiz 0011.0 *Questions*

1. The MS-DOS command to edit a file is:

    A. EDLIN

    B. EMACS

    C. NOTEPAD

    D. EDIT

2. You have changed CONFIG.SYS, adding a line to add a new device driver, but the device is still not recognized. What might be the problem?

    A. Device drivers should be added in AUTOEXEC.BAT, not CONFIG.SYS

    B. There is a typo on a previous line in the CONFIG.SYS file

    C. You have to reboot the machine before the changes in CONFIG.SYS are recognized

    D. You didn't add a matching line in MSDOS.SYS

3. MS-DOS commands for removing files from disk include: (choose two)

    A. Remove

    B. Erase

    C. Scratch

    D. Del

4. The DATE command in MS-DOS is used for: (choose two)

    A. Setting the system date

    B. Setting the system time

    C. Displaying the system date

    D. Setting a time on a file

5. Which of the following is not an external command:

    A. .COPY

    B. .XCOPY

    C. .SETVER

    D. FDISK

Pop Quiz 0011.0 *Answers*

1. Correct Answer: A

2. Correct Answer: C

3. Correct Answer: B&D

4. Correct Answer: A&C

5. Correct Answers: A

IV   FDISK/FAT

FDISK is an external program introduced with **DOS version 2**. It is short for **fixed disk**. Perhaps you may wish to use the following **analogy** when thinking of **FDISK**.

If you were going to setup a **farm** in the 'back 40', you would need a **house** to live in, a **barn** and **fields**.

The **first step** would be to **survey** the **land** and **plant** little plastic **flags** to **define** where the **house** would be **built relative** to the **fields** and the **barn**. FDISK is the **digital version** of **planting** the **survey** flags.

Depending on the version of **DOS** or **Windows** you are using, you may (or may not) get a choice about supporting large hard drives. If you don't get a choice, you are going to create the **digital** version of **planting** survey flags using what is known as **FAT 16**, frequently referred to simply as **FAT**. The **16** means it can **allocate** areas using the 16th **power** of $2(16^\wedge 2)$.

That makes a hard math **limitation** of **4 gigabytes (GB)** of **storage**, assuming each **storage** cluster uses **64 kilobytes (64kb)**. Beginning with **Windows 95 b** (or **osr2**) **FAT** was dramatically improved. Several changes were made to **FAT**. The most important ones include:

Support for up to **2 terabytes (2TB)** per drive partition.

(Terabyte is 1000 Gigabytes GB)

smaller **clusters** sizes, resulting in a 10-15% gain in storage efficiency.

These points and more about the different ways to plant digital survey flags were discussed in the file systems chapter earlier in the book.

FAT 32

FAT32 *can* store the same data using **less space**

NT4 *cannot* **read** FAT32 **drive** partitions

Regardless of which **version** of **FDISK** that is available to you, several items are common to **FDISK**. They are:

FDISK must be run **first.** MS-DOS Prompt - FDISK

DOS must **reboot** for **FDISK** changes to take effect.

Installing DOS

The proper order for installing **DOS** or windows is:

FDISK – reboot – format

☞🏷 **Practice FDISK**

Total Recall

Figure 135 Large Disk Support Message

After you have planted the digital survey flags, construction can begin. The next step in building the **digital house** is the **FORMAT command**. All **storage media** must have some **form** of **formatting** to give it a **structure**. Common drive format structures discussed in the previous chapter include:

FAT (file allocation table 16 bits)

FAT32 (file allocation table 32 bits)

NTFS (new technology file system)

CDFS (compact disk file system)

Once a drive is formatted, **DOS** or **Windows** can be installed. Installing **DOS** can be accomplished **immediately** after **formatting** by using the **/S switch** with **FORMAT**. Simply type A:\>FORMAT C: /S

```
A:\FORMAT C: /S
```

As soon as the hard drive is **formatted**, it will copy **IO.SYS**, **MSDOS.SYS** and **COMMAND.COM** to the hard drive. Specifically, it copies these file to track 0 of either a floppy drive or a hard drive. should you find yourself behind the 8 ball because you were playing with another operating system or caught a digital virus that infects track 0, you can sometime repair by using the **command**,

FDISK/MBR

The **/MBR** *switch* stands for **master boot record**.

Virus Innoculation

If boot sector virus is suspected, try **FDISK/MBR**.

File Transfer

If you need to transfer the three files, **IO.SYS**, **MSDOS.SYS** and **COMMAND.COM** to a drive and you don't want to lose the data that is on the magnetic media, use the **command**, SYS X: (Substitute the **X** for the drive letter)

☞✍ Practice SYS A:

◆ V ATTRIB

FAT (and **NTFS**) have **attributes** telling the **PC** some information about the files that are stored. **NTFS** actually has much more information about the files than **FAT**, and that story has been told in the File Systems chapter earlier in this book.

FAT has **4 attributes** that can be assigned to a file, as we saw earlier. Using the **attrib** command, you can turn these on and off as if each one was a separate light switch on the wall.

ON or **OFF**. The **+** sign means **ON**, while the **—** sign means **OFF**. When you have a moment, go to the **command** line of a **C** drive on a computer. Type the **command, DIR MSDOS.SYS** you will be told, **"file not found"** this is because the file is **hidden**.

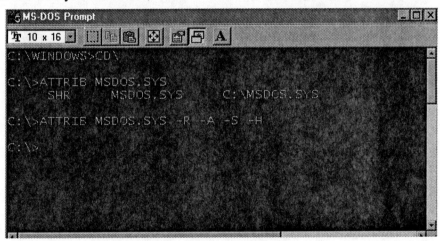

Figure 136 R-A-S-H In DOS

In other words, the **hidden bit,** or **attribute,** is turned **ON** for **MSDOS.SYS**.

You know by now that **MSDOS** has to be there (if it is running **DOS** or Windows 9x). So, it's there. It just isn't visible. Now, type this **command: ATTRIB MSDOS.SYS**

You will be told that the file **MSDOS.SYS** is in fact there, and it has at least **two attributes**. These are the **system** and **hidden attributes**. The **command** may also tell you that the **archive bit** is **ON**. It will inform you of this with the typical terse form of **DOS** with **SHR,** with each letter corresponding to an attribute, as follows:

A=Archive
S=System
H=Hidden
R=Read-only

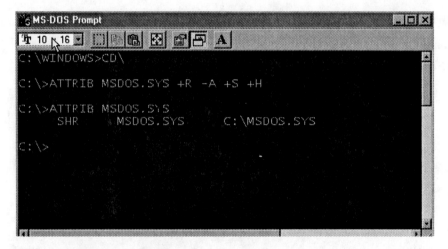

Figure 137 ATTRIB in DOS

☞🖐 Practice ATTRIB

Figure 138 ATTRIB COMMAND

If you want to see the contents of **MSDOS.SYS**, enter this **command**: ATTRIB MSDOS.SYS –A –S –H

Run the **DIR command** as above, and this time, it will be displayed. From here, enter:

C:\>EDIT MSDOS.SYS

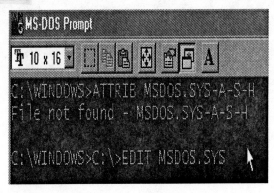

Figure 139 ATTRIB in DOS

Now you will see that **MSDOS.SYS** is a text file and a notation that is must be greater than 1024 bytes in length to keep older **DOS** program happy.

MSDOS.SYS

MSDOS.SYS is a text file that must be greater than 1024 bytes in length. The attributes are **R**ead Only – **S**ystem – **H**idden

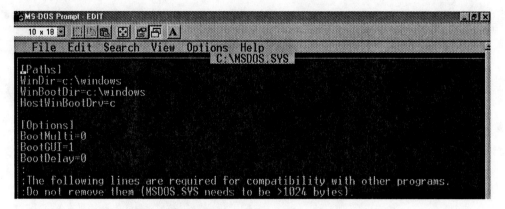

Figure 140 MSDOS.SYS EDIT

BOOTGUI=1

BOOTGUI=O

EDIT MSDOS.SYS

Note: Using the menu options will change the screen and font sizes and colors.

BOOTGUI

Notice the line that states, **BOOTGUI=1** ? If you ever have a client that strongly dislikes GUI interfaces, change this line to **BOOTGUI=0** and save the file. Change the attributes back. Now on the next boot the **Windows** startup splash screen will **appear**, then disappear, going back to a **command** driven interface (**CDI**). You could even **delete** the splash screen, however we do not suggest this. This is because if another user wants to use the **GUI** interface, all they have to type is **WIN** and they will have their normal interface.

☞⚖ **Practice ATTRIB**

ARCHIVE ATTRIBUTE

As with the use of the Archive bit in Windows, the **A (archive bit)** for a file is on (+) and remains so until either it is manually changed with the **ATTRIB command** or the **file is backed up** with either a **full back up** or an **incremental backup**. At this point the **archive bit** is off (-) until the **file is changed** or **manually reset** with the **ATTRIB command**.

☞✓🖱 Practice ATTRIB

BATCH FILES

What is a **batch file**? In short, a batch file is nothing more than a pre-recorded set of keystrokes. This saves time and errors on **boot up**. The conventional **file extension** for a **batch** file is .**BAT**.

When **DOS** boots, it looks for a specially named **batch** file, called **AUTOEXEC.BAT**, and it executes whatever commands are in this file, if it finds it.

Since a **batch file** is nothing more than **pre-recorded keystrokes**, unlike **CONFIG.SYS**, it can be run at anytime, and *does not* require a **reboot**.

Batch Files
AUTOEXEC.BAT runs after **COMMAND.COM** is loaded.
Batch files can be run at *anytime* after **booting**.

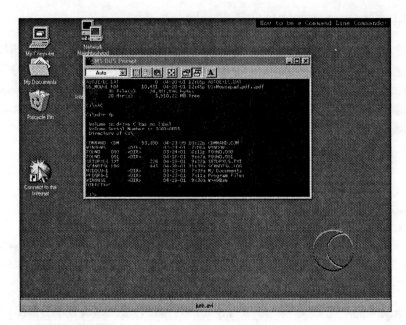

Figure 141 MSCDEX

A common entry found in the **autoexec.bat** file is **MSCDEX.EXE.** This is shorthand for **Microsoft CD extensions**. This **executable** file **extends** the ability of **DOS** to handle the **CDFS (CD FILE SYSTEM)** file **format**.

Several switches are available for **MSCDEX.EXE.**

The **/D:** **switch** is always required. This is because it grabs the **device driver** that was **loaded** in the **config.sys** file. Several *optional* **switches** exist as well. One of our favorites is the **/L:** switch. We like to set it like this: **/L:Z.** This assigns the CD-**ROM** the **drive letter** of **Z**.

> **Drive Letter Assignment**
>
> If you assign a drive letter of z before loading any programs, you will be able to install other devices or assign network drive letters that will come before z. This is cool because many programs remember what drive letter they were installed from. If you install from d drive, then add devices, the cd-rom will get a new drive letter further down the alphabet soup line, and the programs will suddenly get dumb.
>
> **CD-ROM Device Driver Trick**
>
> The OAKCDROM.SYS device driver found in Windows 98 is a protected mode device driver that seems to work with virtually every IDE CD we have tried, including CD 'juke-boxes'. While it won't make a juke-box read every drive letter, it does make the first drive letter available without chasing down some device driver.

Windows setup diskettes assign a 'handle name' in the **CONFIG.SYS** for the **OAKCDROM.SYS** file. If you have to perform a 'quick and dirty', just drop the **OAKCDROM.SYS** driver in the **CONFIG.SYS** file, with **DEVICE= OAKCDROM.SYS**

In the **AUTOEXEC.BAT** file, *type* **MSCDEX.EXE /D:12345678 /D:Z** and you will get virtually any IDE CD operational as a 'Z' drive. Now you can load Windows 2000, Linux, or ? onto a new hard drive from a **command device interface (CDI)** operating system such as **DOS 6.22** (which easily fits on a floppy with all the required support drivers).

☞🗐 Practice Drive letter changing

HIMEM

Another system extending program that comes from Microsoft is the **HIMEM.SYS** program. Back when **DOS** was put together, it was designed for the **Intel** 808x chips.

These "blazing" **CPU's** sported a "whopping" 100,000 instructions per second of **computational** ability. Now the engineers had to draw a line in the silicon somewhere for how much **memory** this chip family could **address**. They went for the "incredible" number of 1,000,000 bytes of **RAM**. Some of this went to read the **BIOS**, and some to the various types of video cards, i.e. black and white or color (with graphics!).

Since the reigning operating system of the day was **C/PM** and it used **64k** in total, granting a limit of **640k** seemed like a great deal of room for growth. Even Bill Gates was impressed, proclaiming, "Nobody could use more than 640k of RAM."

Alas, nature hates a void. The limit was hit, and users screamed for **more**. Without getting into the **HI=MEM** wars of the day, a solution was found by **swapping memory** up above the 'real mode' region, into the **High Memory Area** (HMA) for management and use. This is controlled by **HIMEM.SYS**.

NT/Windows 2000/XP

NT/W2k/XP uses a **flat memory** model, just as Apple has done since almost forever. No need for **HIMEM.SYS** or **EMM386.EXE** to work with **segmented memory**.

MEMMAKER

Tuning what (programs) would go where (in memory) in **DOS** was a fine art that not many folks mastered. With **DOS 5** came **MEMMAKER**. This is a program that automagically tuned what was **loaded high**. This can be seen in both **CONFIG.SYS** and **AUTOEXEC.BAT** configurations with the first line containing the letters, **LH** (**load high**) in **front** of the **device driver** or **program**.

DEFRAG

Earlier in this chapter you learned that **DOS** took away the messy details about **how** and **where** files are stored on a **floppy** or **hard drive**. Now it is time to get a hot tip about how **DOS** does this magic. The truth is, **DOS** is lazy. When you delete a file, it doesn't waste time sending in digital scrubbing bubbles. If it did, Peter Norton wouldn't have made millions with his *un-erase* program.

What **DOS** does do is go through its **index** system, known as the **File Allocation Table** (**FAT**), and erases the **first character** in the **head** of the **index**, and puts a **reserved character** that says it is ok to use this area again. That leaves the **clusters** of **magnetic media** available for **re-use later**.

OOPS! Erased IT!

Un-erase programs from the early days depended on the fact that nothing was re-written to those areas. The program would simply ask for the first character and once supplied, 'magically' the deleted data was restored.

When **DOS** is told to write new data, is simply looks for the closest available magnetically ready media that is available. Given some **deleting** and **re-writing**, a single file can get really **scattered** around on a hard drive. This can slow performance greatly.

This sound like a need, and seeing a dollar to be made, **defragmentation** programs proliferated. Eventually, **DEFRAG** made its way into the **GUI** version of **DOS**, known as Windows. This made third party programmers write even better **DFRAG** programs.3

Performance

A **DEFRAG** program improves **performance** by **re-ordering** programs and **data files** into a **contiguous** order.

SCANREG

SCANREG is a **command** line **utility** that will clean up the **registry**, and allow for backing up of the PC's **registry**. A very nice utility for getting geeks out of hot water with PC's too sick to load the **GUI**.

Registry Help

SCANREG will backup the registry and look for errors.

---

3 our favorite 3rd party defrag program comes from Executive Software, known as Diskeeper.

Registry Extension

Registry files end in the **file extension .REG. double clicking** on a .REG file will automagically **merge** the file into the **registry**.

Figure 142 Registry Merge

DIRECTORY MANAGEMENT

Introduced with **DOS** version 2 is **support** for **hard drives**, sometimes called **fixed disks**. (the latter name come from the fact that they could not be removed, like a floppy could).

As we learned earlier, **FDISK** was needed *before* **formatting**. After a hard disk was **formatted** and contained an **OS** (operating system), a method of creating **virtual floppies** on the **fixed disk** was needed.

These virtual floppies are called sub directories or folders.

There are several reasons for this need. **One** need is a human one. That is to give order to the capability of the fact that **thousands** of **files** could be **stored**.

The **second** reason was a **technical** issue. The **indexing system** that **controlled** where the magnetic bits were that told **DOS** what made up a **file,** was limited to **512 file entries!**

ROOT Limits

FAT 16 is limited to 512 files in the root directory.

ROOTS

In the process of **dividing** up the **drive**, a few **new naming conventions** had to be introduced. This **structure system** calls the **first point** the **root**. The top-most directory in each drive is called the root, and you'll usually see it referred to as **C:** or **D:\.**

An analogy that may help you visualize what is going on would be that of a **tree** that is **upside down**. **Like** a **tree trunk**, the **root** is the **base. Unlike** a **tree, leaving** the **root** going to the **branch system** is referred to as **going down.**(A tree trunk goes up the branches)

Each **branch** is known as a **sub directory**, because it is a **sub** off the **root directory**. When windows and its **graphical interface** became popular, the **sub directory** started to be known as a **folder,** because the **icon** to display the **structure** looks like a **file folder –** hopefully providing an easy-to-remember way for users to think of where they've stored their data.

Like a **tree, branches** can have **branches,** and there can be **more** then **one**1ˢᵗ **level branch** from the **root**. How the **structure** is **created** is up to the user.

Making a **new branch** on any **level** is done with the **MD command**, short for **Make Directory.**

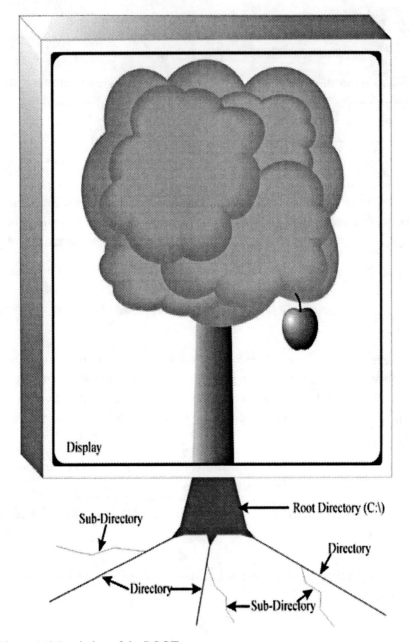

Figure 143 Depiction of the ROOT

To move to a sub directory, use the Change Directory command, which is CD \. To remove an empty folder use the RD (REMOVE DIRECTORY) command.

ROOT Navigation

MD, CD, and RD are navigational commands for managing sub directories.

☞✍ Practice CD,MD,RD COMMANDS

REGISTRY

Figure 144 DIRECTORIES

Did you notice the statement that a folder has to be empty to run **RD**? Sometimes this was a real pain if there were several sub folders running under the first sub folder. You had to go to each folder and **DEL *.*** and confirm with a **Y(YES)** to **empty** *each* **folder** before you could **RD(REMOVE DIRECTORY)**. Later versions of **DOS** acquired the **command DELTREE** that could **delete** a **folder** and all its **sub folders** even if they had data in them. (And still later versions of Windows, like Windows 2000, did away with **DELTREE**, sadly enough).

Copying data from **different folders** and **sub folders** was as equally **painful** as attempting to **delete** old **data**. Each **folder** within a **folder** had to have a **CD command** to the **folder** or called expressly by its **structure** to be **copied**.

To address this, **XCCOPY** was created. **XCOPY** is external to **COMMAND.COM**.

XCOPY is fast, and has a very cool **switch**, which is the **/S switch**. When you use **XCOPY** it is capable of **copying contents** (complete with wildcard arguments.). **XCOPY/S does** the **same** thing, however is will **perform** the **same function** on *all* **sub directories**.

As you may recall, XCOPY is not without its problems when used as a backup utility for your entire system. It is still quite convenient to use when just copying folders ("directory hierarchies") around on disk.

XCOPY

XCOPY only **copies** the **current folder** or the folder that was called. **XCOPY/S copies** all **sub directories**.

☞✎ Practice Drive XCOPY & XCOPY/S

VI ◆ Summary

In this chapter basic commands in DOS were covered. The various utilities that can be used in DOS to help understand the file properties should be explored further. Make use of the help commands to Practice the switches. Many of the commands used in DOS are of serious assist in troubleshooting a variety of issues. You are encouraged to Practice and become familiar with the Disk Operating System.

VII Test for Success Questions

1. A co-worker is updating their computer. Because of this, the recycle bin is at the currently set capacity. As additional files are added to the recycle bin, what happens to the excess files in the Recycle Bin?

    A. Clusters are relocated to a secondary location

    B. The files are moved to C:\Windows\Temp.

    C. Sectors of hard drive are blanked/erased.

    D. Associated entries in the FAT are removed.

    E. File entries are marked with a ~, indicating it is OK to use the space in temporary folder C:\Windows\Temp

2. What program does Windows 95 use, when there is the need to shut down and restart in DOS mode?

    A. COMMAND.COM

    B. CONFIG.SYS

    C. DOSSTART.BAT

    D. AUTOEXEC.BAT

3. When using a multiboot configuration with Windows 9x, the configuration is stored in which file?

A. IO.SYS

B. SYSTEM.INI

C. MSDOS.SYS

D. CONFIG.SYS

4. Select the statements that would be found in the autoexec.bat file? (Choose all that apply)

A. FILES=40

B. PATH=C:\

C. DOS=HIGH,UMB

D. DEVICE=HIMEM.SYS

5. Before installing or upgrading software, what steps would be experienced technician take first? (Choose all that apply)

   A. Copy IO.SYS.

   B. Backup .INI files.

   C. Copy BOOTSEC.DOS.

   D. Confirm OS compatibility.

   E. Determine minimum memory required.

---

6. Using the System Configuration Editor in Windows 9x, what files can be modified? (Choose all that apply)

   A. WIN INI

   B. BOOT.INI

   C. SYSTEM.INI

   D. MSDOS.SYS

   E. CONFIG.SYS

7. After installing Windows 98 on a 11GB hard drive, only 7.8GB is usable. What steps can you take to resolve this challenge? (Choose all that apply)
   A. Reinstall Windows 98 from the OEM CD.
   B. Install Windows98 SE with large hard drive support.
   C. Use fdisk.exe inside of windows 98 from DOS prompt.
   D. Reformat the hard drive overlay that comes with the drive.
   E. Contact the motherboard manufacturer for a BIOS upgrade.

---

8. You need to create a system log. How can you get a printout of your system's configuration on a Windows 9x operating system? (Choose all that apply)
   A. From the System Monitor, click the print button.
   B. From the Device Manager, click the print button.
   C. From a DOS prompt type sys and press <printscrn>.
   D. From a DOS prompt type msdn and press <printscrn>.

9. You are trying to run a DOS application which gives you an error stating that the application does not run under Windows. What should you try first to resolve the issue? (Choose all that apply)

A. Reload the DOS application from the MS-DOS command prompt.

B. Configure the setver command to allow you to run the DOS program.

C. Install a third party program that will allow you to run the DOS program.

D. Select 'Prevent this program from detecting Windows' in the advanced properties of the DOS application.

10. Which of the following can load device drivers in Windows 9x? (Choose all that apply)

A. BOOT.INI

B. MS-DOS.SYS

C. CONFIG.SYS

D. AUTOEXEC.BAT

E. DOS.BAT

11. Of the following choices, which of these files are text files in Windows 9x? (Choose all that apply)
  A. HIGHMEM.SYS
  B. MSDOS.SYS
  C. CONFIG.SYS
  D. SCANDISK.LOG
  E. COMMAND.COM

12. Which files can you edit in Windows 9x in SYSEDIT? (Choose all that apply)
  A. IO.SYS
  B. WIN.INI
  C. MSDOS.SYS
  D. COMMAND.COM
  E. AUTOEXEC.BAT

13. What is the correct order for the DOS-level boot files in Windows 9x?
   A. MSDOS.SYS, IO.SYS, CONFIG.SYS, COMMAND.COM, AUTOEXEC.BAT.
   B. IO.SYS, MSDOS.SYS, COMMAND.COM, CONFIG.SYS, AUTOEXEC.BAT.
   C. IO.SYS, MSDOS.SYS, COMMAND.COM, AUTOEXEC.BAT, CONFIG.SYS.
   D. IO.SYS, MSDOS.SYS, CONFIG.SYS, COMMAND.COM, AUTOEXEC.BAT.
   E. IO.SYS,CONFIG.SYS.MSDOS.SYS,COMMAND.COM,AUTOEXEC.BAT

14. Which switch should you type after a DOS command to get a list of valid switches
   and their **Notes**s for that particular command as well as an **Notes** of what they do?
   A. /?
   B. /#
   C. /*
   D. /&
   E. /Help

15. You are troubleshooting a PC. The user was changing settings, and now you want to replace the current copy of the registry with an older copy. The Windows GUI will not open. Which command should you type at a DOS prompt?
  A. SCANREG/REVISE
  B. SCANREG/RESTORE
  C. SCANREG/REPLACE
  D. SCANREG/REVERSE
  E. SCANREG/UNDO

16. An employee deleted some files from DOS, and was disappointed that they were not placed in the Recycle Bin. What methods should they use to delete files, if s/he wants them backed up in the Recycle Bin? (Choose all that apply)
  A. My Computer.
  B. Windows Explorer.
  C. The DEL command.
  D. The Erase command.
  E. The Deltree command.

17. DOS SmartDrive is replaced by what in Windows 95?
    A. VCACHE
    B. RAM Drive
    C. CACHE95
    D. VDRIVE
    E. VROOM Drive

18. What DOS command would you use to hide a file named PASS.doc in the current directory?
    A. ATTRIB =H PASS.DOC
    B. ATTRIB +H PASS.DOC
    C. ATTRIB -H PASS.DOC
    D. ATTRIB /HIDE PASS.DOC
    E. ATTRIB #HIDE PASS.DOC

19. Which system file in Windows 9x should be kept at a minimum size of 1KB?
    A. WIN.INI
    B. MSDOS.SYS
    C. CONFIG.SYS
    D. AUTEXEC.BAT
    E. USER.DAT

---

20. You want to edit MSDOS.SYS from DOS. What must be run from a command
    prompt first.
    A. RUN SYSEDIT
    B. RUN REGEDIT
    C. ATTRIB -S -H -R MSDOS.SYS
    D. ATTRIB +S +H +R MSDOS.SYS
    E. ATTRIB /S /H /R MSDOS.SYS

21. You suspect registry corruption when your computer will not allow you into Windows 95. What command, entered at a DOS prompt, will attempt to repair a corrupt registry file?

A. SCANREG /FIX

B. CHDKSK /REGISTRY

C. SCANREG / REPAIR

D. SCANDISK /REG

E. SCANDISK /REPAIR

22. COMMAND.COM in the root directory has been corrupted on your Windows 9x computer. Where can you find a duplicate copy of command.com?

A. C:\WINBACKUP

B. C:\WINDOWS\COMMAND.COM

C. C:\COMMAND.BAK

D. C:\WINDOWS\SYSTEM\COMMAND.COM

E. C:\DOS

23. A long file name in Windows 9x can be changed using which method?

    A. In Windows Explorer, choose File, Rename.

    ☞ B. From an MS-DOS prompt, type 'ren <filename> <newfilename>'.

    C. From the Control Panel, click System, then click Rename.

    D. In Windows Explorer, choose Tools, Rename File.

    E. From DOS, choose FILE-REN.exe

---

24. What three places should you check to see where an application is launching from that launches on every Windows boot? You do not want it to load every time. (Choose all that apply)

    A. WIN.INI

    B. Registry.

    C. Startup folder

    D. SYSTEM.INI

    E. MSDOS.SYS

25. COMMAND.COM in the root directory has been corrupted on your Windows 9x
    computer. Where can you find a duplicate copy of command.com?
    A. C:\WINBACKUP
    B. C:\WINDOWS\COMMAND.COM
    C. C:\COMMAND.BAK
    D. C:\WINDOWS\SYSTEM\COMMAND.COM
    E. C:\DOS

26. Your computer will not boot. What command can you use to restore a backup copy of
    the registry from DOS?
    A. CHKDSK
    B. CHKREG
    C. SCANREG
    D. SCANDISK

27. Windows 98 is failing to start for the first time after you see the Starting Windows 98 message. What can you do to troubleshoot this problem? (Choose all that apply)

A. Type WIN.EXE at a command prompt to start Windows.

B. Type WIN/D:M at a command prompt to start Windows in Safe Mode.

C. Run the System Information Utility from an MS-DOS prompt.

D. Run the DOS version of Dr. Watson at a command prompt.

E. Press F8 when Windows is restarting and select safe mode.

Test for Success Answers

1. A co-worker is updating their computer. Because of this, the recycle bin is at the currently set capacity. As additional files are added to the recycle bin, what happens to the excess files in the Recycle Bin?

A. Clusters are relocated to a secondary location

B. The files are moved to C:\Windows\Temp.

C. Sectors of hard drive are blanked/erased.

D. Associated entries in the FAT are removed.

E. File entries are marked with a ~, indicating it is OK to use the space in temporary folder C:\Windows\Temp

Explanation: D. Associated entries in the FAT are removed.

2. What program does Windows 95 use, when there is need to shut down and restart in DOS mode?

A. COMMAND.COM

B. CONFIG.SYS

C. DOSSTART.BAT

D. AUTOEXEC.BAT

Explanation: C. DOSSTART.BAT is the batch file which is run when Windows restarts in DOS mode.

3. When using a multiboot configuration with Windows 9x, the configuration is stored in which file?
   A. IO.SYS
   B. SYSTEM.INI
   C. MSDOS.SYS
   D. CONFIG.SYS

Explanation: C. MSDOS.SYS and BOOT.INI is where the multiboot config information is stored.
In older versions of DOS, MSDOS.SYS was a real executable file. Now it's just a config file. IO.SYS is a binary file. SYSTEM.INI and CONFIG.SYS contain configuration information, but not for multi-boot.

---

4. Select the statements that would be found in the autoexec.bat file? (Choose all that apply)
   A. FILES=40
   B. PATH=C:\
   C. DOS=HIGH,UMB
   D. DEVICE=HIMEM.SYS

Explanation: B. PATH=C:\ . The other statements are config.sys file statements.

5. Before installing or upgrading software, what steps would be experienced technician take first? (Choose all that apply)
   A. Copy IO.SYS.
   B. Backup .INI files.
   C. Copy BOOTSEC.DOS.
   D. Confirm OS compatibility.
   E. Determine minimum memory required.

Explanation: A, B, C, D, E -- All of the above.

---

6. Using the System Configuration Editor in Windows 9x, what files can be modified? (Choose all that apply)
   A. WIN. INI
   B. BOOT.INI
   C. SYSTEM.INI
   D. MSDOS.SYS
   E. CONFIG.SYS

Explanation: A. WIN.INI, C. SYSTEM.INI, E. CONFIG.SYS. You cannot change BOOT.INI or MSDOS.SYS from the System Configuration Editor.

7. After installing Windows 98 on a 11GB hard drive, only 7.8GB is usable. What steps can you take to resolve this challenge? (Choose all that apply)

A. Reinstall Windows 98 from the OEM CD.

B. Install Windows98 SE with large hard drive support.

C. Use FDISK.exe inside of windows 98 from DOS prompt.

D. Reformat the hard drive overlay that comes with the drive.

E. Contact the motherboard manufacturer for a BIOS upgrade.

Explanation: B. Install Windows98 SE with large hard drive support, E. Contact the motherboard manufacturer for a BIOS upgrade.

8. You need to create a system log. How can you get a printout of your system's configuration on a Windows 9x operating system? (Choose all that apply)

A. From the System Monitor, click the print button.

B. From the Device Manager, click the print button.

C. From a DOS prompt type sys and press <printscrn>.

D. From a DOS prompt type msdn and press <printscrn>.

Explanation: B. From the Device Manager, click the print button

9. You are trying to run a DOS application, which gives you an error stating that the application does not run under Windows. What should you try first to resolve the issue? (Choose all that apply)
A. Reload the DOS application from the MS-DOS command prompt.
B. Configure the setver command to allow you to run the DOS program.
C. Install a third party program that will allow you to run the DOS program.
D. Select 'Prevent this program from detecting Windows' in the advanced properties of the DOS application.

Explanation: B. Configure the setver command to allow you to run the DOS program

10. Which of the following can load device drivers in Windows 9x? (Choose all that apply)
A. BOOT.INI
B. MS-DOS.SYS
C. CONFIG.SYS
D. AUTOEXEC.BAT
E. DOS.BAT

Explanation: C. CONFIG.SYS and sometimes **D. AUTOEXEC.BAT** can be used to load device drivers.
Usually only config.sys is used, but some drivers load in AUTOEXEC.BAT as well. BOOT.INI controls multi-boot, MS-DOS.SYS also contains boot parameters.

11. Of the following choices, which of these files are text files in Windows 9x? (Choose all that apply)
    A. HIGHMEM.SYS
    B. MSDOS.SYS
    C. CONFIG.SYS
    D. SCANDISK.LOG
    E. COMMAND.COM

Explanation: B. MSDOS.SYS, C. CONFIG.SYS and **D. SCANDISK.LOG** are text files. HIGHMEM.SYS does not exist. COMMAND.COM is the executable command interpreter.

---

12. Which files can you edit in Windows 9x in SYSEDIT? (Choose all that apply)
    A. IO.SYS
    B. WIN.INI
    C. MSDOS.SYS
    D. COMMAND.COM
    E. AUTOEXEC.BAT

Explanation: B. WIN.INI and **E. AUTOEXEC.BAT.** IO.SYS and COMMAND.COM are binary files, and MSDOS.SYS is not editable from SYSEDIT.

13. What is the correct order for the DOS-level boot files in Windows 9x?
    A. MSDOS.SYS, IO.SYS, CONFIG.SYS, COMMAND.COM, AUTOEXEC.BAT.
    B. IO.SYS, MSDOS.SYS, COMMAND.COM, CONFIG.SYS, AUTOEXEC.BAT.
    C. IO.SYS, MSDOS.SYS, COMMAND.COM, AUTOEXEC.BAT, CONFIG.SYS.
    D. IO.SYS, MSDOS.SYS, CONFIG.SYS, COMMAND.COM, AUTOEXEC.BAT.
    E. IO.SYS,CONFIG.SYS.MSDOS.SYS,COMMAND.COM,AUTOEXEC.BAT

**Explanation: D. IO.SYS, MSDOS.SYS, CONFIG.SYS, COMMAND.COM,
AUTOEXEC.BAT** – remember, file names in order of length!

14.Which switch should you type after a DOS command to get a list of valid switches
and their **Notes**s for that particular command as well as an **Notes** of what they do?
    A. /?
    B. /#
    C. /*
    D. /&
    E. /Help

Explanation: A. /? Is the universal DOS "get me help on this command" switch. The
others have no particular standard significance.

15. You are troubleshooting a PC. The user was changing settings, and now you want to replace the current copy of the registry with an older copy. The Windows GUI will not open. Which command should you type at a DOS prompt?
A. SCANREG/REVISE
B. SCANREG/RESTORE
C. SCANREG/REPLACE
D. SCANREG/REVERSE
E. SCANREG/UNDO

Explanation: B. SCANREG/RESTORE will hopefully restore a working copy of the registry. The other options are not valid.

16. An employee deleted some files from DOS, and was disappointed that they were not placed in the Recycle Bin. What methods should they use to delete files, if s/he wants them backed up in the Recycle Bin? (Choose all that apply)
A. My Computer.
B. Windows Explorer.
C. The DEL command.
D. The Erase command.
E. The Deltree command.

Explanation: A. My Computer, B. Windows Explorer. When the DOS command line is used to delete files, as with DEL, erase and deltree, they are not placed in the Recycle Bin.

17. DOS SmartDrive is replaced by what in Windows 95?
   A. VCACHE
   B. RAM Drive
   C. CACHE95
   D. VDRIVE
   E. VROOM Drive

Explanation: A. VCACHE. The others are not standard components of Windows 95.

18. What DOS command would you use to hide a file named PASS.doc in the current directory?
   A. ATTRIB =H PASS.DOC
   B. ATTRIB +H PASS.DOC
   C. ATTRIB -H PASS.DOC
   D. ATTRIB /HIDE PASS.DOC
   E. ATTRIB #HIDE PASS.DOC

Explanation: B. ATTRIB +H PASS.DOC. To add the "hidden" attribute, you would use the ATTRIB command with a +H specifier. To remove the "hidden" attribute, you would usethe ATTRIB command with a –H specifier. The other options are invalid.

19. Which system file in Windows 9x should be kept at a minimum size of 1KB?
    A. WIN.INI
    B. MSDOS.SYS
    C. CONFIG.SYS
    D. AUTEXEC.BAT
    E. USER.DAT

Explanation: B. MSDOS.SYS. The other system files mentioned don't have a minimum length requirement. The length requirement on MSDOS.SYS comes from the fact that it used to be a binary executable file.

---

20. You want to edit MSDOS.SYS from DOS. What must be run from a command prompt first.
    A. RUN SYSEDIT
    B. RUN REGEDIT
    C. ATTRIB -S -H -R MSDOS.SYS
    D. ATTRIB +S +H +R MSDOS.SYS
    E. ATTRIB /S /H /R MSDOS.SYS

Explanation: C. ATTRIB –S –H –R MSDOS.SYS must be run before MSDOS.SYS can be edited from DOS. SYSEDIT and REGEDIT are not used to edit MSDOS.SYS. MSDOS.SYS starts out life as a system, hidden, read-only file. In order to edit it, you must remove those attributes. Removing attributes is done with the – rather than the + sign. If you wanted to add those attributes to a file, you would use a command line similar to D.

21. You suspect registry corruption when your computer will not allow you into Windows 95. What command, entered at a DOS prompt, will attempt to repair a corrupt registry file?

A. SCANREG /FIX

B. CHDKSK /REGISTRY

C. SCANREG / REPAIR

D. SCANDISK /REG

E. SCANDISK /REPAIR

Explanation: C. SCANREG /REPAIR. The other options are invalid. SCANDISK and CHKDISK check disk and file system consistency, not the registry.

---

22. COMMAND.COM in the root directory has been corrupted on your Windows 9x computer. Where can you find a duplicate copy of command.com?

A. C:\WINBACKUP

B. C:\WINDOWS\COMMAND.COM

C. C:\COMMAND.BAK

D. C:\WINDOWS\SYSTEM\COMMAND.COM

E. C:\DOS

Explanation: B. C:\WINDOWS\COMMAND.COM is where the file is located.

23. A long file name in Windows 9x can be changed using which method?

    A. In Windows Explorer, choose File, Rename.

    B. From an MS-DOS prompt, type 'ren <filename> <newfilename>'.

    C. From the Control Panel, click System, then click Rename.

    D. Windows Explorer, choose Tools, Rename File.

    E. From DOS, choose FILE-REN.exe

Explanation: A. In Windows Explorer, choose File, Rename or B. From an MS-DOS prompt, type 'ren <filename> <newfilename>'.

The other options will not perform a file rename.

---

24. What three places should you check to see where an application is launching from that launches on every Windows boot? You do not want it to load every time. (Choose all that apply)

    A. WIN.INI

    B. Registry

    C. Startup folder

    D. SYSTEM.INI

    E. MSDOS.SYS

Explanation: A. WIN.INI (look for lines starting RUN= and LOAD=), B. Registry, C. Startup folder (which is found under Programs in your Start menu).

SYSTEM.INI isn't used to launch applications, nor is MSDOS.SYS.

25. COMMAND.COM in the root directory has been corrupted on your Windows 9x computer. Where can you find a duplicate copy of command.com?
A. C:\WINBACKUP
B. C:\WINDOWS\COMMAND.COM
C. C:\COMMAND.BAK
D. C:\WINDOWS\SYSTEM\COMMAND.COM
E. C:\DOS

Explanation: B. C:\WINDOWS\COMMAND.COM is the correct location.

26. Your computer will not boot. What command can you use to restore a backup copy of the registry from DOS?
A. CHKDSK
B. CHKREG
C. SCANREG
D. SCANDISK

Explanation: C. SCANREG will do this (when the /RESTORE switch is used). CHKDSK and SCANDISK check the consistency of the filesystem (or underlying sectors) on a disk. CHKREG is not a valid command.

27. Windows 98 is failing to start for the first time after you see the Starting Windows 98 message. What can you do to troubleshoot this problem? (Choose all that apply)

A. Type WIN.EXE at a command prompt to start Windows.

B. Type WIN/D:M at a command prompt to start Windows in Safe Mode.

C. Run the System Information Utility from an MS-DOS prompt.

D. Run the DOS version of Dr. Watson at a command prompt.

E. Press F8 when Windows is restarting and select safe mode.

Explanation: B. Type WIN/D:M at a command prompt to start Windows in Safe Mode, or E. Pres F8 when Windows is restarting and select Safe mode. Both of these actions start Windows in Safe Mode (note: /D:M = start Windows with minimal drivers). If Windows does successfully start up and get past the "Starting Windows 98" message when running in Safe Mode, then you know you have a driver issue, and can start troubleshooting from there.

Let me see something tomorrow which I never saw before.

-Samuel Johnson-

Chapter 0100: New Technology

The objective of this chapter is to provide the reader with an understanding of the following:

◤ Introduction

The interesting and very powerful Operating System known as NT, will be examined in this chapter. The various methods to get to the troubleshooting and administrative tools will be covered. The differences between this Windows operating system (and Windows 2000) and the Windows9x systems will also be addressed.

NT and Windows 2000 are completely different Operating Systems from DOS and Windows 3.x/9.x/Me offerings. When the BIOS examines Track 0 on the hard drive and finds NT the start up process appears similar to DOS in that it is character based, however the similarity ends with appearance.

Getting Ready - Questions

1. The actual physical printer attached to an NT machine is called the:
   A. Print device
   B. Printer
   C. Laserjet
   D. Output device

2. Which of the following is NOT a file required for NT to boot:
   A. NTDETECT
   B. COMMAND.COM
   C. BOOT.INI
   D. NTLDR

3. DRWTSN32 is the command which:
   A. Finds hidden files
   B. Allows the system to record information about errors
   C. Finds and fixes bugs in programs
   D. Looks for large files

4. The "Launch folders in separate memory" option for Explorer might be used to:
   A. Reduce the amount of memory taken by Explorer
   B. Provide more reliability, so that problems in one window don't affect others
   C. Reduce the amount of screen space taken by multiple Explorer windows open at the same time
   D. Allow different users to use Explorer at the same time

5. To adjust the size of the swap file in NT, you would go to:
   A. Control Panel
   B. Settings -> Memory
   C. Disk Administrator
   D. System Manager

Getting Ready - Answers

1. Correct answer: A

2. Correct answer: B

3. Correct answer: B

4. Correct answer: B

5. Correct answer: A

II ◆ Booting

It is the **BOOT.INI** file that tells the **computer where** and **how** to load **NT** (and Windows 2000). This is a **text** file that is marked **Read only**. There are **two** ways to **change** the **BOOT.INI** file. **One** way is **through** the **Control Panel**. The **second** way is to **change** the **Read Only attribute** of the BOOT.INI file and **edit** it with a **plain text editor,** such as **Notepad.** .

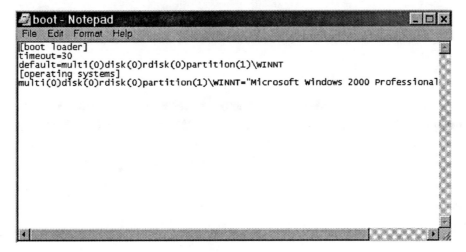

Figure 145 The BOOT.INI file in Windows 2000

```
[boot loader]
timeout=30
default=multi(0)disk(0)rdisk(0)partition(1)\WINNT
[operating systems]
multi(0)disk(0)rdisk(0)partition(1)\WINNT="Microsoft Windows 2000 Professional
```

Figure 146 The BOOT.INI file in Notepad

If you examine the **BOOT.INI** file with a **plain text editor** you will see a long line of **data**, such as **DISK (0)**, **RDISK (0)**, and **PARTITION (1)**.

BOOT.INI

It is beyond A+ to be concerned with the meanings of these values. Briefly, **DISK** is the **physical hard drive**, **RDISK** is the **controller**, and the **first physical device** of each begins with the **value 0**. The **exception** is the **partition** information, which **always starts** with **1**

To edit the BOOT.INI with Notepad, ▱ Notepad go to

☞✍ Practice Exploring System Properties

NT/Windows 2000 Multi Boot

NT/Windows 2000 supports the choice of booting multiple operating systems, and a default choice can be selected with a timeout value in seconds

BOOT.INI waits

Selecting **0** seconds for the default value will force the **boot.ini** file to **wait** for a choice. If multiple Operating Systems are installed, the **default** choice and the **timeout** can be selected from the **Control Panel**.

NT/Windows 2000 differ in many ways from DOS/Windows 3.x/9.x/Me. One huge difference is the fact that NT 3.x/4/W2K are true **32-bit Operating Systems** that use a **flat model** for **memory**. That is to say there is **no HIMEM.SYS or EMM386.EXE,** as there was in DOS and earlier versions of Windows, because there is **no real** and **extended memory**. All **memory** starts at **zero** and just goes up. Applications that are written to operate in a 32-bit memory mode always run in their **own separate memory space**.

Even with this strong distinction between different processes, NT sometimes tries to take a few little short-cuts in the name of efficiency. One of these is that all the Windows Explorer windows you have open, potentially viewing many folders at once, are managed by the same copy of the Windows Explorer program. This is done because it's faster to open a window if you're not ALSO starting up a new copy of a program at the same time. Alas, if Windows Explorer locks up due to a problem in one window, your other Windows Explorer windows also lock up. This is not good for reliability. So, Microsoft provides the option to run each folder window with a separate copy of the Windows Explorer, if you're willing to trade a bit of speed for increased reliability.

To enable this go the **Control Panel** ![Control Panel], open the **Folder Options** ![Folder Options icon]

Folder
Options applet, click the **View** tab and check the

☐ Launch folder windows in a separate process box.

Here are the options you'll see on the **View** tab when you do this:

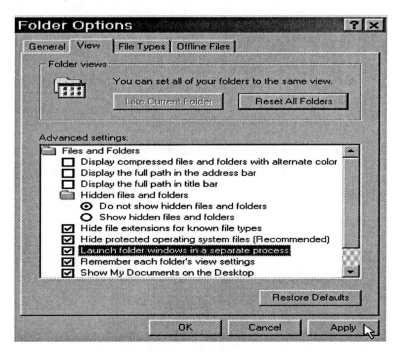

Figure 147 The Launch Folders in separate memory option

Separate Memory

Try running an application it in its own separate (protected) memory, if the application is misbehaving

Shared Memory

16-bit applications can run in shared or protected memory. The challenge with running some applications in protected memory is they may be unable to dynamically share data with another program, say from Word to Excel.

Sharing Downside

The down side of 16-bit programs that run in shared memory is if one application crashes, it will take down all applications that are sharing that memory.

Navigation

From a standpoint of normal navigation, NT4 has a very similar look and feel to Windows 95. At least that is true once a user is logged in. The **login process** is a user's first clue they aren't in Win 9x anymore. Assuming that Win 9x is on a network, a user logging into Win 9x is presented with a name and password prompt. Hitting the ESC key at that point says, "go on and boot without loading the network components". In NT/W2K, there is no such option. No correct name and password = no access, even to local resources (files, printers, etc.).

Network System Design

NT/W2K was designed from the ground up for networking. If you have to install NT on a computer that will truly be stand alone, with no Network Interface Card, you MUST select the "NIC" MS **LoopBack** as a "NIC", or NT will not install. W2K will install this automagically for you at the time of installation.

To log into NT the user must press **CTRL-ALT-DEL** at the same time, which brings up the **WINLOGON applet**. The user MUST present a **valid name** and **password** that has not expired to successfully get into the computer. After any applications found in the start up menu are loaded, NT 4 (and Windows 2000) looks almost exactly like Win 9x.

Control Panel

At first glance, the **Control Panel** looks almost exactly like **Win 9x.** The operative word here is **almost**. One thing that is missing in NT 4 is the **Device Manager** in the **Control Panel**. Sorry, there is no time saving **Device Manager** in **NT**, which was developed before Microsoft thought to add Device Manager to Win9x. Details such as what IRQ are in use, and memory details are quite a bit tougher to find in NT, as they were in Windows 3.1.

In Windows 200 we can find the **System** icon, which can lead us to many troubleshooting and informational areas. These areas are: Network, Hardware, User Profiles, Advanced.

Figure 148 The System Properties Tabs

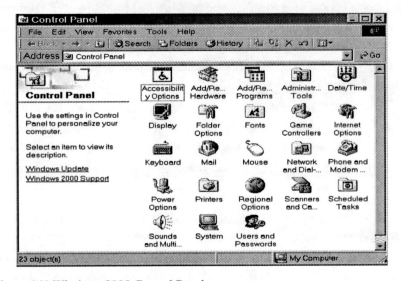

Figure 149 Windows 2000 Control Panel

NT Stability

Many experienced geeks love NT, as it is quite a bit more stable than Windows 3.x/9.x/Me. And most of us miss the details from the **Device Manager**. To offset this missing helper, it is not uncommon to load **Windows 9x** in a small partition of a hard drive with **FAT** to get the **Device Manager**. This can be a critical time saver, even more so if non-Plug 'n Play (legacy) devices are installed.

Memory swap files

NT uses a **swap file**, just as Windows 9x. The **Control Panel** is where the **size** of the **swap file** can be adjusted.

Swap File Sizing

You can increase performance of **NT** by adjusting the **minimum** and **maximum** size of the **swap file** by making each entry the same number. This prevents the system from **dynamically adjusting**. Hard drive space is cheap, so make it one large number. A good rule of thumb is the **amount of ram, plus** some, at least **16 MB more**.

To change the file size in **Windows 2000**, go to **Control Panel,** Control Panel then

System, System then **Advanced**, the following screens will appear.

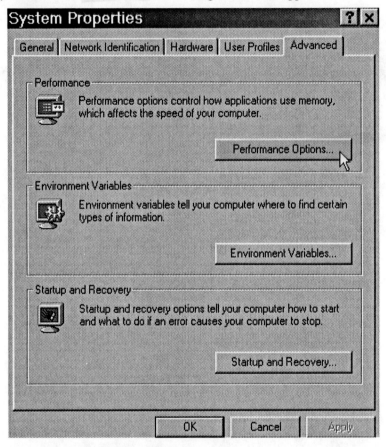

Figure 150 The Performance Options window

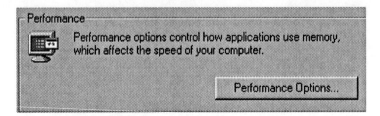

Figure 151 The Performance Options Rationale

Performance Options

Application response

Optimize performance for:

◉ Applications   ○ Background services

Virtual memory

Total paging file size for all drives: 500 MB

Change...

OK   Cancel

Figure 152 Changing the Size of the File

Virtual Memory

Drive [Volume Label]	Paging File Size (MB)
C: [LA 5]	1000 - 1000

Paging file size for selected drive

Drive: C: [LA 5]
Space available: 14533 MB

Initial size (MB):   1000

Maximum size (MB):   1000   Set

Total paging file size for all drives

Minimum allowed: 2 MB
Recommended: 382 MB
Currently allocated: 1000 MB

Registry size

Current registry size: 14 MB

Maximum registry size (MB):   70

OK   Cancel

Figure 153 Set the File Size change

After making the adjustments to virtual memory, be sure to click set then click apply.

* Virtual Mem change   *

ERROR - Virtual Mem Low

III   File structure review

Windows **95 B** (OSR2) introduced **FAT 32** and continued through with **Windows 98** and Me. NT4 was too far along in the development cycle to include support for FAT 32.

NT can't see it
NT cannot see any FAT 32 partitions. NT be installed as an upgrade over Windows 95, if Win 95 was installed on a FAT 16 partition. It is entirely possible to have first installed Win 95 (B) over a Win 3.x with FAT 16, then added a hard drive and formatted it FAT 32, with Win 95 seeing both

partitions. Once NT upgrades Win 95 (B) the newly installed FAT 32 partition would not appear to exist in reality.

Figure 154 File Types Supported In WIN2K

Disk Administrator

NT can be found as an Operating System for users or as the foundation of a server. Because of this, the drive support in NT is much greater. For example, NT will support (in its own software) multiple drives making one volume (spanning), two physical drives backing each other up (mirroring), or stripping data, without or with parity (RAID 0 and 5 respectfully). NT can even support drives without drive letters assigned to them. All these new features needed to be put someplace. That someplace is known as the Disk Administrator.

Disk Administrator

Adding/Changing/Removing/Formatting drives is done with **Disk Administrator** in NT 4

Figure 155 Disk Administrator NT 4

Printing

By now you may have guessed that **NT** is much more powerful than Windows 9x. This heavy weight O/S continues this thought process in printing as well.

Printers & Print Devices

A terminology change occurred with NT, at least as far as Microsoft is concerned. Up until NT, Printers were objects that spit out paper with words on them. Beginning with **NT**, a **printer** is the **device driver** that exists in NT. The **physical machine** that puts words on paper is now in MS terminology a **device**.

If more than one **printing device** can support the same printer (device driver), NT has a feature known as **printer pooling**. This means when you want to print, it will use the device that will happen to print the print job out soonest.

NT will also look at another NT based computer to see if it has a newer print[er] (**device driver**). If so, it will automagically download it and use it. NT will also share its physical device from other Operating Systems if it has the print[er] (**device driver**) installed locally.

Further, NT can support pushing a **print job** for a user or group of users up to the top of the **queue based** on **priority**. And (in NT terms) a **printer** can be set for **availability**, based on time. This means a long print job can be sent to a "printer" that is not available until after hours, hold the **print job** in the **print queue** on the hard drive until it becomes available then spend the night printing.

All these features are really cool, until something blows up. That something is the **print queue**. If the **print queue** corrupts or stalls, no physical printing can occur. To correct a **print queue** that has gone south, go to the **Control Panel**, select **Services**, from this point go down to the **print queue**, then **stop** and **restart** the **service**.

Repairing a Printer

Repair a printer (if devices are no longer printing) by stopping and restarting the Print Queue.

Figure 156 Printers

Maintenance/Clean up Utilities

Even NT isn't perfect. And it seems to be closer to nirvana than most of the applications that run on NT. Sometimes either NT or some application that is running on NT blows up. Compared to Windows 9x, it keeps a very watchful eye on what is going on. Depending on what is selected to monitor, something as minor as changing the time can be logged. Typically, this is a waste of computing resources. And this monitoring can be invaluable to you when you are attempting to figure out what has happened on a PC with NT.

NT has an applet called the **Event Viewer** that will monitor to whatever level it was told to do so. There are **three major logs**, broken down by the names, **System**, **Application**, and **Security**.

Event Viewer

The Event Viewer and its three logs, System Application and Security inform you of what a NT based system has been doing.

The Event Logs can be your eyes that never blink when it comes to system monitoring.

Figure 157 Event Viewer

Task Manager

While Window 9.x has available in some form or another an **agent** to inform you of what a system is doing with an application, known as the **Resource Monitor,** it can't old a candle to what NT can do.

There are **two** different **monitors** in **NT**. The big gun is called **Performance Monitor.** Performance Monitor is wonderful, and it is possible to write an entire book about its use. One challenge with Performance Monitor is it can eat all the computer resources of the PC it is monitoring.

This is where the **second tool** comes in real handy. It is called the **Task Manager**. The **Task Manager** can give you a real time view of **what** is **running,** how much **CPU** tibme is being used, how much **memory** is in use, right down to the details of how **often** it had to go to the **swap file** to continue operations.

Figure 158 Task Manager

There are several ways to get to the **Task Manager**. **Right** clicking the **Task Bar,** pressing **CTRL-ALT-DEL** and selecting Task Manager CTRL-SHIFT-ESC all get you there.

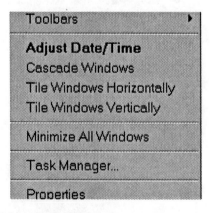

Figure 159 Right Clicking Task Bar Results

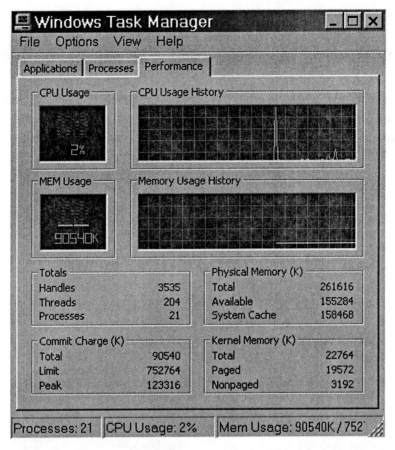

Figure 160 Task Manger Running (Performance Tab)

Task Manager

Task Manager can be opened with CTRL-ALT-DEL and click on Task Manager, or Right clicking the Task Bar, CTRL-SHIFT-ESC.

WIN9X = COMMAND.COM
NT & W2K = CMD.EXE

Command Line Differences

While NT is certainly GUI based, not all functions are run through the GUI. Some utilities must be run through the **CDI** (Command Driven Interface) or text interface.

Windows 9x users would be used to the CDI being Command.com. **That is not the preferred method for NT. While Command.com is available in NT, it is 16-bit based and much more limited than NT's (and W2K's) CDI, which is** CMD.EXE. **To start CMD.exe go to start** 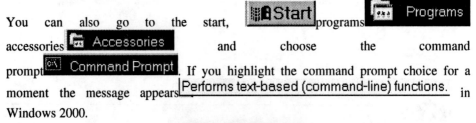 **then run** **then** **type in cmd/or cmd.exe in the**

Start → run → CMD

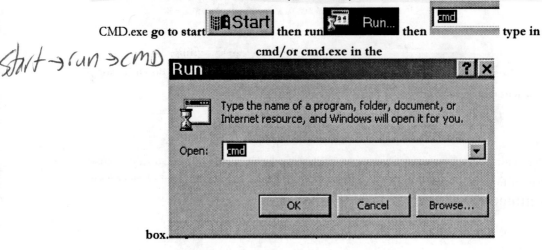

box.

Figure 161 CMD upper or lower case at the run menu

You can also go to the start,  programs accessories and choose the command prompt. If you highlight the command prompt choice for a moment the message appears Performs text-based (command-line) functions. in Windows 2000.

Figure 162 Command-line-Differences

CMD.exe VS Command.com

For NT/W2K, CMD.exe is the interface for text-based communications. Once started, it uses the same commands as DOS and the Win9x Command shell (for the most part).

Networking

As mentioned previously in this chapter, **NT** was **built** with **networking** in mind. To ease **administration** of a **network**, **rights (permissions)** are typically broken down by some **classification** system, which allows **unique users** to be dropped into the **classification system**. At this point the unique user automagically inherits the **rights** of that **classification**. In NT, this **classification** system is known as **groups**.

After setting up all this information on a PC (especially servers), it would be a great waste of time to not **back** it all **up**. **NT** provides a way to do that. To capture the **setup**, run **RDISK.exe**

Figure 163 RDISK.exe

ERD Disk

To create an Emergency Repair Diskette (ERD) run RDISK.exe

Default RDISK

RDISK.EXE only captures the Administrator and guest account. To get all the other users data, run RDISK.EXE/S

There is another form of classification that occurs known as profiles, which is visited next.

Profiles

Historically, people like to set up their PC to suit their own **preferences**. That is what put the P in PC. Without the Personal, it would just be Computer. The **preferences** for a **user** are **stored** in what is called a **Profile**.

Profiles for a user are stored in a **folder**. These **profiles** can be stored on a **server**, and be loaded wherever a user sits down and logs onto the network from any machine. These are known as **roaming profiles**. A company may require standardization of PCs. These are **profiles** that are stored on a **server** and are called **mandatory profiles**.

In all events, a **local PC** stores at least a **copy** of the **profile** at the **local PC (the actual machine)** in a **folder** just for that **user**. When a user makes changes, such as installing a program, its availability is registered with their profile.

Figure 164 Permissions

Administrators Profile

If an **Administrator** logs in to a **local PC** and **effects** changes, such as installing a program, it will install to the **Administrators profile**, making it **unavailable** to the **local user** when they log on.

When running on a network, there are a number of **transport protocols** that are available with NT. Each choice has its own advantages and disadvantages. Today, the defacto standard is **TCP/IP**. That does not mean there are not **other transport protocols** in wide use from networks previously setup. Other popular choices include **IPX** (known as NWLink in NT) and **NetBEUI.** More details on networking appear in the chapter we mysteriously called, networking.

Default Protocols

Default Transport Protocols "Out of the box", NT supports **IPX (NWLink), NetBEUI** and **TCP/IP**

There is a key difference between having **Windows 9x users log** into a **network** and a **NT computer logging** into an **NT server**. The **Windows 9x users** simply use their **name** and **password** for access. **NT clients** (users) use their **name** and **password**, and in addition, a **second** (somewhat hidden) **account verifies** the **request** for **login**.

All **NT systems** have a **special key** called a **Security Identifier** or **SID**. For added security, when one NT system wants to talk to another NT system, the **SID's** must be **registered**. On login, the **SID's** are **compared** in **addition** to the **user name** and **password**.

IV   RAS Remote Access Service

In today's world, we are more productive then ever. Modern devices, such as microwave ovens have reduced the time for basic needs. Instead of more leisure time, we have more time to work to keep improving productivity. Now we get to take our work home without carrying a briefcase.

NT gives us the **ability** to be **remote** from the **network**, and still be **on** the **network**. This is done with the **Remote Access Service (RAS)**. **NT** will use **RAS** in **conjunction** with a **modem** to have all the **rights** (or lack of) and **resources**, just as if you were in the office.

RAS for Remote

NT needs RAS to support Remote Access

Understanding RAS

For some reason, many geeks just don't get RAS. Your authors don't see what is tough about RAS. Sure, if NT is involved, RAS and a modem has to be installed (and that isn't tough). The story that seems to be missed is with RAS, it is just like have a long and skinny network cable attached to the PC that is remote. If you have access to certain printers in the office, you have access via RAS. If you don't have access to the color laser at work, you won't have access with RAS. The only difference between being there and being remote is speed. If you use IPX as a transport protocol at work, then IPX needs to be installed on the remote computer.

Running RAS

Once **RAS** is installed, going to the **desktop** and **launching** the **Dial Up Networking**
Icon Network and Dial-up Connections (through Network Connections or create a

Local Area
shortcut to the connection) Connecti... can **connect** you to the office network. You can
also   go   to   start,   settings,   network   and   dial   up
connections Network and Dial-up Connections in Windows 2000.

Start → settings → network
dial up connections

Figure 165 Dial-Up Networking

Upgrading / Installation requirements

NT may offer some great advantages over Windows 9x, and this comes with some prices
to pay. Computer Resource requirements are higher than with the Win 9x O/S choices.

For example, no video cards standards except VGA are supported. While Microsoft
claims NT will operate on less than a Pentium, don't try it at home or at work. MS also
says NT Workstation has a minimum requirement of 12 MB of ram. Notice they didn't
say it runs on 12 MB.

That is because it doesn't. OK, the computer won't refuse to load, and it won't run either.
The computer would be so slow; you would believe it was frozen.

NT Upgrade
NT will upgrade from Windows 95, provided it is sitting on a FAT 16 partition.

Installation process

Installation of NT can be done a variety of ways. The **CD** is **bootable,** so if your computer supports **booting from CD**, you are good to go. Or, you can load a mini-copy of **NT** with **3 boot diskettes**.

Finally, you can type Winnt.exe /b and it will put the equivalent of the three boot diskettes in a temporary area and install without the diskettes.

Installing NT
WINNT /B will install NT without boot diskettes. NT is a bootable CD.

NT is fussy about hardware. This is because all **hardware calls** must **pass through** the **Hardware Abstraction Layer** (**HAL**).

This **requirement** allows **NT** to be run on different **CPU architectures** than **Intel's**, such as the **DEC Alpha chip** and keeps renegade hardware in check.

NT / WIN 95 Upgrade
NT cannot see any FAT 32 partitions. NT Can do an upgrade install of Windows 95, if Win 95 was installed on a FAT 16 partition. It is entirely possible to have first installed Win 95 (B) over a Win 3.x with FAT 16, then added a hard drive and formatted it FAT 32, with Win 95 seeing both partitions. Once NT upgrades Win 95 (B) the newly installed FAT 32 partition would not appear to exist in reality.

NT uses a **layered structure** for **protection**. An analogy you might think of would be a moat around a castle, with a drawbridge as one of the rings of layered protection. NT uses a number of these layers. Inside the castle walls is called the **kernel (layer 0)**. Like the citizens inside the castle walls, NT is safe if renegades are kept **outside** the **kernel**.

Microsoft made a change when they went from NT 3.x to NT 4. For example, video drivers used to be outside the kernel. That meant that to make the monitor work, all video information had to go through the doorway to 'talk' to the kernel. To make NT respond to the user faster, in **NT 4** they moved the **video drivers** to the **kernel**. That put the pressure on the authors of video drivers to be very careful, lest they crash the kernel.

Should a video driver that is not well behaved get loaded into NT4, the Operating System will go into a fatal tailspin, called a **Blue Screen of Death** (BSOD). This results in a cryptic message at the top of the screen saying something like,

STOP IRQ Less Than or Equal to

Followed by four columns of hexadecimal code all the way down the screen in very small type. You don't need a Doctor to know that NT session is dead. So the question arises, how to get out of this mess?

The answer lies below. NT retains the settings from the last session. During the boot up process a message is displayed that says, "Press the spacebar NOW for the last known good configuration" Pressing this will take you to the configuration that last worked *before* the BSOD due to the video driver. Caution, pressing this before you are sure new installations are working may take you to reinstall not recovery.

BSOD Due to Driver Update

To recover from a bad driver update, press the spacebar when prompted to do so, for "last known good configuration".
NT 4 has a **second boot option** that looks just like the normal boot.

The **difference** is at the **end** of all the **Disk** and **Rdisk** data there are **two switches**. One has **/SOS** which if used replaces the **dots** with an **express call out** of the **drivers** that are **loading**. That is, it lists each driver on the screen as it loads. Watching this as an NT system boots might provide more information about a problem that is keeping the system from booting all the way up into NT. The other **switch** is **/basevideo** which if **used calls** a plain **VGA video driver** that **operates** in **16 colors** @ 640x480 pixels.

Don't charge ahead

A fine way to spend some time reinstalling NT is to ignore a bad driver (assuming NT loaded) and login with CTRL-ALT-DEL and type in the user name and password from memory. NT assumes all went well and will right the configuration down as the last known good.

Figure 166 Invoking Last Known Good

NT Requirements

Previously, this chapter talked about needing three boot diskettes if NT is not installed from the CD. Once NT is installed, it is still subject to failure. NT needs three files to load. They are NTLDR, NTDETECT and the boot.ini file.

Success Tip 1,2,3

NT needs three files to load. They are **NTLDR**, **NTDETECT** and the **Boot.ini**

Booting NT

Actually, IF you used the **default directory, (WINNT)** and the **boot.ini** file is missing, it will take one shot at **booting** by looking for the **WINNT folder. IF NT** is **there**, you will **boot. Otherwise**, the **Boot.ini file** is required. The A+ O/S test simply requires you to know *that all three files are required*.

Dr. Watson

Now that you know about NT and it's layers of protection, it is clear to you that less fatal errors may be contained. For example, lets assume that WinWord.Exe (**892 WINWORD.exe**) dies a horrible death while you are typing an A+ O/S book. (It happens!)

You might want to know what is going on. NT is there to help you. At the point WinWord.Exe dies, a **message** comes up informing you of the **fatal error**. This **message** come courtesy of **Dr. Watson**. This digital doctor will **write out** all sorts of **data** about what was happening to help you figure out what caused the crash of Word. (Generally, it'll be of more help to a program's authors than it will be to you, but it's useful to know how to collect this data in case Microsoft or another vendor asks you to do so.) The **file DRWTSN32.LOG** can be found in the **WINNT folder**. Click **Start,**  then

Run,  and then type **drwtsn32**

Dr. Watson's clues

Dr. Watson will leave evidence of the crime in the file **DRWTSN32.LOG** found in the **WINNT** folder

Using Dr. Watson

Dr. Watson detects information about system and <u>program</u> failures and records the information in a <u>log file</u>. In the event of a program error, Dr. Watson starts automatically.

Open Dr. Watson.

Notes

- To open Dr. Watson, click **Start**, click **Run**, and then type **drwtsn32**.

- Dr. Watson cannot prevent errors from occurring, but the information recorded in the log file can be used by technical support personnel to diagnose the problem.

- For information about using Dr. Watson, click **Help** in Dr. Watson.

Figure 167 Dr Watson from Windows 200 help files

Dr. Watson for Windows 2000 ? ✕

Log File Path:	All Users\Documents\DrWatson	Browse...
Crash Dump:	C:\Documents and Settings\All	Browse...
Wave File:		Browse...

Number of Instructions: 10

Number of Errors To Save: 10

Options

☐ Dump Symbol Table
☑ Dump All Thread Contexts
☑ Append To Existing Log File
☑ Visual Notification
☐ Sound Notification
☑ Create Crash Dump File

Application Errors   [View]   [Clear]

```
c0000005 <nosymbols>(300B9CF8)
c0000005 <nosymbols>(300B9CF8)
c0000005 <nosymbols>(300B9CF8)
```

[OK]   [Cancel]   [Help]

Figure 168 The Dr Watson log file window

```
                                    ┌Program that
                                    │caused the error
App: fault.exe (pid=141) ┐
When: 6/16/1993 @ 15:24:48.15
Exception number: c0000005 (access violation)
                   └_____┘
                                    └Error
                                     that occurred
```

Figure 169 Dr Watson Message Decoded

```
┊ Log File Viewer                                          ✕

  Application exception occurred:
          App:  (pid=892)
          When: 5/11/2001 @ 14:29:15.219
          Exception number: c0000005 (access violation)

  *----> System Information <----*
          Computer Name: NET04
          User Name: LA
          Number of Processors: 1
          Processor Type: x86 Family 6 Model 4 Stepping 2
          Windows 2000 Version: 5.0
          Current Build: 2195
          Service Pack: 1
          Current Type: Uniprocessor Free
          Registered Organization: TcatU.net
          Registered Owner: LA

                        [  OK  ]
```

Figure 170 Actual Dr Watson Log

App: (pid=892)   892 WINWORD.exe

Figure 171 The Error message decoded

Figure 172 Figure 173 Dr Watson

Overcoming Challenges

Throughout this chapter you have seen a variety of issues that can come up, and how to address them. When discussing **Cmd.exe** to grant superior **CDI** access, it was mentioned that some things that are **GUI based** in **Windows 9x** are **CDI based** in **NT**.

This is a point that easily trips up technicians who are used to Windows 9x. Let's look at checking a PC's IP address. In Windows 9x, a GUI based utility called **WinIPCFG** is used. Not so with NT/W2K. They use the **CDI** based **IPCONFIG**.

To start **IPCONFIG** go to the **command prompt** Command Prompt and type in **IPCONFIG.** IPCONFIG The following screen will appear.

```
Command Prompt
Microsoft Windows 2000 [Version 5.00.2195]
(C) Copyright 1985-2000 Microsoft Corp.

C:\>IPCONFIG

Windows 2000 IP Configuration

Ethernet adapter Local Area Connection 2:
```

Figure 174 IPCONFIG at the Command Prompt

IPCONFIG

IPCONFIG is **CDI** (text based), used by **NT/W2K** and is *not* **WinIPCfg**

V   Summary

In this chapter you learned the various properties of FAT and its limitations with NT. You also learned of the FAT capabilities in Windows 2000. Understanding the features and utilities of NT will be assistive in installing and setting up the operating system.

The various print utilities in NT will help in managing document production. The differences in navigation from 9X operating systems were explained. The troubleshooting features found in Dr Watson were covered. Both the powerful NT and Win2K operating systems are complete studies and should be explored in greater detail. This chapter was intended to be an overview to these operating systems and should not be considered complete beyond the scope of the A+ Operating system test. You are encouraged to continue your introduction to NT and WIN2K.

VI Test for Success Questions

1. Your company is upgrading to Windows 2000 Professional. Which of the following operating systems can you upgrade to Windows 2000 Professional? (Choose two)
   A. OS/2
   B. WINDOWS 3.x
   C. WINDOWS 9x
   D. WINDOWS NT 4.0
   E. WINDOWS FOR WORKGROUPS 3.x

2. A customer is running Windows NT and has 20GB of unformatted hard disk space. He wants to format the 20GB drive, move the data from his 5GB drive and label the 20GB drive as drive B. What Windows NT applet can perform all these tasks for him?
   A. File Administrator
   B. Partition Magic
   C. Drive Administrator
   D. Disk Administrator

3. You need to create a Windows NT 4.0 boot diskette. Which three files do you need to copy to the diskette? (Choose three)
   A. NTLDR.
   B. BOOT.INI.
   C. MSDOS.SYS.
   D. NTDETECT.COM.
   E. OSLOADER.EXE.

4. What command creates an Emergency Repair Disk for Windows NT 4.0?
   A. EBD.BAT
   B. RDISK.EXE
   C. ERD.EXE /S
   D. Add/Remove Programs

5. Your computer will not boot, and you think it is because some of your boot files have been deleted. Which files must be present in the root directory of the system partition in order for Windows NT 4.0 to boot?

  A. NTLDR, BOOT.INI, NTDETECT.COM.

  B. IO.SYS, MS-DOS.SYS, NTLDR, SYSTEM.

  C. IO.SYS, MS-DOS.SYS, BOOT.INI, COMMAND.COM.

  D. NTLDR, COMMAND.COM, NTDETECT.COM, BOOT.INI.

---

6. You have a custom application that is conflicting with another application. What can you do to temporarily fix the problem on a Windows NT system?

  A. Run MSCONFIG

  B. Run REGEDT32.

  C. Reinstall the application.

  D. Run the application in a protected memory space.

7. You updated a device driver on a Windows NT 4.0 Workstation, and now the computer fails to boot to the GUI. What should you do?

   A. Reload NT.

   B. Run ScanDisk and Disk Defragmenter.

   C. Press F5 to enter safe mode and delete the last device installed.

   D. Press the spacebar when the Load Last Known Good Configuration message appears.

---

8. When a print job is stalled in Windows NT 4.0, what should you try first?

   A. Restart the PC.

   B. Restart the spooler.

   C. Try another printer cable.

   D. Try another printer driver.

9. An error occurs on your Windows NT 4.0 workstation, and Dr. Watson has created a log file. Where can you find the file to review what has caused the error?

A. C:\

B. C:\WinNT

C. C:\WinNT\system

D. C:\WinNT\system32

---

10. You just received a Windows NT stop error with the full blue screen. How can you print out the error message that was generated?

A. Do a print screen.

B. Reboot and edit the system log.

C. Reboot and open file 0000.chk.

D. Reboot and browse the temp folder.

11. Which utility would you use to get a computer's IP address in Windows NT 4.0?
    A. TRACERT
    B. NETSTAT
    C. IPCONFIG
    D. NBTSTAT

12. Which service must be installed on a Windows NT 4.0 system to allow Dial-Up Networking access?
    A. Net BEUI.
    B. IPX/SPX.
    C. Remote access service.
    D. Dial-Up Networking V 1.3.

13. Which command would you use to remove an NTFS volume from a PC that no longer contains Windows NT 4.0?

    A. MOVE

    B. FDISK

    C. FORMAT

    D. DELTREE

14. You need to create a Windows NT Boot Disk. Which files must you have on the disk? (Choose two)

    A. NTLDR

    B. BOOT.INI

    C. NTFS32.BIN

    D. WINNT32.INI

    E. NTDETECT.COM

15. Windows fails to boot because a customer deleted a file from a Windows NT 4.0 Workstation. Which of the following might have been deleted?
   A. BOOT.INI
   B. CONFIG.SYS
   C. COMMAND.COM
   D. AUTOEXEC.BAT

16. A Windows NT 4.0 command prompt can be invoked with which command?
   • A. CMD.EXE
   B. RUN.COM
   C. COMMAND.EXE
   D. COMMAND.COM

17. A Windows NT 4.0 emergency repair disk can be created using what command?
    A. RDISK.EXE
    B. ERD.EXE
    C. EMERGENCY.COM
    D. FORMAT /ERD A:

18. What will happen if you run 'WINNT /B' from a command prompt on the Windows NT 4.0 installation CD.
    A. 3 NT setup disks will be created.
    B. The Windows NT 4.0 registry will be backed up.
    C. Windows NT 4.0 will be installed without prompting for boot diskettes.
    D. Windows NT 4.0 will be installed and boot diskettes will be created diskettes.

19. While logged in as a local administrator, you install an application on Windows NT 4.0 for an employee of your firm. You test it and it works fine. You reboot and tell her to log in and call you if she has a problem. She calls to report that the application will not run. When you log in, it runs fine. Why?

A. NTFS permissions prevent her from running the application.

B. Incorrect CD Key.

C. The EVERYONE group is missing in the application's security properties.

D. The application was not installed by the user.

20. While booting you receive the following message when booting Windows NT 4.0 Workstation: "NTLDR not found. Please insert another disk". What should you do to fix the disk?

A. Extract the file from the CD.

B. Run the emergency repair process.

C. Copy the file from any Windows system.

D. Copy the file from another Windows NT system.

21. Which OEM installation CD always requires a boot floppy because the CD-ROM is not bootable?

    A. Windows 95

    B. Windows 98

    C. Windows 2000

    D. Windows NT 4.0

---

22. After installing a new hard drive, which Windows NT 4.0 utility should you use to make it usable?

    A. FDISK

    B. FORMAT

    C. DISKEDT32

    D. Disk Administrator

23. Your Windows NT 4 system will not boot. What is the first thing to try?

    A. Format and restore from tape.

    B. Boot to Safe Mode.

   * C. Use the Last Known Good Configuration.

    D. Reinstall NT using three boot disks and the CD.

Test for Success Answers

1. Your company is upgrading to Windows 2000 Professional. Which of the following operating systems can you upgrade to Windows 2000 Professional? (Choose two)
   A. OS/2
   B. WINDOWS 3.x
   C. WINDOWS 9x
   D. WINDOWS NT 4.0
   E. WINDOWS FOR WORKGROUPS 3.x

Explanation: C. WINDOWS 9x, D. WINDOWS NT 4.0 are supported for upgrades, as is Windows NT 3.51. OS/2 and earlier versions of Windows are not upgradeable to Windows 2000 Professional.

---

2. A customer is running Windows NT and has 20GB of unformatted hard disk space. He wants to format the 20GB drive, move the data from his 5GB drive and label the 20GB drive as drive B. What Windows NT applet can perform all these tasks for him?
   A. File Administrator
   B. Partition Magic
   C. Drive Administrator
   D. Disk Administrator

Explanation: D. Disk Administrator is the name of the applet that can be used to format a drive, set the volume label of a drive, and copy a drive's data. Partition Magic is a third-party app. The other choices are not valid.

3. You need to create a Windows NT 4.0 boot diskette. Which three files do you need to copy to the diskette? (Choose three)
   A. NTLDR
   B. BOOT.INI.
   C. MSDOS.SYS.
   D. NTDETECT.COM.
   E. OSLOADER.EXE.

Explanation: A. NTLDR, B. BOOT.INI, C. MSDOS.SYS are used on an NT 4.0 boot disk. MSDOS.SYS and OSLOADER.EXE are not.

---

4. What command creates an Emergency Repair Disk for Windows NT 4.0?
   A. EBD.BAT
   B. RDISK.EXE
   C. ERD.EXE /S
   D. Add/Remove Programs

Explanation: B. RDISK.EXE is used to create an Emergency Repair Disk for Windows NT 4.0. Specifically, you would use the command RDISK.EXE /S, then follow the on-screen prompts. The other choices are not valid ways to accomplish this task. Watch out for "ERD.EXE /S", which sounds reasonable (since the Emergency Repair Disk is sometimes called an ERD, and the switch used on RDISK to create the ERD is /S).

5. Your computer will not boot, and you think it is because some of your boot files have been deleted. Which files must be present in the root directory of the system partition in order for Windows NT 4.0 to boot?

A. NTLDR, BOOT.INI, NTDETECT.COM.

B. IO.SYS, MS-DOS.SYS, NTLDR, SYSTEM.

C. IO.SYS, MS-DOS.SYS, BOOT.INI, COMMAND.COM.

D.NTLDR, COMMAND.COM, NTDETECT.COM, BOOT.INI.

Explanation: D. NTLDR, BOOT.INI, NTDETECT.COM are needed for Windows NT 4.0 to boot.

COMMAND.COM is a DOS command interpreter, which is not a critical component of Windows NT. Similarly, IO.SYS and MS-DOS.SYS are artifacts of the DOS days as well, which aren't relevant to Windows NT 4.0.

---

6. You have a custom application that is conflicting with another application. What can you do to temporarily fix the problem on a Windows NT system?

A. Run MSCONFIG

B. Run REGEDT32.

C. Reinstall the application.

D. Run the application in a protected memory space.

Explanation: A. Run MSCONFIG, which will let you customize the environment, WIN.INI. SYSTEM.INI and startup programs. Reinstalling would only fix the problem if the other application was installed most recently and overwrote something needed by the conflicting application. REGEDT32 might be a way to resolve the problem, but MSCONFIG is a more likely solution. NT runs applications in protected memory space, so you don't need to do anything to cause that to occur.

7. You updated a device driver on a Windows NT 4.0 Workstation, and now the
   computer fails to boot to the GUI. What should you do?
   A. Reload NT.
   B. Run ScanDisk and Disk Defragmenter.
   C. Press F5 to enter safe mode and delete the last device installed.
   D.Press the spacebar when the Load Last Known Good Configuration message
   appears.

**Explanation: D. Press the spacebar when the Load Last Known Good Configuration
   message appears** is how to get the computer back to the GUI after loading a new
   device driver causes difficulty.
It is not necessary to reload NT. Running Scandisk and Disk Defragmenter won't solve
   the problem.

---

8. When a print job is stalled in Windows NT 4.0, what should you try first?
   A.Restart the PC.
   B.Restart the spooler.
   C. Try another printer cable.
   D. Try another printer driver.

Explanation: B. Restart the spooler. If the printer was working before, the cable and
   printer driver are probably not the problem. Restarting the PC that the printer is
   connected to may solve the problem as well, but restarting the spooler is a better and
   more reliable way to do it.

9. An error occurs on your Windows NT 4.0 workstation, and Dr. Watson has created a log file. Where can you find the file to review what has caused the error?

A. C:\

B. C:\WinNT

C. C:\WinNT\system

D. C:\WinNT\system32

Explanation: B. C\WINNT is the folder containing the DRWTSN32.LOG file produced by Dr. Watson. The other choices are not valid.

---

10. You just received a Windows NT stop error with the full blue screen. How can you print out the error message that was generated?

A. Do a print screen.

B. Reboot and edit the system log.

C.Reboot and open file 0000.chk.

D. Reboot and browse the temp folder.

Explanation: A. Do a print screen. Editing the system log won't help. Files named like fileNNNN.chk are from SCANDISK.

11. Which utility would you use to get a computer's IP address in Windows NT 4.0?
    A. TRACERT
    B. NETSTAT
    C. IPCONFIG
    D. NBTSTAT

Explanation: C. IPCONFIG is the most direct way to get the computer's IP address.
TRACERT shows you the path from your computer to another one. NETSTAT shows all
active connections. NBTSTAT shows NetBIOS related status information.

---

12. Which service must be installed on a Windows NT 4.0 system to allow Dial-Up
    Networking access?
    A. NetBEUI
    B. IPX/SPX.
    C. Remote access service.
    D. Dial-Up Networking V 1.3.

Explanation: C. Remote Access Service, or RAS, must be installed.
Dial-up networking appears once RAS is installed. NetBEUI and IPX/SPX are not
required for Dial-up networking to function.

13. Which command would you use to remove an NTFS volume from a PC that no longer contains Windows NT 4.0?
   A. MOVE
   B. FDISK
   C. FORMAT
   D. DELTREE

Explanation: B. FDISK will let you remove an NTFS volume from a PC that no longer contains Windows NT 4.0. Technically, if the PC now contains Windows 2000 or Windows XP, FORMAT would work as well … but it would NOT work on other versions of Windows, which do not understand NTFS partitions. MOVE and DELTREE affect files, and will not remove the NTFS file system.

---

14. You need to create a Windows NT Boot Disk. Which files must you have on the disk? (Choose two)
A. NTLDR
B. BOOT.INI
C. NTFS32.BIN
D. WINNT32.INI
E. NTDETECT.COM

Explanation: A. NTLDR and **E. NTDETECT.COM** are required.
BOOT.INI is normally required, but under certain circumstances you can get away without it. The other choices are not valid.

15. Windows fails to boot because a customer deleted a file from a Windows NT 4.0 Workstation. Which of the following might have been deleted?
    A. BOOT.INI
    B. CONFIG.SYS
    C. COMMAND.COM
    D. AUTOEXEC.BAT

Explanation: A. BOOT.INI may have been deleted.
The other files are not required by Windows NT 4.0.

---

16. A Windows NT 4.0 command prompt can be invoked with which command?
    A. CMD.EXE
    B. RUN.COM
    C. COMMAND.EXE
    D. COMMAND.COM

Explanation: A. CMD.EXE is used to invoke a command prompt on Windows NT 4.0. COMMAND.COM is the Windows 9x/DOS command interpreter. RUN.COM and COMMAND.EXE are not valid options.

17. A Windows NT 4.0 emergency repair disk can be created using what command?

    A. RDISK.EXE

    B. ERD.EXE

    C. EMERGENCY.COM

    D. FORMAT /ERD A:

Explanation: A. RDISK.EXE is the command used to create a Windows NT 4.0 ERD. The other options are not valid.

---

18. What will happen if you run 'WINNT /B' from a command prompt on the Windows NT 4.0 installation CD.

    A. 3 NT setup disks will be created.

    B. The Windows NT 4.0 registry will be backed up.

    C. Windows NT 4.0 will be installed without prompting for boot diskettes.

    D. Windows NT 4.0 will be installed and boot diskettes will be created diskettes.

Explanation: C. Windows NT 4.0 will be installed without prompting for boot diskettes.

19. While logged in as a local administrator, you install an application on Windows NT 4.0 for an employee of your firm. You test it and it works fine. You reboot and tell her to log in and call you if she has a problem. She calls to report that the application will not run. When you log in, it runs fine. Why?

A. NTFS permissions prevent her from running the application.

B. Incorrect CD Key.

C. The EVERYONE group is missing in the application's security properties.

D. The application was not installed by the user.

Explanation: A. NTFS permissions prevent her from running the application. This would explain why you can run it and she can't. Technically, D is the problem, too, but what you really should know about this scenario is that the problem is caused by NTFS permissions.

---

20. While booting you receive the following message when booting Windows NT 4.0 Workstation: "NTLDR not found. Please insert another disk". What should you do to fix the disk?

A. Extract the file from the CD.

B. Run the emergency repair process.

C. Copy the file from any Windows system.

D. Copy the file from another Windows NT system.

Explanation: B. Run the emergency repair process will fix it, by replacing the MBR (Master Boot Record).

21. Which OEM installation CD always requires a boot floppy because the CD-ROM is not bootable?
    A. Windows 95
    B. Windows 98
    C. Windows 2000
    D. Windows NT 4.0

Explanation: A. Windows 95.

---

22. After installing a new hard drive, which Windows NT 4.0 utility should you use to make it usable?
    A. FDISK
    B. FORMAT
    C. DISKEDT32
    D. Disk Administrator

Explanation: D. Disk Administrator can be used on NT 4.0 to prepare a drive for use.

23. Your Windows NT 4 system will not boot. What is the first thing to try?
   A. Format and restore from tape.
   B. Boot to Safe Mode.
   C. Use the Last Known Good Configuration.
   D. Reinstall NT using three boot disks and the CD.

Explanation: C. Use the Last Known Good Configuration. Restoring and reinstalling are drastic steps. If the Last Known Good Configuration doesn't work, try booting to safe mode.

One world at a time

Henry David Thoreau

745

0066-185

Chapter 0101: Networking

The objective of this chapter is to provide the reader with an understanding of the following:

Network components
     Network Topology
     Network models
     Peer-To-Peer
Domains
     Client Server
     Workgroups363
Network Communication
     Adapters364
     Client366
Protocol
     TCP/IP368
     IP369
     DNS and WINS
Network Utilities
     PING374
     TRACERT375
     Dial Up Networking
     Sharing377
     Printer and File Sharing
Troubleshooting

Introduction

The details of Networking will be reviewed in this chapter. The fundamentals of how a network accomplished everyday task such as file sharing and printing will be covered. The process of networking with regard to basic operating system functions will be addressed.

This portion of operating systems will cover Networking and the Windows Operating Systems family. The first question to answer is what is a Network?

A network by definition is an environment that allows 2-way communication between computers. You may have only one computer available to you, however when you connect to the Internet you are part of a Network.

That process of connection and the communication process are the network components. The study of networking is complex and by nature is more comprehensive than the compounded overview offered here. This section is intended to provide a working knowledge of a network.

Getting Ready - Questions

A client can ping the resource server by its IP address but not by its URL. What is the computer not set up to use?
   A. ARP
   B. DNS
   C. WINS
   D. DHCP

2. Which command is used to display network configuration information in Windows 98?
   A. IPDETECT
   B. IPCONFIG
   C. TRACERT
   D. WINIPCFG

3. The network topology in which each machine validates users against a password file local to that machine is:
   A. Hierarchical
   B. Domain
   C. Secure
   D. Peer-to-peer

4. The "Launch folders in separate memory" option for Explorer might be used to:
   A. Client for Novell Networks
   B. NFS
   C. FTP Server
   D. Client for Microsoft Networks

5. A benefit of DHCP is:
   A. Allows network mapping
   B. Allows name resolution on the network
   C. Reduces the number of IP addresses needed for a network
   D. Reduces bandwidth used by the network

Getting Ready - Answers

1. Correct answer: B

2. Correct answer: D

3. Correct answer: B

4. Correct answer: A&D

5. Correct answer: C

◆ II ▶ Network components

A network requires a number of components to be functional. Those components are referred to as the media or the communication method.

They are the computer, the means of communication, such as a modem, cable modem or DSL connection or a wired or wireless media (structure) to support the communication method.

Network Topology

Each network regardless of size has a schematic. This network design or layout is known as the topology.

The equipment in use and the desired form of communication determines the network topology. Factors such as what the network users will require assist in determining how the network will be laid out, simply put the purpose of the network has high impact on the design.

The factors involved will include, desired speed, file transfer and storage needs, size of the layout and number of users involved.

Network models

Each network type is based on a model. This means that based on the **topology** chosen, factors, which may work for or against the intended result, are put into play. Beyond the **topology** chosen, there are additional considerations, which are examined next.

Peer-To-Peer

In a small network, the **peer-to-peer** model is a typical choice. This model is generally favored in small networks because it does not require much in the way of additional resources (money spent) beyond the computers that are already in use.

The implementation of a **peer-to-peer** network, beyond the computers used by the users, is done with a **Network Interface Card** (**NIC**) installed in the users computers, and **cable** to connect them together. Depending on the cable choice, one additional component may be required. Currently the most popular cable choice in the wired world for a network in a geographical area measured in room (s) is **Category 5** (**CAT 5**) **Unshielded Twisted Pair** (**UTP**).

Its popularity is based on the balancing of performance verses price. If only two computers are to be **joined** (networked) a piece of cable is the only additional requirement beyond the **NICs**. More than two computers using this cable require some tying **device** such as a **hub** or **switch**.

Networking typically has some sort of **authentication** scheme in place, and this holds true with the **peer-to-peer** model. Authentication means that the **users** right to **participate** or **log** on to the **network** is **validated**. The most common way to **authenticate** is to supply a **name** and **password**.

In **peer-to-peer**, each **local machine** contains a **name** and **password** list and a limited set of choices for allowing what that **user name** can (or not) do with the **data** and other **resources** on that **computer**. These choices are known as **permissions.** Note that this means the same user can have different passwords on different computers on the same network.

That brings us to the down side of a **peer-to-peer model**. If you think about several dozen computers tied together, and each one had its own **name-password-permission list,** an unwieldy situation is in your face. This brings into play the other very common **format** for a **network,** the **domain.**

III ▶ Domains

The **domain** is the **Windows NT or 2000 network** to which your **computer** will be talking. Think of a **domain** like a family. In a family we have **members**. To talk to a **domain** you must become a **member**.

In a typical **domain** there are also **subsets** of the **family** that can be thought of like **cousins**. These **subsets** are known as **groups.** Picturing a family tree will assist in understanding the concept. In a **family tree** there are main or immediate family members. There are also **branches** of the family. These branches are the **groups.**

A **domain** can also be thought of like an **area code**. To an **area code** we **add prefixes** to further **identify** a **local calling area**. To this number we typically **add** another 4 digits to **identify** the **specific line** or **computer**.

A **domain name** is used in a **client server** model.

Client Server

The **client/server** is used in larger environments. The concept of **name/password/permissions** is the same, however this list is stored on a **single computer.**4

The advantage of this model beyond the fact that it can support a larger number of users is finer **control** of **security**. The down side is, that this **model** requires a **separate computer** and **software** (such as Netware, NT/W2K Server).

Workgroups

In a **domain**, some domain name is assigned or entered, such as marketing, or Seattle. The **default name** in setting up a domain with Microsoft Server products carries the catchy title of **DOMAIN.**

Typically, a **workgroup** is setup with a minimum of fuss (and frequently a similar minimum of technical knowledge) so it is not uncommon to see the person who set up the **peer-to-peer** network with Microsoft's default name for this type of network, with the equally catchy title of **WORKGROUP.**

---

4 A+ does not focus on the technical issues of networking at the enterprise level. Therefore the discussion of multiple servers with separate permission lists and how they interact is off-topic for the purpose of this book.

IV   Network Communication

Another consideration of setting up a **network** is, determining how the data will get from one place to another? Somehow, it must be **transported**. And without **agreement** on how to **transport** it, the **data** isn't moving.

Since the word **protocol** is frequently used to **describe** a **series of events** that need to make something successfully happen, it has been adopted by the network world as well, to describe the structure of the conversation used to transfer data back and forth among machines. In particular, the term **transport protocol** is bantered about, to refer to the basic member of the protocol family (a group of network protocols) that is being used to transport the data.

Protocols are **installed (included)** by **default** when you **install** the operating system, if a **NIC** was present. (On newer versions of Windows, they may automagically install when you install the NIC hardware itself.) The **protocols installed** are then **chosen** from a **list** to determine which ones you will use for **network communication**.

Protocols by Default

By **default, Windows 2000** uses the protocol family **TCP/IP**, Transport Connect Protocol/Internet Protocol.

Adapters

An adapter is the network card (NIC). The NIC (network interface card) has a number of properties.

Simply put, you must **configure** the **card** to **talk** after **installing** the **card** physically.

The **settings** and the information used for **configuration** are **dependant** on the **communication method** chosen for the **network**.

Typical settings for most **network adapter cards (NIC).**

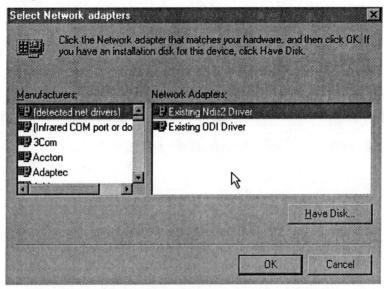

Figure 175 Selecting the adapter card to configure

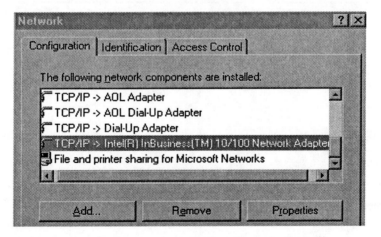

Figure 176 Note the TCP/IP setting for the NIC card

Client

Currently, there are **three** different **models** for **communication** between file servers and clients. Keep in mind this viewpoint has nothing (much) to do with the **transport protocol**. They are:

Network File System (NFS) – The default choice for UNIX/LINUX.

Netware Core Protocols (NCP) – The default choice for Novell through Netware 4.x

Server Message Block (SMB) – The default choice for NT/Windows.

Informed & Armed
A+ (and even many Microsoft tests) do not require knowing NCP/SMB/NFS. This data is presented so that you can quickly understand there are three different 'styles' of communication between a file server

and client PC's, making it clear that you must install the correct client software for the type of server you are attempting to communicate with.5

---

5 Microsoft by default uses SMB on both the client and server. Most Microsoft O/S that are intended to be used on the client side also includes the NCP client (Client for Novell Networks). Some versions of MS software may not have either NCP or SMB available in consumer level O/S choices, forcing the use of client software from the Network O/S vendor. NT/W2K has either NCP client or NCP gateway software in the Server versions.

The **client** that must be chosen is the **method** for **connecting** to the **network**. There are 2 (MS) choices installed by default when the **operating system** is installed.

The choices are:

Client for Microsoft Networks

Client for Novell Networks (NWLink client for IPX/SPX)

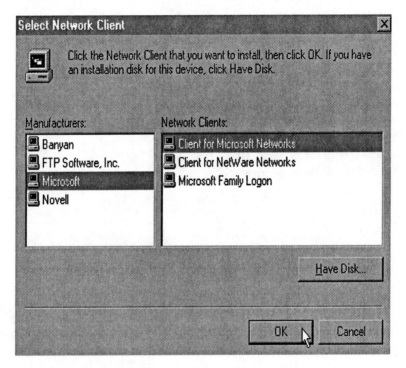

Figure 177 Note the choices from the Select Network Client

◆ V   Protocol

The **protocol** that will be **installed** is **dependant** on the **method** of **communication** chosen for the network. The **protocol** must be properly **configured** to get the **computer** to talk to the network. The operating systems installs by default the **protocols**. They are:

Windows 95 NWLink (IPX/SPX), NetBUEI

Windows 98 NWLink (IPX/XPX), NetBUEI

TCP/IP (Available in 95, installs in 98)

Windows 2000 TCP/IP

Available in:
Windows 9x, NT4 WS, W2K Pro:
NetBUEI, NWLink (IPX/SPX) TCP/IP
(W2K Pro <u>only</u>) AppleTalk.
NT4 Server/W2K Server:
NetBUEI, NWLink (IPX/SPX) TCP/IP, AppleTalk.

TCP/IP

TCP/IP is rapidly becoming the standard protocol for networking. One common error is to call **TCP/IP** the **transport protocol**. Actually, **Transmission Control Protocol (TCP)** and **User Datagram Protocol (UDP)** are the two protocols that are used for the actual transport.

The reference to **TCP/IP** is more accurately a **reference** to the **networking suite** or **protocol family** that contains other **protocols** useful for everything from **transferring files** with **File Transfer Protocol (FTP)** to overcoming challenges with tools like **PING** and **TRACERT**. That leaves the **IP** part to explain, which is examined next.

IP

Internet Protocol (IP) is the naming scheme that gives each device on a **TCP/IP network** a **unique descriptor**. Because unique identification is the only way to find a device, such as a PC, there is a mathematical limit to the number of **unique** devices that can exist on the mother of all networks, the **Internet**.

Now when **TCP/IP** was developed, it was for military use, and the idea of several or even dozens of devices that would need unique numbers in every home and business in the world (and beyond) was not a consideration. Yet, that is where we are going, and several workarounds have been developed to handle the limitation of only so many numbers being available to give out publicly.

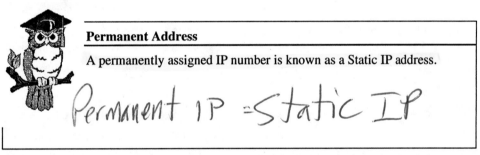

Permanent Address

A permanently assigned IP number is known as a Static IP address.

Permanent IP = Static IP

One workaround was to take **three number groupings** and declare them **private**. That means you are free to use them on your network at home or work, without directly being part of the Internet. They will never conflict with the numbers assigned to anyone else's computers on the Internet, because by definition, they are private to the individual's or company's own network, and not shared with the Internet.

This allows re-use of the **same set** of **numbers** without **conflict**. To make each network using the same numbers privately have Internet access, the **network** uses a **single** public number that is **unique** as the doorway or **gateway** to the **Internet**.

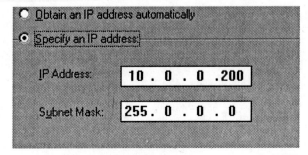

Figure 178 Example of a typical IP address

A process known as **Network Address Translation (NAT)** takes all requests from the **private numbers** and sends them through the **unique** and **public IP** number. This would be called the **gateway**.

The second workaround that **conserves** the **available numbers** is to *loan* a **publicly** available **number** only for as long at the **connection** to the Internet is **required**.

For example, think of an **Internet Service Provider (ISP)** such as Earthlink. They may have 200 modems available to accept calls from the customers in Seattle. That would mean they need **200 IP numbers**. And if they had 200 modems, they probably have 2,000 customers. Not all the customers could or typically would want to dial in at the same time.

When a customer connects to a **modem** at Earthlink, the customer would be *loaned* an **IP number** from a **computer** setup to manage this process. That computer is running a **Dynamic Host Control Protocol (DHCP)** server. Like a file server, whose purpose is to hand out files to clients, the purpose of a DHCP server is to hand out IP addresses to clients.

The **DHCP server** would in effect, allow the **clients** to **borrow a cup of IP**. As soon as the **customer** hangs up, the **unique number** is **returned** (**lease cancellation** or **expiration**) to the **available set** of **numbers**, for **reuse** by another **client**. This is another **conservation** workaround.

DHCP

Reduces the demand for unique numbers.
Leases a **IP number** *temporarily*

DHCP doesn't address the fact that **IP numbers** such, as **10.9.8.2** are not very easy for humans to remember. It wouldn't make a great commercial to hear a jingle telling you to visit www.192.168.254.168.com

The solution to the fact that humans are more math challenged than computers is next.

DNS and WINS

When you hear the commercial asking you to visit **somesite.com** or **yoursite.net** (and you actually do so) your request by the more **human name** gets passed on.

When you're on the Internet, the request is passed to a **computer** running **Domain Name Service (DNS)** that **looks up** the friendly (to humans) name and finds out what the **IP number** is for that site, and that tells the equipment on the Internet you are looking for that **IP number**.

Now that is great for the **Internet,** and doesn't do much for computer that have names in your office, where Microsoft's local network naming system rather than DNS is usually in effect. Think of how many computers are out there with names such as Sales, or Accounting. (The exception here is Windows 2000, which will use DNS for your local network as well.)

The humans in the office as compared to computers are as math challenged in the office as they are at home. To solve this issue in the office, **Microsoft** provides a way to **resolve the names** of the **computers in the office** to **unique IP numbers** with software called **Windows Internet Naming Service (WINS).**

The successful A+ technician would understand one more part of **IP**.

The **IP number** a **computer** or other **device** uses, **consists** of **4 sets of numbers**, which must range from **0 to 255** and the **4 sets are separated by periods**. Technically, they are called **octets**. (Refer to the A+ core book for more details).

A **second set** of **numbers** that follow the same rules must be part of the **IP number**; this set is known as the **subnet mask**.

IP Address:	10 . 0 . 0 .200
Subnet Mask:	255 . 0 . 0 . 0

Figure 179 IP Address Example

In effect the **subnet mask** takes the **IP number** and **splits** it into a **family name** for the **network,** and a **first name** for each **device** on the **network.** The **generic name** for each **device** is known as a **HOST.**

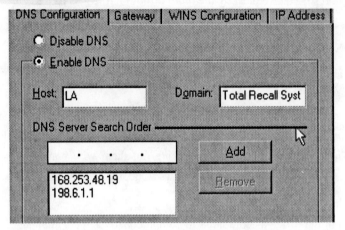

Figure 180Host Name and Domain

Figure 181 Computer Name and Workgroup

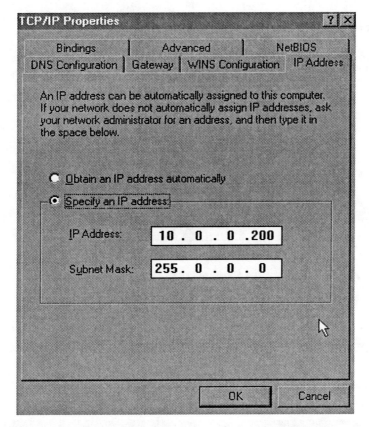

Figure 182 TCP/IP Properties Window

VI   Network Utilities

The **network** pericodically may have communication, speed or other issues. There are **utilities** built in to the **Windows** family to help gather information on the **network condition.**

PING

An **IP** number or **NetBIOS** name,can be tested by invoking the **PING (PACKET INTERNET GROPER) command** from a **command prompt**.

PING IT!
Using the **PING** command will tell you if a **TCP/IP** based **device** is **functioning**.

The example shows this request timing out meaning the destination is unreachable, and a request that is invalid due to an invalid IP address.

```
C:\>ping 10.0.0.1

Pinging 10.0.0.1 with 32 bytes of data:

Request timed out.
Request timed out.
Request timed out.
Request timed out.

Ping statistics for 10.0.0.1:
    Packets: Sent = 4, Received = 0, Lost = 4 (100% loss),
Approximate round trip times in milli-seconds:
    Minimum = 0ms, Maximum =  0ms, Average =  0ms
```

Figure 183 Ping from the Command Line

Note: ping can be run from the command line. Go to start run then type in ping and the address to ping.

```
C:\>ping 127.0.0.0

Pinging 127.0.0.0 with 32 bytes of data:

Destination specified is invalid.
Destination specified is invalid.
Destination specified is invalid.
Destination specified is invalid.

Ping statistics for 127.0.0.0:
    Packets: Sent = 4, Received = 0, Lost = 4 (100% loss),
Approximate round trip times in milli-seconds:
    Minimum = 0ms, Maximum =  0ms, Average =  0ms
```

Figure 184 PING with invalid IP address

TRACERT

Sometimes while you know that things are blowing up, but you don't know where. The cousin of **PING, TRACERT** will show you where the hang up is. This means that if you are not getting a connection to something or someone out there on the **INTERNET** or even on the **network** the **TRACERT** command can tell you if the **address** will be **resolved** to a **hostname** and if it is timing out or getting to the destination.

```
C:\>tracert

Usage: tracert [-d] [-h maximum_hops] [-j host-list] [-w timeout] target_name

Options:
    -d                 Do not resolve addresses to hostnames.
    -h maximum_hops    Maximum number of hops to search for target.
    -j host-list       Loose source route along host-list.
    -w timeout         Wait timeout milliseconds for each reply.

C:\>_
```

Figure 185 TRACERT at the Command Prompt

Dial Up Networking

When connecting to an **ISP (Internet service provider)**, typically the **Dial-Up**

Dial-Up
Networking panel is used. Networking Double-clicking My Computer directs you to the

icon.

Clicking on **Dial-Up-Networking** will take you to the **Make New Connection**

Make New
Connection
icon. It is here where we configure the modem device or even dialing into the Office network (VPN) services. We choose a name for the connection, the device and then how the dial-up service will be configured.

The purpose for all of this is to utilize **RAS (Remote Access Service)** or to use our **ISP dial-up services** from a number other than what we would typically use. For instance your authors travel a great deal and need to connect to the office network or dial in to Internet mail services when away.

Commonly this is where laptop users set the configurations for communicating while on the road.

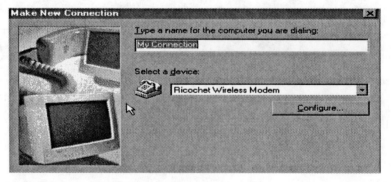

Figure 186 Make a New Connection screen

Once the configuration is set you are not limited to the one. As many connections properties as needed for each situation can be made, simply name each one differently.

Sharing

The main purpose of a **network** is to share information. Knowing how to share and when to protect information is key to successfully managing files in the **network environment.**

Printer and File Sharing

The files we share may contain information we only want to be viewed not changed in any way. We already covered the file properties such as **read only.**

We want to make certain when giving access to information that the proper properties or permissions are assigned to the folder or file. Right clicking on a file or folder will allow us to set those permissions or change them at anytime.

To share a printer we must choose the **sharing** option under properties. There are several ways to do this. The first is to go to start, **Start** , settings **Settings** printers, **Printers**. The second way is to go to the control panel **Control Panel** and choose the printer shortcut icon.

Printers. We can also right-click or double-click to open my computer, **My computer** to take us to the printers **Printers** folder The following screens will walk you through the adding a shared printer process.

The screen you see will show all the printers available to you or installed. If your printer is there then right click properties for that printer to open the sharing dialog.

If the printer you wish to print to, is not listed there are several ways to add it to your printing options.

One method is to use the **CTRL + P** and bring up the printer screen and tab thru the printer choices to see if your printer is listed there and make sure you are printing to the correct printer.

Printer		
Name:	Default Printer	Properties
Status:	Idle	
Type:	Brother MFL Pro Printer II	
Where:	LPT2:	Print to file
Comment:		

Figure 187 Choosing the printer to print to

This is the tab next to the **properties** tab, notice the location of the **printer** and the **printer name** is listed, as well as the **port**.

Another method is to **map** to the **network drive** where the printer is located and click on the printer you want to print to when you see it.

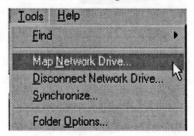

This is done by either right-clicking My Computer or by b right clicking on the start and then choosing explore. You can also get to **Explorer** by going to **start, programs, Windows Explorer**.

Once there chose from the menu, tools, then **Map Network Drive.**

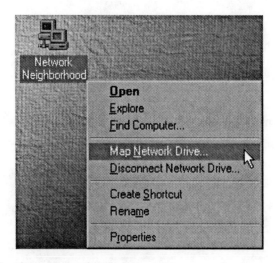

Figure 188Choose Map to Network Drive

Figure 189 Mapping a Network Drive

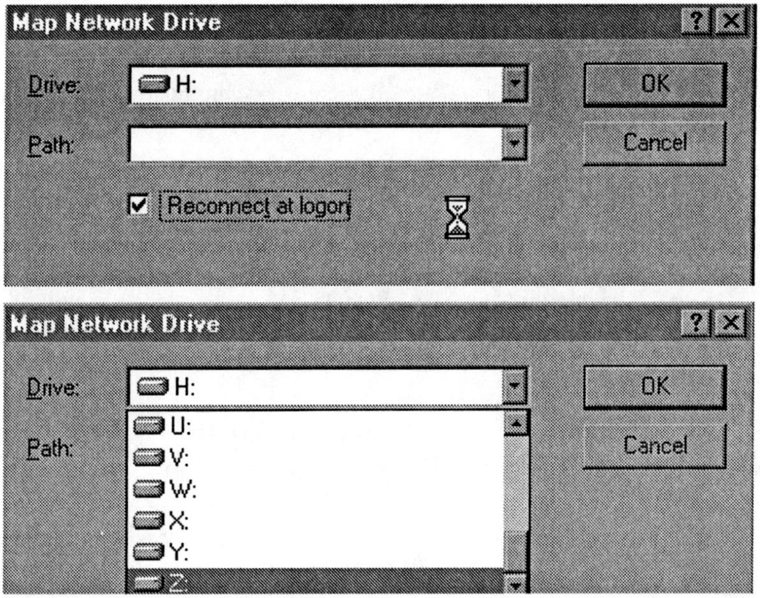

Figure 190 Choosing the Drive to MAP to

Note: it must be already shared for you to access it.

Once you see the drive that has the printer attached to it, then **Map** and be sure and click on the **Reconnect at logon** box. This will allow you to stay or reconnect to the printer or drive where a folder is shared, and then make it easier for you to locates it graphically on your **local machine.**

The other method is to browse the network and when you see a shared printer , then click it on to print to it. If a special driver is needed for that printer it will install for you across the network.

VII   Troubleshooting

So when you see the error message "see the network administrator" and you are the administrator what to do??

YOU ARE IT!!!!!! ☺

This section is designed for you to take and make notes on your own questions and scenarios!

VIII Summary

In this chapter you learned the basic of a network. The various components, the areas where the information is entered to make the computer work on a network were covered.

There is much more to learn about networking than is covered in this chapter. We encourage you to continue your studies and pursue the Network+ certification to learn even more.

IX   Test for Success Questions

1. The program System Monitor that is found in Windows 95 will display data on?
   (Choose all that apply)
   A. Anti-virus applications.
   B. Virtual memory.
   C. Interrupt settings.
   D. Hardware compatibility protocol.
   E. Network clients and server information.

---

2. You are running a small training class for end users who must demonstrate a product.
   What two ways would you show them to rename a shared network printer, using a
   GUI approach in Windows 9x? (Choose all that apply)
   A. My Computer, Printers.
   B. Start, Settings, Printers.
   C. Start, Accessories, System Utilities, Printers.
   D. Start, Programs, Accessories, System Tools, Printer Setup.
   E. My Computer, Control Panel, System, Device Manager, Ports, Printers.

3. As a field technician you have just installed a new modem under Windows 98 and can no longer connect to your Internet service provider with through Dial-Up Networking. What is the next step you take?

A. Change the string to ATZ in modem properties.

B. Call your telephone company to report a dead line.

C. Configure the modem to use Dialup Networking.

♦ D. Select the new modem from the Dial-Up Networking connection's properties.

4. You have just completed installing Windows 98 to a computer on your network. In your testing you discover that you can't browse the network. You check for Client for the Microsoft networks and find that it is installed. What is you're next step to address the challenge?

A. Enable File and Printer sharing.

c B. Verify the workstation's IP address.

C. Enable Browsing Services in the Control Panel.

D. Enable NetBIOS support.

E. Enable Network support in the PC BIOS.

5. You are installing a network card in a Windows 98 computer, and the computer will not connect to the network. What should you do to find out if the device is functioning correctly?
   A. Run net config.
   ♦ B. Look at the Device Manager.
   C. Check Network Neighborhood.
   D. Check Dial-Up Networking properties.
   E. Run NetFix

---

6. Where in Windows 2000 can you change your network identification?
   A. Device manager.
   ♦ B. Network properties.
   C. System properties.
   D. Network and dial up connections.
   E. Disk Administrator

7. On a Windows 2000 client computer, how can you map a drive letter? (Choose all that apply)
   - A. Right click My Computer.
   - B. Right click Control Panel.
   - C. Right click My Network Places.
   - D. Right click Network and Dial-up Connection.
   - E. Right click Start

---

8. If you configure a Windows 2000 system is TCP/IP with DHCP, but does the computer doesn't find a DHCP server when booted, what will happen?
   - A. Windows 2000 will not be able to start the network.
   - B. System will switch automatically to Net BEUI protocol.
   - C. Automatic private IP addressing will be used to assign an address.
   - D. System will listen to the network (using BOOTP) to discover what range of addresses is being used and will assign an address in this range.
   - E. BOOTP will automagically find an IP address, if it has been installed.

9. Which network protocols are included with Windows 2000? (Choose all that apply)
   A. XNS
   B. DECNET
   C. NWLINK
   D. NETBEUI
   E. APPLETALK

---

10. You need to prepare a laptop or an employee spending much of their time out in the field. Which service must be installed on a Windows NT 4.0 system to allow Dial-Up Networking access? (Choose all that apply)
   A. Net BEUI
   B. IPX/SPX
   C. Remote Access Service
   D. Dial-Up Networking
   E. TCP/IP

11. A user on your company's network has worked for several hours on a document that was retrieved from the network. The document was saved several times by clicking the Save icon. After returning from an absence, the user finds his computer indicating a fatal write error. Why? (Choose all that apply)

   A. The network drive is read only.

   B. The user's hard drive has crashed.

   C. The file is restricted to administrative use.

   D. The users disconnected from the network drive.

   E. The network drive is off line running a backup.

---

12. You have just installed a new PC on a network that has file and print sharing enabled, and it can be seen in the Network Neighborhood by other computers. Unfortunately, other computers cannot connect to resources on your computer. Why?

   A. You have not shared any directories.

   B. Shared directories are password protected.

   C. Other computers are using the ROM protocol.

   D. Other computers do not have file and print sharing enabled.

   E. The system administrator does not have this permission turned on.

13. You are being trained by an ISP to provide tech support. A user calls your mentor, and complains that his password is repeatedly rejected when trying to connect. Your mentor tells him to run Defrag and Scandisk while waiting on the phone. What would be the purpose for giving this instruction?

A. To fix a malfunctioning modem.

B. To fix a corrupted password file.

C. They suspect an upper memory problem.

D. They expect the network to be functional by the time Defrag and Scandisk are done.

E. The mentor suspects there is an error in the registry.

14. How can a user on a Windows 9x workgroup find a network printer?

A. By protocol

C. By cable name

D. By manufacturer

E. By NetBIOS name

F. By type of printing method (Laser or Inkjet)

15. Why would File and Print Sharing for Microsoft Networks be unchecked on a laptop which uses a network adapter and NetBEUI?

    A. TCP/IP must be added.

    B. File and Print Sharing will only work with Windows NT.

    C. File and Print Sharing for MS Networks receive server must be added.

    D. File and Print Sharing must be enabled on the network

    E. Interface card.

---

16. With which network protocols can share a printer in Windows 9x? (Choose all that apply)

    A. PTP

    B. IPX/SPX

    C. TCP/IP

    D. NETBIOS

    E. NETBEUI

17. In Windows 98, which of the following devices can you share via the network?
    (Choose all that apply)
    A. Printer
    B. Modem
    C. Monitor
    D. CD-ROM
    E. Keyboard

---

18. Where would you go to capture a printer port for a network printer in Windows 9x?
    A. Printer palette, File, Properties, Details.
    B. Printer applet, File, Properties, Details.
    C. Network Applet, File, Properties, Details.
    D. Add/Remove Program applet, Properties, Details.
    E. Start, Settings, Control Panel, System

19. To add a computer to a domain on a network running Windows 2000 you should:

    A. My Computer, Tools menu.

    B. Open Control Panel, Network icon.

    C. Right click My Computer, Properties, and Network Identification.

    D. Right click My Network Places - properties, right click Local Area Connection - right click properties.

    E. Right click Desktop, right click on properties.

20. What kind of network can 10 Windows 98 computers provide?

    A. WAN

    B. DOMAIN

    C. PEER-TO-PEER

    D. CLIENT SERVER

    E. Metropolitan Area Network (IEEE standards)

21. Why would you add an IP address to a DNS Server search order?

    A. It restricts browsing to the DNS Server.

    B. It overrides the local system's IP address.

    C. It tells the DNS server the location of the local system.

    D. It tells the local system the location of the DNS server.

    E. It is mandatory to make the network function correctly.

---

22. Every time you reboot, a successfully mapped network drive disappears. Why?
(Choose all that apply)

    A. The computer you have connected to has moved.

    B. 'Reconnect at Logon' is not checked.

    C. A map statement is not in the autoexec.bat file.

    D. The last drive is not set correctly.

    E. Domain name is incorrectly set.

23. Any network requires what components to be installed and configured correctly? (Choose all that apply)

    A. Client

    B. Protocol

    C. Server

    D. Resource Sharing

    E. Adapter

---

24. A user clicks on the Print icon within an application, and their print job is sent to the wrong printer. What can you do to assure that your print job is sent to the correct printer? (Choose all that apply)

    A. Change printer drivers.

    B. Reorder the printer entries in the Printers folder.

    C. Select File, Print to set the desired printer for the application.

    D. Change the desired printers location on the network.

    E. Set the desired printer as the default printer.

25. In Windows, which network components must be present to make a dial up
    connection to the Internet? (Choose all that apply)
    A. TCP/IP
    B. DHCP
    C. Client for Microsoft Networks
    D. Dial-Up Adapter
    E. NetBEUI

---

26. In a peer-to-peer network, printing has slowed the network performance. What can
    you do to quickly remedy the problem?
    A. Install more memory on the network printers.
    B. Disable network printing on one of the computers that never prints anyway.
    C. Run print jobs after hours when there is less network traffic.
    D. Configure one computer as a network print server.
    E. Install a hardware print buffer

27. In the Windows 9x Network applet, you can add which of the following? (Choose all that apply)
   A. Client
   B. Protocol
   C. Service
   D. Printer
   E. Adapter

28. Where in Windows 2000 would you go to connect or disconnect a network printer?
   A. Start, Settings, Task.
   B. Start, Settings, Printers.
   C. Start, Settings, Network.
   D. Start, Settings, Connections.
   E. Start, Printer Wizard

29. You have multiple folders shared successfully. When you create a new shared folder, it is not displayed as a shared folder. Why is this problem occurring?

    A. Disk quotas.

    B. Insufficient hard drive space.

    C. Insufficient RAM.

    D. More than 300 shared folders already exist.

    E. Insufficient access rights. See the network administrator.

30. In Windows 9x, where would you go to find out the type of network adapter that is installed?

    A. Control Panel, Ports.

    B. Control Panel, Network.

    C. Control panel, Adapters.

    D. Network Neighborhood.

31. In Windows 2000 where do you go to add your computer to a workgroup or domain?
    (Choose all that apply)
    A. Device Manager.
    B. System Properties.
    C. Membership Manager.
    ★ D. Network and dial up connections.

32. A customer has received their username, password, and dial up numbers for his ISP.
    What should they do first to set up their computer to use the ISP for Internet access?
    A. Obtain an ISP account after installing PPT and Dialup Networking.
    ↲ B. Install Dial-Up Networking and TCP/IP and set up all appropriate settings.
    C. Install PPT and Dialup Networking after establishing a new account with the ISP.
    D. Obtain an account from an ISP then reinstall the modem TCP/IP and Dialup
    Networking.
    E. Reinstall the Operating System

33. What does a WINS Server do on the network?
    A. It assigns IP addresses.
    ↳ B. It assigns computer names.
    C. It resolves NetBIOS names to IP addresses.
    D. It allows dual booting between operating systems.
    E. It resolves NetBEUI names to IP addresses.

Test for Success Answers

1. The program System Monitor that is found in Windows 95 will display data on?
   (Choose all that apply)
   A. Anti-virus applications.
   B. Virtual memory.
   C. Interrupt settings.
   D. Hardware compatibility protocol.
   E. Network clients and server information.

Explanation: B. Virtual memory

---

2. You are running a small training class for end users who must demonstrate a product. What two ways would you show them to rename a shared network printer, using a GUI approach in Windows 9x? (Choose all that apply)
   A. My Computer, Printers.
   B. Start, Settings, Printers.
   C. Start, Accessories, System Utilities, Printers.
   D. Start, Programs, Accessories, System Tools, Printer Setup.
   E. My Computer, Control Panel, System, Device Manager, Ports, Printers.

Explanation: B. Start, Settings, Printers

3. As a field technician you have just installed a new modem under Windows 98 and can no longer connect to your Internet service provider with through Dial-Up Networking. What is the next step you take?

A. Change the string to ATZ in modem properties.

B. Call your telephone company to report a dead line.

C. Configure the modem to use Dialup Networking.

D. Select the new modem from the Dial-Up Networking connection's properties.

Explanation: D. Select the new modem from the Dial-Up Networking connection's properties.

---

4. You have just completed installing Windows 98 to a computer on your network. In your testing you discover that you can't browse the network. You check for Client for the Microsoft networks and find that it is installed. What is you're next step to address the challenge?

A. Enable File and Printer sharing.

B. Verify the workstation's IP address.

C. Enable Browsing Services in the Control Panel.

D. Enable NetBIOS support.

E. Enable Network support in the PC BIOS.

Explanation: A. Enable File and Printer sharing

5. You are installing a network card in a Windows 98 computer, and the computer will not connect to the network. What should you do to find out if the device is functioning correctly?

    A. Run net config.

    B. Look at the Device Manager.

    C. Check Network Neighborhood.

    D. Check Dial-Up Networking properties.

    E. Run NetFix

Explanation: B. Look at the Device Manager will tell you whether the device is functioning properly.

Net config lists the available services (not hardware). Network Neighborhood relies on both the device and software configuration. Dial-up networking is not involved with network cards. NetFix is not a valid option.

---

6. Where in Windows 2000 can you change your network identification?

    A. Device manager.

    B. Network properties.

    C. System properties.

    D. Network and dial up connections.

    E. Disk Administrator

Explanation: C. System properties, available from the Control Panel.

7. On a Windows 2000 client computer, how can you map a drive letter? (Choose all that apply)
A. Right click My Computer.
B. Right click Control Panel.
C. Right click My Network Places.
D. Right click Network and Dial-up Connection.
E. Right click Start

Explanation: A. Right click My Computer, C. Right click My Network Places are two locations in which you can do this.

---

8. If you configure a Windows 2000 system is TCP/IP with DHCP, but does the computer doesn't find a DHCP server when booted, what will happen?
A. Windows 2000 will not be able to start the network.
B. System will switch automatically to Net BEUI protocol.
C. Automatic private IP addressing will be used to assign an address.
D. System will listen to the network (using BOOTP) to discover what range of addresses is being used and will assign an address in this range.
E. BOOTP will automagically find an IP address, if it has been installed.

Explanation: C. Automatic private IP addressing will be used to assign an address

9. Which network protocols are included with Windows 2000? (Choose all that apply)
    A. XNS
    B. DECNET
    C. NWLINK
    D. NETBEUI
    E. APPLETALK

Explanation: C. NWLINK, D. NETBEUI, E. APPLETALK

---

10. You need to prepare a laptop or an employee spending much of their time out in the field. Which service must be installed on a Windows NT 4.0 system to allow Dial-Up Networking access? (Choose all that apply)
    A. Net BEUI
    B. IPX/SPX
    C. Remote Access Service
    D. Dial-Up Networking
    E. TCP/IP

Explanation: C. Remote Access Service

11. A user on your company's network has worked for several hours on a document that was retrieved from the network. The document was saved several times by clicking the Save icon. After returning from an absence, the user finds his computer indicating a fatal write error. Why? (Choose all that apply)

A. The network drive is read only.

B. The user's hard drive has crashed.

C. The file is restricted to administrative use.

D. The users disconnected from the network drive.

E. The network drive is off line running a backup.

Explanation: E. The users disconnected from the network drive

---

12. You have just installed a new PC on a network that has file and print sharing enabled, and it can be seen in the Network Neighborhood by other computers. Unfortunately, other computers cannot connect to resources on your computer. Why?

A. You have not shared any directories.

B. Shared directories are password protected.

C. Other computers are using the ROM protocol.

D. Other computers do not have file and print sharing enabled.

E. The system administrator does not have this permission turned on.

Explanation: A. You have not shared any directories

13. You are being trained by an ISP to provide tech support. A user calls your mentor, and complains that his password is repeatedly rejected when trying to connect. Your mentor tells him to run Defrag and Scandisk while waiting on the phone. What would be the purpose for giving this instruction?

A. To fix a malfunctioning modem.

B. To fix a corrupted password file.

C. They suspect an upper memory problem.

D. They expect the network to be functional by the time Defrag and Scandisk are done.

E. The mentor suspects there is an error in the registry.

Explanation: D. They expect the network to be functional by the time Defrag and Scandisk are done

---

14. How can a user on a Windows 9x workgroup find a network printer?

A. By protocol

C. By cable name

D. By manufacturer

E. By NetBIOS name

F. By type of printing method (Laser or Inkjet)

Explanation: E. By NetBIOS name

15. Why would File and Print Sharing for Microsoft Networks be unchecked on a laptop which uses a network adapter and NetBEUI?
   A. TCP/IP must be added.
   B. File and Print Sharing will only work with Windows NT.
   C. File and Print Sharing for MS Networks receive server must be added.
   D. File and Print Sharing must be enabled on the network
   E. Interface card.

Explanation: D. File and Print Sharing must be enabled on the network

---

16. With which network protocols can share a printer in Windows 9x? (Choose all that apply)
   A. PTP
   B. IPX/SPX
   C. TCP/IP
   D. NETBIOS
   E. NETBEUI

Explanation: B. IPX/SPX, C. TCP/IP, E. NETBEUI

17. In Windows 98, which of the following devices can you share via the network?
    (Choose all that apply)
    A. Printer
    B. Modem
    C. Monitor
    D. CD-ROM
    E. Keyboard

Explanation: A. Printer, B. Modem, D. CD-ROM

18. Where would you go to capture a printer port for a network printer in Windows 9x?
    A. Printer palette, File, Properties, Details.
    B. Printer applet, File, Properties, Details.
    C. Network Applet, File, Properties, Details.
    D. Add/Remove Program applet, Properties, Details.
    E. Start, Settings, Control Panel, System

Explanation: B. Printer applet, File, Properties, Details

19. To add a computer to a domain on a network running Windows 2000 you should:

   A. My Computer, Tools menu.

   B. Open Control Panel, Network icon.

   C. Right click My Computer, Properties, and Network Identification.

   D. Right click My Network Places - properties, right click Local Area Connection - right click properties.

   E. Right click Desktop, right click on properties.

Explanation: C. Right click My Computer, Properties, and Network Identification

---

20. What kind of network can 10 Windows 98 computers provide?

   A. WAN

   B. DOMAIN

   C. PEER-TO-PEER

   D. CLIENT SERVER

   E. Metropolitan Area Network (IEEE standards)

Explanation: C. PEER-TO-PEER.

In order to provide client/server or domain-based networking, there would have to be at least one NT server. WAN and Metropolitan Area Network are also possibly correct, but in this situation, peer-to-peer is the most correct answer.

21. Why would you add an IP address to a DNS Server search order?

    A. It restricts browsing to the DNS Server.

    B. It overrides the local system's IP address.

    C. It tells the DNS server the location of the local system.

    D. It tells the local system the location of the DNS server.

    E. It is mandatory to make the network function correctly.

Explanation: D. It tells the local system the location of the DNS server.

---

22. Every time you reboot, a successfully mapped network drive disappears. Why?
    (Choose all that apply)

    A. The computer you have connected to has moved.

    B. 'Reconnect at Logon' is not checked.

    C. A map statement is not in the autoexec.bat file.

    D. The last drive is not set correctly.

    E. Domain name is incorrectly set.

Explanation: B. 'Reconnect at Logon' is not checked.

23. Any network requires what components to be installed and configured correctly?
(Choose all that apply)
A. Client
B. Protocol
C. Server
D. Resource Sharing
E. Adapter

Explanation: B. Protocol, E. Adapter.

---

24. A user clicks on the Print icon within an application, and their print job is sent to the wrong printer. What can you do to assure that your print job is sent to the correct printer? (Choose all that apply)
A. Change printer drivers.
B. Reorder the printer entries in the Printers folder.
C. Select File, Print to set the desired printer for the application.
D. Change the desired printers location on the network.
E. Set the desired printer as the default printer.

Explanation: E. Set the desired printer as the default printer. In the case above, the user doesn't select a printer, and that means that their job is going to their default printer. If that isn't the printer the user really wants, the answer is to change their default.

25. In Windows, which network components must be present to make a dial up
   connection to the Internet? (Choose all that apply)
   A. TCP/IP
   B. DHCP
   C. Client for Microsoft Networks
   D. Dial-Up Adapter
   E. NetBEUI

Explanation: A. TCP/IP, D. Dial-Up Adapter

---

26. In a peer-to-peer network, printing has slowed the network performance. What can
   you do to quickly remedy the problem?
   A. Install more memory on the network printers.
   B. Disable network printing on one of the computers that never prints anyway.
   C. Run print jobs after hours when there is less network traffic.
   D. Configure one computer as a network print server.
   E. Install a hardware print buffer

Explanation: C. Run print jobs after hours when there is less network traffic.

27. In the Windows 9x Network applet, you can add which of the following? (Choose all that apply)
   A. Client
   B. Protocol
   C. Service
   D. Printer
   E. Adapter

Explanation: A. Client, B. Protocol, C. Service, E. Adapter

28. Where in Windows 2000 would you go to connect or disconnect a network printer?
   A. Start, Settings, Task.
   B. Start, Settings, Printers.
   C. Start, Settings, Network.
   D. Start, Settings, Connections.
   E. Start, Printer Wizard

Explanation: B. Start, Settings, Printers

29. You have multiple folders shared successfully. When you create a new shared folder, it is not displayed as a shared folder. Why is this problem occurring?

A. Disk quotas.

B. Insufficient hard drive space.

C. Insufficient RAM.

D. More than 300 shared folders already exist.

E. Insufficient access rights. See the network administrator.

Explanation: C. Insufficient RAM.

---

30. In Windows 9x, where would you go to find out the type of network adapter that is installed?

A. Control Panel, Ports.

B. Control Panel, Network.

C. Control panel, Adapters.

D. Network Neighborhood.

Explanation: B. Control Panel, Network

31. In Windows 2000 where do you go to add your computer to a workgroup or domain? (Choose all that apply)

A. Device Manager.

B. System Properties.

C. Membership Manager.

D. Network and dial up connections.

Explanation: B. System Properties

32. A customer has received their username, password, and dial up numbers for his ISP. What should they do first to set up their computer to use the ISP for Internet access?

A. Obtain an ISP account after installing PPT and Dialup Networking.

B. Install Dial-Up Networking and TCP/IP and set up all appropriate settings.

C. Install PPT and Dialup Networking after establishing a new account with the ISP.

D. Obtain an account from an ISP then reinstall the modem TCP/IP and Dialup Networking.

E. Reinstall the Operating System

Explanation: B. Install Dial-Up Networking and TCP/IP and set up all appropriate settings.

33. What does a WINS Server do on the network?

A. It assigns IP addresses.

B. It assigns computer names.

C. It resolves NetBIOS names to IP addresses.

D. It allows dual booting between operating systems.

E. It resolves NetBEUI names to IP addresses.

Explanation: C. It resolves NetBIOS names to IP addresses

Index of Tables and Figures

Index of Tables

Index of figures

Index

"I have offended God and mankind because my work didn't reach the quality it should have."
--Leonardo da Vinci

Other CompTIA Certification books by TotalRecall Publications

InsideScoop to Network+

TotalRecall Certification System

ExamInsight Network+

TotalRecall The IT Insight Book Series

ExamWise Network+

TotalRecall The IT Question Book Series

InsideScoop to A+ Operation System Technology

TotalRecall Certification System

ExamInsight A+ Operation System Technology

TotalRecall The IT Insight Book Series

ExamWise A+ Operation System Technology

TotalRecall The IT Question Book Series

InsideScoop to Security+

TotalRecall Certification System

ExamInsight Security+

TotalRecall The IT Insight Book Series

ExamWise Security+

TotalRecall The IT Question Book Series

Money Back Book Guarantee

This guarantee applies only to books published by TotalRecall Publications, Inc.! We are so confident in our products, we are prepared to offer the following guarantee to YOU our valued customer: If you do not pass your certification exam after two attempts, we will give money back!

Visit www.TotalRecallPress.com
Select "Money Back Book Guarantee" for details.

Registered book purchasers will receive
    1. Receive a 50% cash refund of purchase price
OR
    2. Receive a free TotalRecallPress.com book of less or equal value.

To qualify for this www.TotalRecallPress.com Guarantee you must meet these requirements and perform the following tasks:
    1. Register your purchase at www.TotalRecallPress.com web site before taking the Real Exam.
    2. Fail the corresponding exam twice (No time Limit)
    3. Contact TotalRecall for the RMA # and to claim this guarantee
    4. Send a notification email to Guarantee@TotalRecallPress.com
    5. Subject must contain your Membership # or Registration #

Ship the following to claim your refund.
    1. RMA # from returned email
    2. Documents of exam scores (Copy) for both failed attempts
    3. Return the Book to the following address

TotalRecall Publications

Attn: Corby Tate

1103 Middlecreek

Friendswood, TX 77546

888-992-3131 **bfquiz@swbell.net**

281-992-3131 **http://www.BFQOnline.com**

281-482-5390 Fax**http://www.BFQ.com**

It's a **Passing** day here at the BeachFront.
Thank you for using the TotalRecallPress.com Success Program.
Bruce Moran President

CompTIA 220-232 Operating System Practice Exam Purchase

BeachFront Quizzer, Inc. (BFQ) version 4.0

With the purchase of this book you qualify to purchase a Beachfront Quizzer Practice exam at a $20 discount.

Visit www.TotalRecallPress.com for details.

Register your book purchase at
www.TotalRecallPress.com

Your Registration Code # = EI-22232-9000

System Requirements   Microsoft Windows OS Workstation Product line with a minimum of 6 MB hard disk space and 16 MB RAM

Call: 281-992-3131

Good Luck with your certification!

Your Book Registration Number is EI-22232-9000

You cannot go wrong with this book because it is GUARANTEED:

See details at www.TotalRecallPress.com